the
living faith

the

LLOYD C. DOUGLAS

living faith

FROM HIS SELECTED SERMONS

HOUGHTON MIFFLIN COMPANY BOSTON

THE RIVERSIDE PRESS CAMBRIDGE

acknowledgments

Grateful acknowledgment is made to the publishers for permission to quote from the following works:

"The Mind" by Edward Lee Thorndike from *Exploring Your Mind with the Psychologists* by Albert Edward Wiggam. Copyright 1928. Used by special permission of the publishers, The Bobbs-Merrill Company, Inc.

"The Idol-Maker Prays" from the book, *Death and General Putnam and 101 Other Poems* by Arthur Guiterman, copyright, 1935, by E. P. Dutton & Company, Inc.

"Critique of *The Scarlet Letter*" by Newell Dwight Hillis from *Great Books*, used by permission of Fleming H. Revell Company.

table of contents

publisher's note

ALL THE SELECTIONS in this book were written by Lloyd C. Douglas. The great majority of them are sermons. A few are addresses given before groups other than church congregations. But whether he was in church or not, when he delivered these speeches, Dr. Douglas was speaking as a minister. Where the information is available, we have given the date and place he delivered each of these selections. The fragments that follow some of the sermons are taken from prayers that Dr. Douglas wrote for his Sunday Services.

In the thirty-two years that he was an active minister, Lloyd Douglas preached many hundreds of sermons that illuminated the Christian faith in a new way. We have chosen sermons and arranged them to give the highlights of Dr. Douglas' philosophy of life.

In the first section, "The Christian Adventure," the sermons describe his ambitious view of what the church ought to be and do. In "The Bible Speaks to Us," he gives some modern applications of familiar Bible stories that for too long have been set aside as religious museum pieces, to be admired but not touched. The title of the third section, "How a Christian Lives," is self-explanatory. If people knew that, and acted accordingly, the rest would take care of itself. Dr. Douglas would have considered this the most important part of the book.

BOOKS BY LLOYD C. DOUGLAS

MAGNIFICENT OBSESSION

FORGIVE US OUR TRESPASSES

PRECIOUS JEOPARDY

GREEN LIGHT

WHITE BANNERS

DISPUTED PASSAGE

HOME FOR CHRISTMAS

DOCTOR HUDSON'S SECRET JOURNAL

INVITATION TO LIVE

THE ROBE

THE BIG FISHERMAN

TIME TO REMEMBER

THE LIVING FAITH

part one

THE CHRISTIAN ADVENTURE

part one

the gallantry of galilee

THE OTHER NIGHT, as I sat at dinner in a semi-public dining room of exceptional beauty, my attention was directed to the tiny scarfings on the surface of the concrete pillar hard by our table. The eccentric tracings were as if some Lilliputian hand had written the history of an empire on the pillar, in elaborate hieroglyphics. Or, as if a multitude of busy Lilliputian feet had crossed and recrossed their own tracks, bent on who-might-know what important errands. But, on more minute inspection, the strange pattern on the pillar turned out to be *imitation worm-holes.*

The pillar was meant to be an exact replica of a huge sustaining post in an ancient Spanish house; a post that had been there so long that it showed every savage inroad that Time and the elements would make on it. It was ashen-gray; it had been ineffectually gnawed at by generations of ambitious little wood-worms; but, here it was — scarred, discolored — proudly announcing, in its own silent eloquence, that it had proved infinitely superior to its enemies.

Doubtless there had been a day when the aspiring little wood-worms had planned a vast campaign to eat the pillar up, and have done with it. Then the house would fall down, and they could eat that up, too, at their leisure. It was an ambitious program, which did much credit to the whole kingdom of wood-worms, and instantly placed them, for sheer audacity, alongside

the historic fly on the chariot wheel who remarked, self-appre-
ciatively: "See what a dust I am stirring up!"

And now, there is no better way for this brand-new reproduction of the ancient Spanish house to carry off its intention to
look old — and therefore valuable — than to perpetuate in cold,
hard concrete the ugly stigmata, the scars, the weatherbeatenness
— the wormholes — which testified that the structure was sound
beyond impairment.

The pillar stands there, comfortingly saying: "I have been
here always. I mean to stay here. You need not be fearful, in
this house. It will abide. I have suffered many attacks, but, as
you see, I have been more enduring than my foes. Handle me
and see! Put your fingers on the print of my scars, and be reassured."

Now, as a typical representative of that large lay public which
pretends to no expert knowledge of things architectural, I may
be willing to accept the testimony of that recently cast concrete
pillar, and believe the evidence of its imitation wormholes. An
experienced builder of houses, however, might not be quite so
easily satisfied as to the soundness of it by the testimony of these
scars. He might, indeed, have his suspicions aroused by the in-
finitude of labor and ingenuity spent by the architect to make
the outside of the pillar resemble that of the ancient log which
gave the original structure its unquestioned solidarity. It might
occur to him that the pillar was hollow; that the cost of imitating
wormholes, on the outside, may have been paid out of substantial values omitted from the inside.

And if you were to find him overly suspicious and supercriti-
cal, and say to him: "You never heard of an architect doing such
an unconscionable thing," he might be likely to reply: "But
there was Saint Paul's Cathedral, you know, in which even so
eminent a builder as Sir Christopher Wren spent so much on
decorations that he had to take it out of the pillars, which he
filled with rubble; you remember, don't you, how dreadfully

it cost and how much labor was required to take those tired old pillars down, and replace them with enduring stone?"

But we find this crotchety old builder too querulous for us. We have our precious wormholes; and that means the pillar is sound to the heart!

Something of this same psychology is observable in our estimate of traditional Christianity. If one may, by accommodation, consider it for the moment as an edifice, it is not unfair to say that our appraisal of it rests mostly on what we see of it from where we sit, devoutly, albeit comfortable, in the pew — not judging it as to its structural soundness, nor considering whether its massive pillars may be hollow, or filled with rubble — but reassured of its trustworthiness by the antiquity of the faded paintings on its walls; the aesthetic, time-haunted value of what we see of Old World color sifting through its stained windows, the pictorial reminders of its cherished sacraments, reposeful in the shadowy nooks of the chancel.

These hallowed relics signify that Christianity is here to remain. It is of the eternal. No swinging pendulum ticks its life away. It has no traffic with time, beyond its sonorous chant that it belongs to yesterday, today, and forever.

As we sit in these venerable places (for they are venerable, if for no better reason than because they have been Home to many a heart, and a Rock of Refuge for many a life otherwise quite too difficult to be lived, at all) we completely lose consciousness of the practical fact that these houses of worship, this modern edifice of Christian thought, is, after all's said, but our own attempt to reproduce, in our generation, the cultus of ancient Galilee.

We forget that what we emulate, as Christianity, has traveled a long way, across the miles and years since Jesus walked the narrow, dusty roads of an obscure Roman province, conversing with simplehearted people about the terms of the life everlasting.

As for the plastic and graphic decorations of that gospel, we have been at much pains to preserve every valuable tradition associated with the memorabilia of the early church. We have been careful to retain the local color and flavor of rural Galilee, where Jesus lived. We have reproduced him in his seamless robe and sandals. We have been zealous for his unshorn hair. We have posed him sitting gracefully on a hillside, with his classic draperies arranged just so; his long, slim, artist's hand upraised in tranquil benediction before a multitude of eager faces, alight with a sublime discovery.

Among the most charming of the decorations in our modern edifice of Christian thought are the pastoral scenes traditionally associated with the Master's birth. How delightfully these incidents lend themselves to art! Magi, from the mysterious East, in gorgeous apparel, ride majestically on the sky line of the desert's waste, the rhythmic stride of their tall camels symbolic of that slow but steady advance of the world's Wise Men to the light of Christ's larger understanding. Shepherds, emblematic of that vast, unidentified, social miscellany of the earth, whom Jesus had particularly on his heart, when he declared he had been ordained to preach the gospel to the poor and bring liberty to the oppressed — these shepherds bow, bewilderedly, before the Infant who is to give them new hope and better fortune in the world that had always considered first the welfare of the well-to-do.

With reverence and ingenuity we have brought all these delightful pictures of Palestine, in the Augustan age, to adorn our newer structure of Christian belief and aspiration; and it is to our credit that we still find, in these ancient allegorical themes, a measure of spiritual satisfaction; and he would be no friend of Christ, who, by hint or gesture, minified the quite significant value of such traditions.

With even more earnest zeal — for the climax of Jesus' career deserves a soberer treatment than one's thought of the Nativity — have we reproduced those tragic trappings of Calvary. The pillars of modern Christianity are given an air of verisimilitude, ornamented as they are by scars — scars of a thorn-crown; scars of nails; scars of a scourge; scars of a lance; honorable scars; scars of puny weapons in the hands of puny men, ineffectual scars: scars testifying to the essential strength of that which they futilely strove to destroy: old, dried, healed scars signifying that the opposition to Jesus is over; that his enemies have given it up; that all is clear sailing with him now.

And I should want to be among the last to take umbrage at those blessed scars, or to speak lightly of them, or to deal with them otherwise than with the deepest reverence.

The truth remains, however, that while we have devoted the best of our Christian zeal to the task of reproducing as much of the mood and color of the Master's life as may be gleaned from the traditions of an early church, whose passion for dramatics not infrequently devoured her interest in plain facts, we have been more punctilious about the incidental circumstances of Jesus' career than the essentials of his faith, or the driving motive of his character.

Of all the world's great teachers, none has been so lovingly extolled as to his own moral grandeur. But of all the world's great teachers, none has left a body of moral injunction so feebly practiced by his devotees.

Christmas approaches, and in thousands of churches the Sweetest Story Ever Told will be offered again through the media of the art-forms. Once again, the Word will be made flesh, to dwell among us; and the angels will sing of peace to the world; and the wise will come with their gifts. No detail of that Nativity pageant will seem too trivial to be omitted, for it behooves us to be faithful to our good tradition; and that is right.

But, I wonder what the Christ-spirit really thinks, and whether he does not regard us with an unspeakable sorrow when he sees at what pains we are to reproduce the pictures of his infancy, and how easily we forget the principles of his valor.

I wonder which of those superb qualities of the Galilean mind have most attracted you. Perhaps, if one knew, one could almost tell what manner of person you are, on the inside. Might it be his gentleness? His unfailing courtesy? His sympathetic understanding — his capacity for forgiveness?

I wonder if we have thought with sufficient earnestness about his gallantry? Among all the massed splendors of his idealism it seems to me his steady, unswerving intrepidity is the most appealing virtue he possessed. From the day that he walked out of the little carpenter shop in squalid Nazareth to espouse his mission, until the hour that he hung bleeding slowly to death upon his cross, his life was filled with gallant deeds.

One marvels at it. One does not marvel at the dreaming youth who, disillusioned by men's petty greeds and the tragic merchandising of life's most beautiful opportunities for service and happiness, scorns his own adolescent visions, and plunges into the welter to get what he can — scornful of the shining city of his dreams.

One does not marvel at the pietist, who, disgusted with the apparently incurable jungle-fever of humanity, betakes himself to some monastic seclusion and walls himself in against a world he can neither lead nor follow.

But one does stand in amazement at the gallantry of Jesus who, himself unimpeachable, deals with the willful, half blind, blundering, self-infatuated men surrounding him, in the utmost of courtesy and consideration — quite as if they were entitled to his friendship.

You call the roll of the people he was obliged to confront daily, and see who they were.

There was little, greedy Judas: Judas of the money-bag; Judas, the penurious, the parsimonious; Judas the penny-counter, drawing a long face and trying to look pious over his job as the steward. Jesus permitted himself to walk in that fellow's society for three and a half years — graciously, courteously — aware that when the time came for loyalty to the cause for which the new gospel stood, Judas would flunk it.

There was the loud and swaggering Simon Peter, never quite normal of temperature, given to fevers of affection which embarrassed more than they pleased, and chills of doubt and pessimism, calculated to dampen the spirits of the whole party. And Jesus permitted himself, for three years and a half, to endure Simon Peter, aware that when the hour struck for a big test of devotion, the fisherman would, likely as not, deny any acquaintance with him.

Call the roll of them: John and James, whose only thought, at the last minute, was to secure good seats for themselves in glory; and Thomas, whose faith oozed out of him at a crucial moment; and Philip, who, at the last supper, announces that he really doesn't know what the gospel was about — after three years and a half.

So much for Jesus' close companions.

Look over the list of the religious leaders of the time — the priests, the scribes, the Pharisees with their pretensions; their hypocrisies; their tiresome mummeries.

Take a glance at the public he faced. Why, at the very moment he was talking to them about the majesty of comradely helpfulness and affection, they were tramping one another down, in the crowd, to find better places to see and hear.

One marvels that a man of Jesus' valor, and love of the finer graces of life, did not turn away from the whole greedy, grimy, gluttonous outfit of them, and leave them to wallow in their own stupidities.

But what does one find him saying to such as these? Pretending he does not see how little they were, he continues to talk in terms of a great idealism; what it costs, in courage, to live supremely; underlining the difficulties of discipleship — warning them of its price, as if they were big enough to rally to such a call!

And somehow (I make no pretense of understanding how this was) somehow his very gallantry so impressed a few of them that, when he died, they started out to spread his gospel; and they told their story so convincingly that men are still telling it.

At the moment, however, it must have required a sublime faith to believe that anything could ever accrue from an investment of imputed valor in the lives of so unpromising a crew of blunderers.

Of course, Jesus had some excellent precedents for his hope. Many, many centuries before, in the ancient city of Ur in Chaldea, a little family of passionate dreamers, sickening of the grossness of life in that degenerate place, resolved — not unlike the Pilgrim Fathers, thousands of years later — to cut clear of it all, and find a land where they could breathe unpolluted air, and build their lives over. Without a thought for their risk, and with all attention focused on their visionary goal, they set out to find their dream-country.

It was a long journey, and it took a long time. Young heads that had dreamed that dream turned white, and still they had not found their country. Young faces that had been full of eager longing became seamed and lined and leathery, and still nothing had come to them; not a foot of land. They owned nothing but some purchased graves. But, undaunted, they continued to hope. God, their Father, was in charge of them and their fortunes.

The majestic old book of Hebrews says of them: "They died in faith — not having received the fulfillment of their hope — God having provided that their faith must be vindicated by ours."

Jesus knew that story. Doubtless it helped to sustain his own gallantry. In spite of all the sorry appearances of the world, it was worth saving.

He said there would be a few who would appreciate the necessity of his gospel. They would be the salt of the earth to keep the whole social order from putrefying. It doesn't take much salt to arrest a considerable volume of decay. He said those few would be as a light to the world; and it really doesn't take much light for men to see by — and the darker the world is, the fewer lights are necessary to point the path.

One marvels that he fed his courage on such frail evidences as appeared in the character of his companions. And, as if it were not enough to trust the fortunes of his gospel in their hands, he announced that if he should some day be hustled and pushed and slapped to a gallows-tree, he would draw all men unto him. That remark was the highest compliment ever paid the human race — Jesus' belief that men would have the fine idealism and spiritual discrimination to be lured into moral splendor and high adventure by the appeal of a man on a cross!

He predicated that faith upon the heroic idealism of a few valiant souls, in every age and country, who would believe what he believed — that the world was worth saving: that the world could be saved.

I believe that the strongest pillar that supported the edifice of the original Galilean Christianity was this inextinguishable hope of Jesus — and firm belief of Jesus — that, somehow, in God's good time, the thing could be accomplished!

Exactly at that point — and only at that point — does our confidence in the modern conception of Christianity reside. A hasty survey of our turbulent, discordant, fussy little Christian organizations, in America, is sufficient to show that in our attempted restoration of the gospel edifice, on this soil, some of the pillars — however they may be decorated to give the impression that they are the original, authentic, everlasting underpinning of Christ's culture — are hollow.

And, unfortunately, the general public has found that out. In vain do we call attention to the hallowed antiquity of our Christian traditions. In vain do we mouth euphonious phrases about the church as an anvil that has worn out many a hammer. In vain do we point to the imitation discolorations on the walls, and the imitation wormholes on the pillars, and the sword cuts, scourge welts, chain ulcers, and all the scars of holy martyrdoms — the public has heard a rumor that most of these massive structural supports of the modern Christian church are *hollow*.

They have a fixed ideal connoted by the name of Jesus. They forget all about him for days and weeks and months. They make no profession of trying to follow him. But, deep in the heart of them, they know exactly what Jesus willed for his world; and if they do not obey that will it is not because they think him mistaken, but because they find themselves unable to pay the price of such discipleship. They look longingly toward the churches, and make tours of them, hopeful of at least looking in upon people who are able to pay that price and conform their living to that ideal; somewhat in the mood of the uncourageous little chap who goes to the theater to watch a really whopping hero disposing of his enemies, and calmly stepping over his difficulties. But, mostly they are disillusioned. It is their observation that, taking them by and large, professed Christians in the churches are not much less unhopeful than themselves; not much less uncharitable in their estimates of one another; not much less unkind in what they have to say about other people; not much less prone to quarrel; and bicker, and gossip, and rejoice in iniquity.

And we may talk to that general public all we like about the artistry and ingenuity with which we have restored the symbolisms and sacramenta of the past: they know that many of the pillars of the modern edifice of Christianity are hollow — unsafe — shaky — likely at any moment to come tumbling down!

Do they not read it in the papers? Do they not hear it in the streetcars; at the bridge table, on the golf course — rumors that people in churches behave, in the main, about the way people behave out of the churches? the only difference being that it looks worse, in view of the Christians' professions of merit.

But, one pillar remains that is not hollow — the pillar of Gallantry; the everlasting continuation of Christ's belief that, in spite of our blunders; in spite of the poor material we offer to the ennobling influence of the gospel; in spite of the doubts of the gloomy Thomases, and the unsteadiness of the noisy Simon Peters, and the smug selfishness of the Johns and Jameses, and the stupidity of the Philips, and the treachery of the parsimonious little Iscariots — *if Christ be lifted up, he will draw!*

If that was Jesus' firm belief, it can also be ours. If, from his lonely cross, he can be hopeful of an ultimate victory for idealism, that hope can also be ours. It is not a triumph that may be expected in a day, a decade, or, perhaps, a millennium — but it is on the books that the triumph will eventually arrive! It will not come by might, nor by power; but by his spirit, resistless as the tides.

That idealism is a thing too lofty to be realized by all the people, or by any considerable number of people, in any given age. Humanity has come a long way, since its jungle days. When Jesus encountered it, he was as a light shining into an uncomprehending darkness. Even his own race received him not; knew him not. But, always there were a few who recognized him for what he was.

And as many of them as received him, people who had come into that understanding; not by birth into any special tribe or country; not by the will or persuasion of men, but by the resistless lure of his godly character — to them he gave the right to be known as the Children of God — joint heirs with him of the ancient promises — chosen souls to whom he expects to say, in some shining hour: "Well done, good and faithful, competent in a few things, enter into the joy of your Lord."

Los Angeles
December 9, 1928

the Bethesda pool

NORTH OF THE TEMPLE in Jerusalem there was a gate in the wall through which the shepherds from the hills drove their flocks to the market. It was known as the Sheep-gate. Near it, there was a spring called the Pool of Bethesda. This spring was thought to possess, at times, strange healing qualities.

I have said it was "thought to possess," because I am persuaded that the tradition which made this pool famous had little to commend it but the interest attaching to any ancient and mysterious tale.

The story concerning the spring was to the effect that at certain seasons a kindly disposed angel, whose name nobody seemed to remember, stirred the water, investing it with remedial qualities. Immediately after the visitation of the angel, whoever first stepped down into the pool was cured of whatever disease he had.

There is little doubt but very many people in Jerusalem believed implicitly in this legend, believed in the angel, believed in the pool, and, in the strength of that sincere belief, may have been benefited by plunging into it.

I should dislike to be misunderstood here. There is no mental state which I am quite so free of coveting as that of the skeptic. If there were the slightest warrant for belief in the efficacy of this Bethesda Pool, I should want to be among the last to discredit the legend concerning it. But everything is against the integrity of the legend. Therefore, I do not feel called upon to subscribe to it as an article of my faith.

In the first place, I cannot believe there was any healing quality in that spring because the thoughtful people in Jerusalem evidently did not believe it. They had, indeed, built a pavilion over the pool. This was not because they wished to encourage popular interest in the place but because such a swarm of the sick and wretched continually crowded about it, in the hope of securing help, that common humanity suggested a shelter for them. If the people who built the pavilion had thought there was any actual therapeutic value in this water, they would have stationed some man there to conduct these woebegone wretches down into it. They would have passed a regulation enjoining all the deformed and paralyzed who lay in the streets — a public expense and a public nuisance — to go to that pool and take their turns at being healed.

That quite a delegation of Jerusalem's misery did go to this pool, day after day, waiting for the "troubling of the waters," does not add much, in my opinion, to the authenticity of the legend or the healing virtues of the spring. When, indeed, has not the sufferer of an incurable disease crawled and groped and dragged his weary way from river to spring, from quack to charlatan, from shrine to tomb, searching for physical redemption? It does not require much of a legend to excite the interest of such a man! There is a vast difference between the rational beliefs of a normal man and the last despairing hope of a helpless invalid. The drowning man, "catching at straws," is not to be called absurdly superstitious. His "catching at straws" may not represent a deliberately conceived confession of faith in straws as life-preservers. With him, it is merely the last, blind, fierce struggle to set himself right. I dare say the Pool of Bethesda meant just about as much to the conglomeration of woe that crowded about its slippery ledge, waiting the return of that whimsical, albeit generously inclined angel.

In the second place, I cannot believe that there was any healing virtue in the spring because Jesus did not believe it. He had come to provide health and peace and life. He was not known to have refused a single call for help. He was moved to compassion by the sorrows of his people. He only healed a few of them, comparatively, for they spread over a far-reaching area and his life was so short. But he was touched to sympathy by their woes. If he had believed there was any healing virtue in that spring, he would undoubtedly have recommended it. Once, he visited the pool. He conversed with a man there who for thirty-eight years had been invalided. The sick man complained, bitterly, that he had come there daily, expecting a restoration. Always, somebody less ill than himself leaped into the pool before he could drag his enfeebled body to the edge. Consequently, for want of a friend to lead him into the pool, he stayed there, wretched as ever. There was a pleading tone in his tale which hinted that perhaps this stranger might be the friend he had longed for. Jesus was only too willing to accept the position as friend to a man who stood in need of one. But, instead of waiting with the invalid until the angel came, Jesus healed the man with a word. He had listened in silence to the sufferer's story about the marvelous power of the pool. He spoke no word, he made no sign that would indicate any belief in his own mind concerning the value of this water. And as for healing, he totally ignored this pool and healed him.

As the man departed, carrying his rug, he was halted on the street by a party of citizens who demanded to know why he was carrying his bed on the Sabbath. A Jew dared not carry anything on the Sabbath but his self-complacency.

Now, these law-keeping Jerusalemites had serious objections to any form of employment on the holy day. And if that mysterious angel, who "troubled the waters" of Bethesda, had ever wrought a real miracle on anyone on the Sabbath Day, they would have disapproved of his services. Doubtless it was not unlawful for these sick people to lie about on the flagging all through the Sabbath Day, waiting for a cure, for they were not employed, in the strict sense of the term.

But I fancy it was a rare sight to see people coming away from the Pool of Bethesda carrying their cots. It was rare enough to excite the interest of this man's fellow citizens. They were eager to know how he had been cured. They did not leap to the conclusion that the charmed waters had effected it. They only wanted to know the name of the man who had proved so successful a physician to the long-standing disease of this joyful man who was carrying his bed on the seventh day of the week.

Taking all of these things into consideration, I am unable to believe in the Pool of Bethesda as a healing agent.

But, for the sake of argument, let us agree that this pool was all that the superstitious claimed for it. Let us say that there was an angel hovering over it and that at times he did dip the tips of his wings into the water and that whoever stepped in immediately thereafter was cured of whatever disease he had. Does that not place a heavy burden of responsibility upon these good people of Jerusalem for failing to provide some means of making a fair and just distribution of this healing among the afflicted? Let us admit that this pool was just the place to go for help; was it not monstrously unfair that the persons who had the least ailment should be the most likely to receive a cure while those who were wretchedest of all had the least possible chance ever to gain access to the medicinal waters?

Somehow, I believe that this pool was a fair example of the type of spiritual healing the Jews believed in. The man who, apparently, had the least trouble in his soul was always the man who had first access to the benefits of their religious system. The rich Pharisee, who made a business of his religion, could wade into that elaborately appointed Temple Pool every hour of the day, offer his sacrifices, and absolve himself by all the various expedients which were thought to shrive one of sins. The poor hill-dweller, coming in occasionally with a lamb to offer, was invariably informed that the lamb was blemished and that he had better go to the dealers in the temple corridor who would provide him with a lamb that had been OK'd by the priests. (It was for this knavery that Jesus drove the butchers out of the temple. And it was no wonder the priests were so enraged, for the sacrifice-brokers were handing them a percentage on all such sales. If ever there was a rotten piece of graft, the begowned and bespangled priests in that temple answered for it!)

But, after all, is it not the man who has the least need of healing who always gets into the pool first? I own that this is a pessimistic remark. I wish somebody could successfully challenge it.

Some of our churches are like that Pool of Bethesda. They are equipped handsomely. Nobody can say that considerable care has not been exercised in making them commodious and comfortable. Some of them have "five porches," and most of them have cushioned pews. But there seems to be such a noticeable lack of provision for bringing in just the people who are in such obvious need of its curative agencies. How frequently is it the case that each Sabbath Day finds the same people wading into the pool who have been going there weekly, throughout their lives, passing on their way scores who have no notion of its benefits!

You say, "But the churches are open to all! The people in the churches are only too glad to welcome the very lowest and poorest and give them a word of cheer!" Very well; if you can make out a good case, I will most cheerfully withdraw my motion, assured that my second consent with tears of thankfulness in his eyes. I agree with you that the churches are open. There seems to have been no admission fee at the pavilion with five porches that was built over the Bethesda Pool. I am sure the gospel is offered without money and without price. It appears that no charge was made for entrance into the mysterious pool. But are we solving, in any adequate measure, the problem of leading into the pool the people who seem to be most in need of its healing power?

You say, "It's their own fault! We have built the churches. We are digging deep into our pockets to provide for its maintenance — and the upkeep of the modern church institution is not a problem in pennies and nickels! We have auxiliaries without number trying to interest the public in our work! What more shall we do?"

I don't know, I'm sure. If I did know, by next week I would be figuring in headlines an inch high in a thousand metropolitan papers. I am not laying it to the charge of any man or any system that this state of affairs exists. I am only soliloquizing upon the fact that it does exist. We have the pool and we have the pavilion but, for some reason utterly inexplicable, the very people who ought to go into the pool first are not going in at all.

Jesus strolled down to the Pool of Bethesda on the Sabbath Day. We are not told why he went there. We overhear his conversation with the impotent man and see the latter, a few moments later, going away with his bed on his shoulder, while Jesus is retreating in another direction without pausing further to investigate the pool or wait for an interview with the angel, whom he probably would have known, since it was a good angel.

If he were to approach one of our pools on the Sabbath Day, I do not know just what attitude he would assume toward them or toward the pavilions we have built over them. I have often wondered just what he thinks of our churches. Of course, it is the badge of a wicked and perverse generation to seek after a sign; but I am almost ready to submit to that classification, for myself, and desire the sign anyway. I wish he would give us some notion of his estimate of our work. That we are failing to solve our problem successfully ought to be obvious to every man who has to do with church endeavor.

Would it not be a hard blow to our pool and our pavilion and our angel if he should happen by, some Sabbath, and, without taking our institution into the slightest account, relieve some man of his distresses for whose case we had made no provision?

This is a long story in The Book. It shall be a short one here.

The Jews were enraged because Jesus had wrought this cure on the Sabbath. Oh, but they were so easily enraged! They were forever rending their robes and pouring ashes on their heads and tearing out their beards whenever anybody succeeded in accomplishing anything worth the mention! They found Jesus and questioned him. He replied in an address of some length. In the course of this speech, he said, "Search the Scriptures!" I can easily imagine the weary look on his face and the gesture which accompanied the words. "Search the Scriptures! In them ye think ye have eternal life; and they indeed testify of me! But ye will not come unto *me* that ye might have life!" He was saying, in substance, "Ye study about me; ye philosophize concerning me; ye dogmatize over me; ye theorize upon me; ye do everything but come unto me!"

Now, he might be inclined to say much the same thing to us. "Ye have my Book on your pulpit, my cross on your altar, my portrait on your windows, my paten and chalice, my crown of thorns, my royal purple, my white burial sheet. Ye have everything that belongs to me except myself!"

This angel that visited the Pool of Bethesda seems to have been irregular in his attendance in this congregation of suffering. Nobody knew but he would come three times today and absent himself for a week. This undoubtedly had the effect of keeping the sick people everlastingly on the lookout for him. I suppose they never felt at liberty to take their eyes off that water. And immediately upon seeing the waters move, there was a grand scramble for the steps. How strange an angel!

There is a bit more system about our pool. There are "certain seasons," to be sure, but they are always announced in the papers and posted on the bulletin board. There is Lent, and the revival services, and the Week of Prayer, and any number of special occasions when our pool seems invested with more virtues than upon ordinary occasions.

In this respect, our heart-sick and soul-sick have the advantage of those poor invalids crawling about on the flagging at Bethesda.

But it seems to make little difference. Even at that, the most wretched of all are not going down into the pool. Now, if you have a remedy for this condition, just state it and you will be famous by tomorrow noon.

Luther Place Memorial
Washington, D.C.

Inspire us to be grateful for our heritage, and mindful of our duty to preserve it.

Forbid that through any selfishness or slothfulness we should let slip the priceless bequest of freedom and fellowship.

nevertheless

He said unto Simon: "Launch out into the deep, and let down your net."
And Simon answered: "Master, we have toiled all night, and taken nothing: nevertheless at thy word I will lower the net."
— Luke V: 4,5

CERTAIN OCCUPATIONS — especially those which grapple with Nature at close grips — are bounded by traditions and superstitions not easily cast aside.

One of these vocations is fishing. You do not make a successful fisherman by reading scientific books on the subject. You have to be born to it. It is necessary that your father was a fisherman, and his father, and his great-grandfather. The feel for it has to be fixed in the blood stream.

The fisherman needs but few instruments of precision in his business. He gets on without a barometer. His bad knee will tell him when the glass is low; or, if he is too young and vigorous to have acquired a bad knee, his father's will do just as well.

He comes to have a well-developed sixth sense for judging the exact direction and velocity of the wind. He knows all about the moon. He can tell you next day's weather from the shape and color of the clouds. If you ask him to write down a page of signs and symptoms by which these matters are to be determined, he will not be able to do so. His knowledge is intuitive, rather than rational. And because that is true of his knowledge, there is no use talking him out of it; for *What he knows does not respond to argument.*

He knows what he knows, though he knows not why.

One has to remember all this about Simon Peter and his trade, if one wants to understand exactly what it cost him — that day — to say: *"nevertheless."*

Not meaning that "nevertheless" is an easy word to pronounce — even for other people than fishermen — as we shall see; but meaning that it is an especially difficult word for those *who have come by what they know . . . through inherited traditions.*

Simon was a fisherman, as had been his father Jonas before him. Simon never asked himself, when he climbed into his boat: "Well — where shall we fish today?" For wind and weather, sign and season, sky and sea, determined his course.

Even at that — there might be some disappointing hitch in the proceedings . . . for there was the problem of sheer caprice to be reckoned with. You obeyed all the rules. Sometimes you caught fish: sometimes you didn't.

Life was a good deal like that. You could obey all the laws from your youth up, and still feel, sometimes, that you'd missed the mark; that you'd left something out: that you hadn't arrived at the main thing.

But . . . here were the rules. And you'd better follow them. . . . For example: it was better to fish in shoal water. That was what old Jonas' father had believed and practiced. He had had it from *his* father. And who was Jonas that he should venture to introduce a new method? And who was Peter, that he should break a sound old tradition like that?

Doubtless Peter wondered, sometimes, as old Jonas had wondered, whether there might not be some very good, very large, very valuable fish out in the deeper water; but, as everybody knew and had always known, proper, orderly, orthodox fishing was restricted to the shallows; so . . . *Peter kept to the shallows.*

Perhaps one should be prudent about inviting a little story like this to deliver up a profound ethical doctrine; but is it not a fact that a very great deal of our exploratory efforts in trying to lay hold on life's desirables are restricted, by custom and tradition, to the mere shallows of experience?

Of course, we have a notion, in our time and industry, that we are quite valiant with our pioneering. The modern equivalent of Old Jonas not only expects but hopes that his son Simon Peter will leave all this soggy, smelly business of catching fish . . . and find a nicer, cleaner job in town; a profitable little silk shop, maybe; and Old Jonas will boast to inquisitive tourists: "Yes . . . my boy Simon. . . . He's doing well in trade . . . down in Jerusalem. . . . You couldn't keep that boy in the country. . . . No, sir!"

But this urbanity, that we've made so much of, does not mean we've left off fishing in the shallows of life. . . .

Consider, for instance, our *intellectual pursuits.* How shallow they are; for the most part! For the vast majority of us, the scope of our reading is narrowly bounded by the passing news of the moment; the current sensation; the latest fear; to-day's alarm.

As for the wider, deeper information concerning *life* — not in its merely acute mutations and pulsations — but in its general trend of relatively permanent progress — we are largely unaware of it.

As for the possibilities of our emotional life, we hardly scratch the surface of it; hardly know what our souls are good for; rarely put them on their mettle; possess only a bit of routinish knowledge of their *shallows;* know next to nothing about their *depths.*

One would have thought that some fine day, young Simon Peter, gripped by an inquisitive mood, would say to himself:

"I'm going out to try it in deep water: black water: and see what comes of it." . . . But he never did . . . because it wasn't customary.

One morning, as Simon returned to his usual location on the beach, after a whole night's unsuccessful fishing, he saw quite a crowd collected. Doubtless it was that young Nazarene, again, who had such a captivating way with him. Simon could have wished that he might be able to unload a good catch from his boat; it was rather humiliating to come in, empty-handed.

However, he was no worse off than the others. His was not the only empty boat, that morning. Simon might be unsuccessful; but he had plenty of company. And perhaps he found some consolation in *that*. Most people do. When they reflect that they are not getting anywhere in the business of living, they glance at their neighbors and say: "Oh, well — I'm no worse off than the rest of them," which, in the main, is true, but does not solve the problem proposed by our dissatisfied souls.

Again, we must be cautious here about overemphasizing the details of this story; but it is almost impossible to pass by one little remark in the narrative as reported by Luke.

The fishermen (Simon, as usual, most conspicuous of all) drew up near shore and began washing their nets. That explained what kind of fishing they had been doing. They had been raking their nets through the weeds and the muck of their favorite shoals.

The crowd swarmed down to the water-edge, and Jesus stepped into Simon's boat; and from that vantage continued his talk to the people. We are not explicitly informed about the subject of the address, but it is not unreasonable to conjecture that the talk had to do with the larger issues of the spiritual life.

One of the distinguishing features of the greatest preacher who ever taught was the ease and skill with which he adapted the little commonplaces, at hand, to purposes of illustration. Jesus always knew what the crowd was thinking about, and chose his luminous parables from such materials.

A throng of hungry thousands in the desert — to whom the uppermost thought is "What shall we eat?" — is challenged to solve its own problem by a spectacular feat of sharing what little there was at hand.

A company of irascible nationalists, hoping to get Jesus into trouble with the Romans, invites him to discuss the problem of taxation; and he says: "Hand me a coin." And he talks about the coin.

When his disciples comment about a barren fig tree, the episode is good for an intensive discussion of responsibility in bringing forth fruit commensurate with one's capacity.

How natural indeed, if, today, while Simon and Andrew, and John and James threshed the water with their muddy, weed-tangled nets, in full view of this audience made up of persons presumably acquainted with the fishing industry — *how natural* if Jesus were to use these muck-stained nets as his point of departure.

That was the trouble *with our Life; wasn't it?* We never really got out into it far enough . . . Always too close to the shore . . . The deep things of the spirit were usually left unexplored. Why did we not get along better with our neighbors? Why did we allow little worries to menace our peace and poise? Why did we depend upon hard-driven bargains and short weights to furnish our prosperity? Why did we argue and haggle and *generally scour* the mucky shoals of life looking for values . . . and lack the courage and the faith to let down the net into deep water? Always looking for good purchases of things that the moth and rust would devour — but rarely searching for the sublime treasure deep in the heart of a friend. Always concerned about the wheat crop, but almost never pausing to consider the lilies of the field — how they grow. Always thinking of life in terms of appetite, and almost never thinking of it in terms of *aspiration.*

Now, had Jesus been himself a fisherman, perhaps it would have been easier for Simon to listen to this kind of talk. Simon was entirely respectful, but it is easy to see he took no stock in the deep-water theory. He says: "We have toiled all night and have taken nothing" — and I suppose we are at liberty to suspect that the rest of the sentence, which he *thought* but did not *say,* for courtesy's sake, may have run something like this:

"If *we,* who have grown up on this lake, and learned to fish when we were little boys, and know all the habits of the fish, and where they are likely to be found at given times and under certain weather conditions, have nothing to show for a whole night's work — it goes without saying that a carpenter, who never caught a fish in his life, would be a poor counsellor. Nevertheless," said Simon, "if you say so, we will put the nets down deeper."

It was this "nevertheless" of Simon Peter's that made a great man of him, in the days that were to follow.

"Nevertheless" is a very important word in the vocabulary of heroism. Later, when the great crowds of curiosity-seeking country people, having heard Jesus propose a way of life so exacting that they began to leave, by scores, and it seemed as if the Master had undone his influence over them (and even the little group of disciples, themselves, were disturbed, bewildered, and disappointed), it was Simon Peter's rallying cry that saved the day for them. Things looked bad for the new gospel, that afternoon, and we appeared to be losing ground, but, *nevertheless,* "Thou art the the Christus. Thou hast the words of eternal life."

It's a word that carries the tang of high adventure; reckless valor; and the faith that overcomes the world.

"If it be possible," prayed Jesus, "let this cup pass — nevertheless. . . ."

"We are creatures of blind fate," growls the cynic, "and it's silly to look for divine guidance." "Nevertheless," replies the voice of faith, "we are in our Father's care."

"You cannot change God's plans for you," shouts the cynic. "Your prayers are ridiculous." "Nevertheless," replies the confident voice, "I shall continue to ask in faith, believing."

"What's this nonsense about finding prosperity by giving one's hard-earned things away," sneers the cynic, "and winning battles by refusing to fight — and seeking a crown by bearing a cross?" "Nevertheless," answer the adventurers. "*Nevertheless.*"

"You have fished the shoals all your life," shout the fishermen. "You know there's nothing out there in the dark water." "Nevertheless," says Simon, "at his word I will lower the net."

So — according to Luke's account — Simon Peter moved out into deeper water . . . Contrary to the best traditions among fishermen, there was a great catch out in the deep water — so great that all the other boats in the vicinity were hailed to come and help drag in a net that wasn't used to such prosperity.

Of course, there is always a temptation to make a scriptural narrative seem to mean a great many things that may or may not have been intended. In this misfortune the Bible shares honors with Shakespeare, who probably never meant to be as canny and omniscient as one is led to believe by the younger crop of Ph.D.s.

We mustn't try to load this episode about the good day's fishing with modern instances whose relations thereunto may be of the sketchiest sort. However, the comment of the Master, himself, quite justifies our feeling that there is a significant allegory here. When the jubilant fishermen — flushed with success — have returned with their cargo — Jesus says: "Henceforth ye shall fish for *men.*"

If one takes a steady look at the twelve disciples — under the guidance of Jesus — they are seen to represent, in miniature (as to volume) The Church of Christ, as its Author would like to see it operate. Not as to incidental details, perhaps, which belong to a given time and country — but as to essential motives and ultimate aims.

These untutored country men, going out to win the interest of their neighbors in a saving deal, were in the business of making popular a new social commonwealth of the spirit. They were to be fishers of men. The processes of the Church have been changed, somewhat, to be made adaptable to progress and the varying demands of a civilization infinitely more complex than at the beginning of the Christian Era; but the Church's business remains the task of winning wistful humanity to a more abundant life here and hereafter.

May it not be conceivable that in our endeavor to win the support of men for this world-saving ideal, we have been fishing too close to the shore, and relying too heavily upon traditions which may have little to warrant them beyond the fact that we have grown accustomed to them — and have ventured upon no experiments which might dispute them?

Lately we have been passing through a perplexing period which we have often characterized by the phrase, "deep water." "We have come into deep water," we say. Very well — what's to come of it? Is this deep water a threat or a promise? Assuming we are in deeper water than we are quite accustomed to — what are we out here for? — To sink, or to fish? To worry or to work?

In normal times, churches may very well pursue the processes best know to them. They help support the missionary and philanthropic work of their sect. They bring their own children up through the church school, and frequently write a few new names on the church roster. Critically examined, a great deal of this work is the mere conservation of *that which is already theirs*.

In a time like ours, we are quite justified in putting our nets down into the deeper water. We should be able to offer — in these problematical days — a message of hope and courage and faith that will appeal to a larger and more remote constituency composed of people whom we had previously thought inaccessible to us. In fact, we have thought very little about them. Now and again we have lumped them all into one big, loose category, and have referred to them as "the unchurched" — as if they all had the same reasons for taking no interest, and were — in their lack of spiritual curiosity — as nearly alike as peas in a pod; whereas their apparent lack of interest has to be accounted for on almost as many different grounds as the number of such individuals.

It hasn't been so very long since we used to stage an annual evangelistic revival — which was gradually abandoned when it was seen that a strictly sentimental appeal, while it *did* capture and retain a small percentage of the people stirred by it, only amounted to a transient psychosis in the experience of the majority.

But unless we can think of some saner, more steady and permanent method of fishing in deeper water, we are very likely to see a *return* to this emotional appeal, with all the attendant hysterias and extravagances which — unfortunately — are inevitable to any wild dissipation in sentiment — no matter how good, in itself.

The much better method is for individual Christians, who honestly believe that the gospel is able to reconstruct our disordered society, to make a consistent effort to bring that fact to the attention of friends not already under definite religious influence.

As the matter stands, while our churches are doing an intensive work with a fair degree of success, our methods are quite inadequate to reach the much larger public. We must recover from the idea which many of us hold — that the apparently irreligious — who go to the movies on Sunday instead of to church; and do not even own a Bible, much less read it; and have no interest in the conventional forms and observances of the church — are, by these tokens, of a different order of humanity from ourselves.

These people have the same problems that *we* have, for the reason that they are living under the same conditions, so far as active, secular life is concerned. They hurry to catch the same trams that we try to catch; and come downtown to do much the same kind of work in which we are engaged — encountering the same physical and moral difficulties and anxieties that *we* have.

When we contrive to get acquainted with them — well enough to win their confidence — we discover that, underneath a quite transparent film of assumed bravado (which is only a form of whistling in the dark) they are just as clamorous for a driving motive and the achievement of a better inner contentment, as we are. All that we have known of them is the mere weedy, sandy shoals of their lives: their *depths* are as *our depths*.

One of the most interesting incidents of this Galilean fishing experiment occurs when Simon Peter calls to all the other boats to come and help draw in the laden net. It would take a very unusual occasion to make a fisherman quite so magnanimous. Simon Peter doesn't ordinarily invite Zebedee and his sons to hurry over and share his catch . . . Indeed, when James' and John's anchor drags and their boat drifts a little too close to Simon's, there are a few remarks exchanged which add nothing to the sum of human felicity. But when the catch is so impressive that one can afford to forget all the little parochial restrictions, and call to the neighbors to come and load their boats, there is some promise of a genuine organization of fishermen who have forgotten their little rights to fish in the far bigger job of actually *Catching fish*.

We have had a good deal to say, lately, about the Unity of Christians, the abandonment of denominational party-cries, the pooling of our interests for the sake of the larger task. We will get that when somebody's net is full to the breaking-point.

We will rid ourselves of the constraints which keep us apart, and mutually suspicious — *when we have decided to lower the nets into deeper water.*

St. James United Church
Montreal
November 20, 1932

> *However precious may be to us the measures we have taken for our own spiritual culture, may we, like the obedient fisherman of Galilee, be willing — nevertheless — to obey our Master's word.*
>
> *Make us discontented with the shallows, when we might invade the deep.*

the task of the church
in this generation

I PRESUME the average layman, whose interest in the church as an institution — if it may be predicated of him at all — is purely casual, would regard the topic of this sermon with some impatience. Says he: "After two thousand years of activity, the Christian Church, one would think, ought to know by this time exactly what it is trying to accomplish." He regards the question as absurd.

Were the church a brand-new something that had sprung up a week ago last Tuesday, the matter would be different. But here we have the oldest organization in the world — from point of consecutive and sequential history — still defining and redefining its aims — still asking itself what its chief business is — still inquiring which, of its many versatile interests, is entitled to the bulk of its time and effort.

But, on a second glance, the query is not so absurd or self-indicting as it seems. For, on examination, the question does not have to do with the generic ideal but with the technique by which that generic ideal may most readily be reached.

When Christopher Columbus crossed the Atlantic Ocean in 1492, his sole ambition was to discover a western passage from Europe to Cathay. The discovery of America, in the course of that adventure, was either accidental, incidental, or providential, accordingly as the individual views such famous by-products of important quests. I do not pause to debate this matter with you, just now, for my business with the circumstance does not happen to lie in that quarter, today.

Enough to say that however more rewarding may have been Christopher's voyage — in the light of a failure rather than a success to achieve his original goal — he did not find that shorter western passage to Cathay. And the reason for his failure was the fact that the American continent presented a solid front of impenetrable coast, clear to the Horn, thus making imperative a trip of far greater length than the old route eastward.

Still hopeful, however, of making portage across the narrow neck of land which united the two great Americas, early navigators and explorers turned their attention, at once, to the problem of thrusting through that slender barrier with their boats.

In 1550, a Portuguese engineer published a book in which he demonstrated the feasibility of a canal. Within two years a memorial was presented to Philip the Second, urging that the work be attempted without delay.

In 1698, work was actually begun, and continued until the problem became too serious, economically, for practical solution.

In 1771, the Spanish government ordered a survey, looking toward resumption of the work. Political difficulties in Europe frustrated the endeavor.

In 1808, Alexander von Humboldt carefully examined the situation, and reported that the project *could* be put through. After that, at intervals of two or three years, various governments took the matter up — and always postponed action.

Came then the epidemic of gold fever, breaking out on the west coast of the United States — bringing renewed fervor to the hope for that necessary canal. In the course of the explorations which followed, nine separate and distinct courses were platted. The navy sent experts, the army sent experts, private engineering concerns sent experts. Everybody was agreed that there had to be a canal. Nobody was agreed on where it should be put through, or how it should be put through, or *who* should put it through. Except for these minor obstacles, the canal was going forward splendidly.

In 1879, an International Congress, with delegates from all the great world Powers, convened in Paris to talk canal. After a two weeks' session it was determined that France should be permitted to build it, at once, under the management of Ferdinand de Lesseps. The organization bought out all the previous concessions for ten million francs, and went to it — failing three times to raise enough money to start the project — but finally gaining enough momentum to justify an actual beginning. After two years of surveys, de Lesseps launched a task estimated at eight years' hard digging and the cost of six hundred fifty-eight million francs. In six years, the company had taken out seventy-two million cubic yards of dirt, had spent a billion and a quarter francs, and had gone hopelessly bankrupt.

A new company took over the machinery and the ditch, refinanced the undertaking, and went at it again.

The story is getting too long. May it be sufficient to say that — at length — after failure had been piled upon failure until the whole enterprise became a huge international joke, heavily saturated with tragedy, our own government attempted to do this thing. We couldn't, because the old problem of *labor* was as serious with our engineers as it had been with all their predecessors. Men could not work down there. They grew sick, and died like flies.

Then we found out that we must keep the workmen well, else the canal could never be dug by *any*body. We found that it *wasn't* an engineering problem, at root. It was a problem of health. So we sent medical men. They found it was a problem in malaria, caused by insect bites. We sent entomologists and chemists. They hunted down the insect responsible for the infection. They found it and exterminated it; and so, we built the canal.

Now; all the time, these various groups of hardy and heroic adventurers — from a dozen nations, and stretching over a period of at least four hundred years — knew in a general way *what* they were trying to do. They were still actuated by the Christopher Columbus motive — to find a short route to the West.

It was a sheer matter of technique — what route was best; what policy was most expedient; what method was most practicable. In the end, the whole difficulty was simmered down to the apparently trivial business of *killing mosquitoes.*

I have spent a lot of time reviewing this old tale — but I believe it was worth the bother if it helps anybody to understand *how* and *why* the ancient quest of the Christian Church, to thrust its way through to a more abundant life for an increasingly larger number of people, is constantly undergoing fresh appraisal, as new generations of idealists attempt to solve the problems incident to this task.

According to the crude and vague map in the mind of Columbus, all he had to do, to reach the extreme western world, was to sail west. At length he would find it. All he had to do was sail on.

According to the mind of the early Christian Church, the problem of arriving at the actual goal of their endeavor was a simple matter of waiting patiently until the Ultima Thule was sighted from the crow's nest. They expected the end of the world in their own time. They were sure that the world was due for a gigantic and dramatic wind-up, while they lived.

There was no need for social service — or the practical cleaning-up of their poverty-cursed communities — for the end was in sight — and in the great Assize, all the grime would be washed away, the diseases healed, and the redeemed of the Lord *saved,* by some miracle of grace, for the enfabled delights of a world to come.

But, presently, it became apparent — as it came to Columbus that he had not found his goal, but only a tremendous obstacle to that goal — it became apparent that the world was to go *on*. There were no mysterious signs in the sky. The moon had not turned to blood; and the stars had not fallen as blasted figs; and the mountains had not tumbled into the sea. Every morning brought the dawn, and evening the twilight; spring brought flowers, summer brought fruit, and winter brought snow. The world was going on.

The whole Christian enterprise had to be reappraised on a new basis.

It was still intent upon the ultimate goal — a splendid life in a better world — but, prefatory to that splendid life, arrangements must be made for carrying on *here*, as happily and effectively as might be. So — there was a sudden flare of interest in the *organization* of Christian idealism. About this time a powerful emperor embraced the new cultus — and lent to it not only his prestige, but all the machinery which was then considered indispensable to massed power.

And if anybody had inquired (as doubtless the thoughtful *did* inquire) in the second, third, and fourth centuries, exactly what was the task of the Christian Church — I dare say the reply would have been phrased in an eloquent gesture toward the huge religious monarchy which — dictating policies to temporal kings — and laying down terms to secular armies — surely spoke for itself in the extent and degree of its power.

Once a forward-looking apostle had said of Christ: "And he must reign until he hath put all enemies under his feet." The thing was coming true! Christ was a King. The church was his army. He was going to pound his gospel into the world until there wasn't an agency in the world so audacious or impertinent as to question the absolute sovereignty of this Heaven-guaranteed social state.

But too much authority, distilled and concentrated and focused in the lives of a few, usually leads to disaster; and the very success of the thing came to be its own chief menace.

Whatever of sincerity had escaped the blighting influence of a parading and swanking Christianity, all togged out in cloth of gold and exotic decorations — slipped quietly out into the hills and prayed for a return to the stately simplicities which had dignified his life who spoke to the multitudes in the calm of the Galilean hillsides.

And had one asked — in those days — what was the distinctive *task* of the church, the noblest spirits in it would have pointed to the humble monasteries, in the mountains, where the pick and flower of the Christian system wrestled in penitence and prayer for a re-illumination of the church, and a rehabilitation of its spiritual life.

The time came when not all that monasticism and pious penury could do to beguile the organization from its money-mad and power-hungry course, was any longer considered practicable. A definite break must be made from the old machine — and it came in the form of a reformation. It was a sort of combination reformation, revolution, renaissance, iconoclasm, and secession — which filled the air with a clamor of discordant voices, all aiming, doubtless, at one ultimate goal, but proposing scores of diverse routes presumably leading to it. The reforming tendency contrived to break itself into fragments.

If one may hark back, for a moment, to the great canal project — the motive of which was to open the way to the Western World — there was a time when men became so contentious for their individual opinions as to the best route, that they completely lost sight of the ideal.

There was a time when the engineers quite left off talking about the sublimity of their common hope to reach Cathay — and were battering each other over the head on the score of their differences as to whether the best route across the isthmus was via Nicaragua, Panama, San Blas, Caledonia Bay, Darien, the Atrato River, or the Truando, or the Tuyra. I have left out some sixteen other routes, partly because I hope I have made my case, and mostly because I can't pronounce their names.

Had you asked any one of the contenders for these separate routes how he felt about the whole canal business, he would have replied that the canal could and would be dug, when and if some country was able to show sufficient sanity to go across by the particular route to which he was committed. He wasn't trying to open up a way for the east and the west to clasp hands: he was trying to demonstrate the superiority of digging through by way of Nicaragua, or Caledonia Bay, or Darien — or whichever of the score of projected passages happened to appeal to his mood, temper, and understanding.

Keep it in mind that — in the end — the question wasn't whether it was a better way to go by Caledonia Bay, or San Blas, or the Atrato River. The problem, in its last analysis, was: *who* can kill the mosquitoes? Let us have the mosquitoes killed, and we can go across *any way* — by the Atrato, or San Blas, or Darien — or what-have-you.

It wasn't long after the reforming parties got under full momentum that the task of the church — had anyone paused to ask about it — was not, apparently, a concerted effort on the part of a unified mass of people, to strive for a more abundant life; but a mere tumult of pious engineers, each contending for the supremacy of the route his surveying gang had staked off.

To one group, the thing was to be baptized by a special, certain technique. Unless you had your baptism that way, you weren't baptized, at all. To another group, the thing was to construe the Lord's Last Supper according to a certain formula. If you took it that way, you were in line for a conferment of grace. If you had it some other way, it not only did you no good: you were a humbug into the bargain. Sects were differentiated from one another on such major points as having an organ or not having an organ in the church building; having a cross on the altar or not having a cross on the altar; allowing only ministers to speak who had experienced ordination at the hands of certain ecclesiastical dignitaries, or letting anybody speak who thought he had something to say; churches that read prayers from a book, and churches that composed them on the spot; churches that conducted high-pressure revivals, brimming with hysteria and mob-complexes, and churches that approached the subject of religion in the calmness of approximate sanity; churches that held to feet-washing as a sacrament, and churches that didn't; churches that said "you" and churches that said "thou"; churches that denounced fiddles and theatres, and churches that thought fiddles and theatres might be all right.

But the racket was so tremendous that the original idea of trying to open up a new way into an undiscovered world was drowned in the clamor about the routes thither.

Today; we are still inquiring about the church's distinctive task. Let us see if we are agreed among ourselves as to the nature of that endeavor.

A common expression among us, when the subject of religion is touched upon in a group where are assembled representatives of various cults, is: "Oh, well; we're all bound for the same place. It matters little what we believe, so long as we are sincere." That statement is good enough to use as a plug to stop up a sudden leak in the controversial plumbing of a much mixed assembly; but, in actual fact, it lacks a great deal of the truth.

We are *not* all going to the same place, if the various statements of our hopes and beliefs concerning a future life mean anything at all. The Catholic is going into a sort of purgatorial vestibule of Heaven, where he must tarry until enough credits have been deposited to his account — either accrued from his own estate — or provided by his heirs and assigns — to justify his promotion into something better. Due to the special spiritual activity of the saints and martyrs — and the prayers of the faithful — there has been created a general sinking fund of merit which can be drawn upon, through masses and private pieties, and thus transferred to the account of the individual who lingers in purgatory, awaiting his clearance papers.

When, therefore, my good friend the Catholic remarks to me — apropos of our unity in the generic elements of Christianity — "Oh, well; we're all going to the same place," I smile and nod my head — obviously rejoicing that we have no quarrel about the *fundamental* things — but, in very truth, I am not intentionally booked for any such adventure; and if I thought my future welfare depended upon the caprice of friends, left behind — rather than upon a fair and just appraisal of my own spiritual status — I should consider the whole celestial arrangements a mere tangle of accidents and injustices in a land of scientized topsy-turvydom.

Mind; I do not say that these people are wrong, and I am right, for nobody knows, certainly; and we are all *guessing*, with the best intentions in the world, and according to what light we have. I am only saying that — so far as Hope and Expectation are concerned — the Catholic and I are not bound for the same place, at all. And if I ever arrive where he says he is bound for, I shall be not only disappointed, but disillusioned and dismayed.

Furthermore; when a man says, "It makes little difference what we believe, so long as we are sincere" — I have to remember that a farmer may be no end honest and industrious in planting his fields — but the nature of his harvest does depend, very heavily, upon the type of seed he sows. I do not mean that any one seed is — at all points — superior in value to every other seed: I only mean that if a man sows clover seed, he mustn't try to cultivate it with a plough, or harvest it with a corn-husking machine.

> *Our little systems have their day;*
> *They have their day and cease to be:*
> *They are but broken lights —*

All well and good; but, so long as we have our little systems let us try to make them as consistent as possible to their own specific aims and processes.

If the Catholic wants to look forward to a future life more or less commercially arranged for, out of the sinking fund bequeathed from the saints and martyrs — let him put himself into the good graces of said saints and martyrs, while he lives — so that he may stand a good chance of a favorable hearing, when the time comes that a receivership is appointed for his soul, in purgatory, and negotiations impend for the adequate settlement of his affairs.

Let him stick to his text; and make all his theories fit together. I respect him for them; and I wish him well in his practice of them. He might do worse. He has a lot of tradition back of him; and whoever sneers at his superstitions would do better to spend some time and bother examining his own.

I have no objection to make to the belief of people who stake their claims upon the textual accuracy of a Holy Book — ours, or any other. There is a good deal to be said in behalf of a faith that has absolute and unquestioned authority for its claims. It entitles the believer to a certain sense of ease and surety and finality, which must — to the one who can hold to it, honestly and without effort — bring a peace and satisfaction assuredly not to be had by people who candidly assert that they are *seekers for the truth.*

The literalist is not a seeker for truth. He has no need to be a seeker. The truth is all there, before him, in the Book. Let him be able to *read:* that is all the machinery he requires; or, if he cannot read, let him be able to *listen.* It is an easy road, because it is surveyed — every step of the way: and the signboards are posted so that the wayfaring man, though a fool, need not err therein.

Now, this literalist — who stakes his all on the accuracy and infallibility of a Sacred Book (the Bible, we will say) — should concentrate his attention at that point, and be in every way consistent with the ethics, and natural philosophy it teaches. He should be wary of extraneous issues which cloud his final authority. Strangely enough, the typical literalist of the day is an advocate of a curious jumble of doctrines, many of which have no background in the Bible, at all; but are the deliverances of ecclesiastical councils, resolved upon in an age when the Bible was not the seat of final authority, but subsidiary to the decrees of the church.

With persons of our type and training, the church is a school for spiritual culture. And, that being true, our chief task is to conduct the church on the same basis as any other educational institution. We may not say of any particular textbook — not even the Bible — that it contains *all the truth;* for education understands that truth is being constantly modified by accretions of fresh knowledge.

Even in the ethical field, where, one might think, an adequate moral code for one generation should be equally serviceable to all other generations — it is to be discovered that new occasions teach new duties.

The Christian's duty to the state may be one thing — when everybody believes that the end of the world is imminent, and Judgment Day is at hand — and quite another thing in an age when practically everybody believes that the world must carry on, indefinitely. . . . For, whereas the problems of social justice, international peace, the healing of diseases, the reformation of delinquents, and the proper training of youth for citizenship were of no concern to a generation which expected, at any moment, the climax of all mundane activities — such matters must loom large in the mind of a generation which believes the world is good for another million years or so.

To the church that considers itself a school for spiritual culture, it is important that it keep itself adjusted to the ever changing demands of an ever changing civilization.

So; our first desire is for *more light.*

There is a type of faith that confesses itself a bit skeptical about more light. It feels that day-by-day information concerning the world is too secular, too materialistic, too earth-earthily close to the ground to fit into a mystical Hope that believes without proving, and trusts without query. Such a Faith has frequently been pointed to — even by commercial interests — seeking reasons for blocking the progress of advancing techniques in civilization.

For instance — when it was proposed in New York, to install gas lighting on the streets, the *Koelnische Zeitung,* a German daily which apparently had some vital interest in keeping the old oil-lantern system in vogue, editorially stated its objections to a more adequate process of lighting — the first paragraph of which read: "Artificial illumination is an attempt to interfere with the divine plan for the world, which has preordained darkness during night-time."

Now if the church that considers itself a school, wishes to maintain a position of self-respect, it must do a minimum of talking about the things and conditions which it believes are preordained. People who declare that they know what things are preordained prove nothing but the dismaying extent to which human impertinence can go in exalting private guesses to the estate of general forecasts.

The task of the modern church is to give every light-producing agency in the world full liberty to demonstrate its hope that all men may see clearer — and understand better — the road over which our common pilgrimage must be made.

It is the modern church's business, for example, to know something about science: not in the capacity of a school of science, to be sure, for it hasn't the facilities to do that, if that were its function — but it must have a care to avoid staking the elemental hypotheses of its faith upon postulates which the tireless students of the material world have proved untrue — and must have an equal zeal to recognize and applaud every discovery of science — leading to increased knowledge — even if such discoveries are disconcerting to traditional beliefs, and insistent upon revisions of our ancient and hallowed phraseologies.

We have no quarrel with the literalist who proceeds on the assumption that the truth about God, and Man, and Nature is all in hand: People who can derive spiritual satisfaction from that position should be unmolested. Our controversy with them begins only when they forsake their attitude of *ignoring* science, and themselves turn scientific — endeavoring to show — as the New York *Koelnische Zeitung* endeavored to show — that a better lighting system for the world is an attempt to interfere with the divine plan which preordained darkness at night.

It must be remembered that some very excellent people have gone in wholeheartedly for the demonstration of a pet theory, to the complete obscuration and neglect of everything else. Even so zealous and valorous an old Christian soldier as Paul, for example. This man gets himself into an "other-worldly" state of mind to the exclusion of every earthly urge men were experiencing — in the hope of making this life more pleasant, profitable, and effective.

In Paul's time, experiments had already been made by inquiring physicists, looking toward mechanical aids to improve the human vision. Cicero had written in his essays — when Paul was a little boy — concerning the great comfort he took in his new reading glass. In the ruins of Herculaneum, which went out of business before Paul was born, there was found a microscope with a focal length of nine diameters. But Paul did not know — or if he knew he did not care — that men were trying to see better with their eyes. When he wrote — apropos of mysteries — "For now we see, as through a glass, darkly," he was thinking of the traditional glass of the days before contemporaneous science had gone to grips with that problem of a cloudy and dark glass — and had solved it, too, in an amazing manner. Paul wasn't interested in clearer glass. He was concerned only with a clearer mystical vision of a future world.

Not in a single instance is there a Pauline allusion to the intellectual progress of his day. He grills the metaphysicians on Mars Hill, on the ground of their superstitions; but — in his letters — he never speaks of the advancements made in the fields of scientific thought, although such progress was in motion all about him.

In that first century of the Christian Era, when Paul was at the very height of his missionary career, Hero of Alexander invented a turbine engine; Galvani had produced an electrical spark; Ptolemy's work in mathematics was at the elbow of all students; Aristotle had opened a university offering advanced courses in botany, paleontology, and what passed for biology; but if Paul and the other New Testament writers knew anything about these advances in civilization's mental progress, they considered these matters too trivial to talk about; for they were in quest of eternal life in another world — and the business of making *this* world more comfortable and wise and happy was apparently beside the point.

So; however regretfully one may say it — and hoping it is not construed as a belittling reflection upon one of the world's most sacrificial martyrs and prophets — we have but little to learn today from a Pauline Christianity that gazed aloft, ignorant of and indifferent to the re-shaping of human society in the interest of a better social order.

The task of the modern church — when seeking some adequate basis of authority — definitely enjoins it to get back — back of creeds and councils — back of Peter's unsuccessful communistic sociology — and Paul's jurisprudential metaphysics — and John's symbolic dreams of celestial pageantry — *back* to the footpaths along the lake shore in Galilee, where the majestic figure of Christ stands pleading for more light: better eyes: broader vision. We find him saying: "The light of the body is the eye. If, therefore, thine eye be single, thy body shall be full of light; if thine eye be clouded, thy body shall be full of darkness; and if the *light* that is in thee be Darkness, how great is that darkness." We find him saying to the people who sat blissfully reciting the ancient texts of the traditional parchments: "*Ye* search the scriptures, thinking that in them ye have eternal life. Ye would not come unto me, that ye might have life."

There was a certain Aristotelian spirit of inquiry in the heart of Christ which urged him to lay hold upon — and test — every alleged fact on a basis of "know the truth, and the truth shall make you free." Constantly they were bringing him to task for not talking enough about the Old World prophets. The typical congregation wanted to snooze through a homily in which their dreams would be punctuated with well-remembered classic quotations from Moses and Elijah. They felt that orthodoxy and religion were in safe hands, so long as the preacher kept repeating what Moses said about this, and what Elijah said about that, and what some other man — a thousand years dead — had remarked about something or other.

And when Jesus began to talk about exorbitant rents charged poor people for their residence in hovels; and ten per cent interest at the bank on money that was only worth six; and courts that were so partial to rich men and so hard on poor men that if a man sued you for your coat, you'd better give it up — and your overcoat, too, rather than get yourself in the toils of a machine that would strip you stark before everybody had enough; AND a caste system that would permit a dying beggar to lie gasping at the very lodge gate of the prosperous; when Jesus began to talk about such matters, the conservatives said: "How come you never talk about Moses? Or Elijah? Great people, they were. Let's hear a little more about *them*."

No; the people of the day — except the very downs-and-outs

— and persons who had some urgent need of actual, temporal, immediate, earth-earthily help — were quite fearful of Jesus' modern church; so fearful of it, indeed, that they thought of disposing of it by disposing of *him.*

I presume our task is to attempt to redefine that Galilean Spirituality in terms applicable to the day in which we live. It is a gospel slightly harder to preach than the traditional lore, because it is so much more likely to be misunderstood. So much more likely to be construed as a mere irreverent dismissal of the prophets and a nonchalant skepticism of dogmas valued by our fathers.

The other day, in Cleveland, I met a very much travelled man who had just come back from Syria. Speaking of conditions there, social, political, and economic, he said that Syria's great problem today is not the issues involved in the French mandate, or her defenselessness in the face of predatory neighbors — her trouble was due to her conservative reluctance to accept the new gifts of the twentieth century. For three thousand years she has been ploughing an outworn soil with a light wooden plough, which penetrates the ground to the depth of about four inches. Century after century, the same old ploughs have scratched the same old four inches of dirt. To raise six bushels of wheat to the acre, is to have produced a fine crop.

The western world has sent in steel ploughs equipped to turn up a hitherto undiscovered soil. But the Syrian does not like the idea. He thinks it a rank affront to the wisdom of his father, his grandfather, and his great-grandfather, clear back to Adam, to change his agricultural technique. So; the difference between poverty and prosperity in Syria is just a matter of four inches of dirt. We can educate, missionize, hospitalize, convert, clothe, feed, and lug along the people of Syria — from now on to the end of time — but the only thing that will solve their problem is their consent to use a plough with a longer blade!

Differing from the Syrian mind in degree — but not in kind

— huge masses of self-admittedly civilized people of this country would rather hang on to grandfather's metaphysics than accept the new ideas which make for a better world. Even in this highly developed part of the country where *we* live, the amount of mental adhesions per thousand of population ranks alarmingly high; with the bulk of the churches quixotically tilting at ancient windmills, and preaching a reactionary gospel encrusted with fears and phobias, ever on the alert to strangle a new idea in the name of the Lord.

In the midst of this reactionary tendency, there stand a few — a *very* few churches conscious of their responsibility to make Christian truth consonant with modern life. This church is one of them. I pray that through the coming days, and through the future years, this institution may be known as an agency of knowledge and a power-house for the generation of new light in this community.

So that — a quarter century from now, when the historians smile wryly over the prevailing state of mind of this general locality — back in the nineteen-twenties, pointing to the fact that this zone was modern in all its ideas except for the really *important* ideas — your own children will be able to lay a detaining hand on the chronicler's pen, and say:

"Just a minute! There were a *few* people — in those days — who wanted the freedom of the truth."

They will be proud of their heritage. They will have respect for the faith bequeathed to them.

To prepare that legacy for the next generation is our supreme task.

September 26, 1926

the fundamentals

It has occurred to me that on the last day of my ministry here I might venture to review my own philosophy of religion, and the features of faith which I consider as of major importance.

Not that I shall be saying anything I have not previously said to you, many times; but only that the order of arrangement in presenting these thoughts may have a more logical sequence than is possible when one views the separate items of faith singly, or to point some specific moral.

This is to be in the nature of a survey of one man's evaluation of the fundamentals.

The first problem of religious faith IS the human estimate of God.

There is no disagreement in the minds of thoughtful people on the primary importance of this belief. It is significant that the opening words of our Bible are: In the beginning *God.* . . .

At this point, all religious faith stakes off its initial claim; and unless and until a man has arrived at something like a satisfying theory concerning *God*, any further explorations into the mysteries of religion are as futile as if a child were set to do problems in algebra before he had learned to count on his fingers.

Perhaps it is exactly for this reason that so many persons find the emblems and symbols of Christian faith meaningless. . . . These symbols are the algebraic signs of a body of beliefs. They signify very little to the mind that has not learned how to handle the actual Arabics for which they stand. No religious philosophy can proceed until it has made sure of its own ideas concerning God. Its ideas may eventuate in the declaration that God is an inscrutable mystery: but at least, He will have been postulated.

Simply stated, the problem is as follows: We human beings find ourselves living, for a little while, on a revolving sphere. Were we possessed of no physical wants — and had nothing to do but speculate upon the mystery of our brief existence — Life would be a vastly different institution than it is. Occasionally, every normal man and woman pauses to reflect upon this problem — but so urgent are the demands of our everyday life that we quickly resume attention to the immediate duties incident to our physical welfare.

Whether — if we had nothing to do but think about the world's origin and probable destiny — and our own eventual stake in it — we would have become wiser than we are — or mad as the Hatter — is an open question. It is a question we don't *have* to answer, because our lives are too crowded to permit any continued concentration upon this riddle. I get to thinking earnestly about it all — and then somebody wants me on the telephone.

On the brief occasions when we *do* give ourselves to philosophizing on this greatest of all mysteries, our opinion is practically unanimous that a world so intelligently designed could not have come to pass without an Intelligent Designer.

The easy and primitive method of accounting for the world as the product of a Great Designer is to presume that it was created by *magic*. Thus the early Hebrew poets and prophets envisaged a Jehovah who said: Let there be light — and there was light . . . Let the land be separate from the seas — and it was so. And if a man has no inclination or opportunity to inform himself concerning the things definitely known about the age-long processes of Nature which have given the world its present appearance, perhaps this conception of the earth's creation by *magic* must suffice.

The trouble has been that because this magical theory of creation was set forth in the Bible, and the Bible was offered, by the overwhelming majority of the churches, as the authentic word of God — equally inspired in all its parts, and divinely revealed through men who wrote as they were directed by the Holy Spirit — an increasing number of persons who have had access to the findings of scientific research have felt obliged to abandon this Book as an infallible guide to an adequate philosophy of life.

Having then been left to go their way, un-led and unattended by an authentic declaration of God, in respect to His creative methods and intentions, a considerable number of intelligent people are seriously bewildered about the very first step to be taken in formulating a system of religious beliefs.

For the moment, then, let us leave out of consideration the primitive ideas of these Hebrew shepherds, who lived thirty centuries or more ago, and inquire of ourselves what *we* think about the origin and apparent purpose of the world.

The student of geology and biology finds himself vastly pleased by the information handed him during the first few weeks of his course of study. He learns that the same dynamic elements which, in various relationships, provide the activity of the earth, are also present in the sun. He is willing to believe — for it sounds reasonable — that this earth and the other planets of our solar system are all derived from the same source. When informed that all of these bodies were thrown off from one parent-star — owing to some terrific upheaval — he understands.

Our earth, then, began to take on, gradually, the aspect it ultimately exhibited, by the operation of elements resident in it when it was violently set adrift to fend for itself. Molten rocks cooled and the surface of the earth was shrunk, wrinkling as it contracted, which accounted for the mountains . . . The rocks crumbled and eroded; vegetation began to find sustenance in this soil; out of tiny, rudimentary forms of life, various types of animals, adapting and readapting themselves to a changing environment, found the earth a home for themselves.

In the course of time, one family of these creatures — which the student is informed was the *genus homo* — became possessed of more inquisitiveness than the other animals; learned how to use its fingers (the fingers becoming more and more dextrous, through versatile experience); learned how to tan pelts for clothing, how to sharpen stones for tools and weapons, how to hunt and trap for food; how to make a boat, a wheel, a pulley, a microscope, an airship, a radio. And the essential germs of all this multiform activity — if you will believe it — was once resident in the central sun from which our earth, and everything it evolved, had been pitched off.

Now this knowledge is very important; and, in its essentials, may be considered true. The only difficult thing about it is: that the inquisitive young student is, for the time, so carried away with its purely phenomenal aspects that he does not immediately pause to inquire where these dynamic forces *came from, in the first place.*

He sees the world carrying on under its own steam, so to speak. He observes the procession of the seasons. The heat of the sun evaporates the water of the lakes and streams. The vapor rises and forms clouds. When the clouds are chilled, the water falls. The grass and flowers receive their nourishment. . . . The soil serves as a laboratory vessel containing nitrogenous properties capable of feeding the plants; and the animals eating the plants get their necessary chemicals for the making of flesh and bone.

It is all very simple, indeed; and explains itself quite nicely.

And you would think that almost anybody should be contented with the hypothesis that the whole institution is self-contained, self-restorative, and independent of creative personality.

But — not so. The normal human is not satisfied with this theory. He takes up a flower. The hard, woody stalk he thinks he understands. There was something in the soil that produced this stalk . . . There was some chemistry in the soil that gave the stalk its outer covering of green. Whatever it is, in the soil, that produces color, the color is green. So much for the stalk of the plant. We are getting on quite nicely.

But now we come to the blossom; which, in this case, is composed of pink petals, and white stamens, and purple pistils; and the theory that this particular patch of soil is loaded with a chemical productive of green goes on the rocks.

But another theory also — much more significant — has now gone aft agley. Why is it you are not contented with the naturalistic explanation? What makes you want to know who or what is back of all this?

Why should *you* bother your head about the variegated color of the flowers, and the stripes and spots and shapes and sizes of the animals living side by side in the same forest, feeding on the same foods? What makes you think it's *your* affair? Why not just let the whole question take care of itself?

There isn't anything you can do about it; is there? Even if you knew. Suppose there was or is a super-intelligence that designed the Universe . . . how does that affect *your* life?

Yet — throughout the ages — men and women have believed that it was, somehow, their affair.

They never thought they were responsible for things being as they are, on the earth, and they weren't so impertinent as to think they might alter the processes of Nature — in the long run — *but they always felt themselves peculiarly related to the source of it all.* Early, they began to search for the super-intelligence who, they stoutly believed, must be postulated as the *cause* and *motive* of the world.

At first, lacking any instruments of materialistic research, they contented themselves with the magical theory. Jehovah had said: Let there be light; let there be land; let there be vegetation; let there be animals; let there be Man. . . . And it was so, and it was good.

A God who worked magic was to be feared . . . The people feared Him. They felt that it pleased Him to be feared. They felt that He resented any effort of theirs to find out the secrets of the earth. It was quite enough to know that He had planned all things wisely.

However — they saw that the only dissonant note in the universal symphony was produced by *themselves*. Everything that God had made played its destined part according to the rules — all but man. Man was the one type of creation that refused to conform to the otherwise harmonious scheme.

Surely God must be perpetually indignant and annoyed over the delinquencies, the vandalisms, and the violent unrest of this creature man. So they assumed that He was angry over their inquisitiveness; their struggles to probe His secrets; their high impudence in considering themselves superior to the world they lived in, hopeful to be, at length, well out of it — and its uncertainties and its jeopardies — into another, better, *more stable world.*

Why couldn't they be contented to live like the other animals who apparently took this world for granted, accepting it for what it is worth at today's quotations, and willing — when the time came — *to die and stay dead;* and not talk wildly about living with God?

They evolved systems of worship conformable to their abasement in the sight of God; and wrote it in their holy books that *the fear of God is the beginning of wisdom.*

Came then a day when one arose who completely abrogated this theory. He did not abrogate man's restless ambition. He lifted it from the category of the impudences, and gave it divine sanction. God did not want to be feared, but loved. Man, if he wished, could be God's friend; could consider himself God's child.

The Father God was not angry over the inquisitiveness of His children. He had meant them to be inquisitive. If not — He would never have gifted them with the spirit of inquiry. He was pleased when they explored. He liked it when they made demands for further knowledge.

Said this far-seeing prophet: "Ask, and ye shall receive; seek, and ye shall find; knock, and it shall be opened unto you." Which was indeed a far cry from the primitive picture of a Garden with certain trees in it which no man might touch — lest he become wise as Jehovah.

And thus it was that the gospel of the Great Galilean reappraised the conception of God — and it is of colossal importance to notice that the progress of civilization has been in the hands of the people who adopted this Christian thought of God as a Being who expected and hoped that His Children would become more and more aware of the world in which they lived — realizing that the more they knew about it, the more they would know about *Him* — and that the more they knew about Him, the more eager they would be to possess His wisdom. This is not impertinence, but aspiration.

Under the old theory of a *Jealous God* — so resentful of human inquiry that He would confound their speech to keep them from building a record-breaking tower — men grovelled and burnt their lambs and cried for mercy.

Under the new theory of a *Loving God* — eager to see his secrets learned — men last night dared to reach out into the blue and light their little pageant at a celestial torch so far remote in space that the ray they captured had been en route for forty years.

Now there is a very strange thing about this liberating gospel of Jesus. If you will make a serious study of the Old Testament Scriptures — as the finest example of men's earlier philosophy of religion — you will be struck by the frequent changes of thought, as the generations passed. Every great prophet enunciated a philosophy based on that of his predecessors, but modified by the current circumstances of life.

For a long time, religion was a nationalistic, tribal affair. Zeus was concerned only with the affairs of the Greeks; Jupiter was Roman; and Jehovah was a Jew . . .

The God of Jesus was not a partisan or a national; and whenever modern men have made an effort to enlist God in their respective armies, and impute to Him a higher degree of interest in and regard for themselves and their well-being than in the affairs of other peoples, they have completely detached their philosophy from authentic Christianity — and reverted to the paganism which antedated the Gospel.

You see — you cannot have the Jesus-philosophy unless you are willing to be consistent in accepting it. It is all very comforting to say that Jesus disposed of the old idea of a God who wanted to be feared, and introduced the idea of a God who wanted to be considered the Father of Mankind — but you cannot have this newer, more lovely, thought of God as humanity's Father, unless you permit Him to be humanity's Father, which, naturally, includes the whole world.

This may be a rather rough way to express it — but if God is not the Father of *all*, He is not the Father of *anybody*. In other words: here is the Jesus philosophy concerning the Fatherhood of God. You may take it, or leave it; but you may not modify it to suit occasions, or racial superiorities, or preferred creeds.

This does not mean that the heathen in his blindness is, in all respects, our equal in intelligence, or social consciousness; but it *does* mean that the potential divinity invested in him is of the same category and as valuable qualitatively as *ours*. In respect to origin, we are brothers derived from a common Father. If we are not akin — no one of us is related to God by any more personal ties than a zebra or a chrysanthemum.

It must be remembered, however, that the gospel of Jesus was rather a great ideal — than a code of laws. The full understanding and acceptance of that gospel was a goal to strive for, rather than a destination arrived at.

You will have noticed, in the ancient scriptures of all earlier peoples (notably in the Old Testament, with which we are most familiar) a decided shift of views, from the era of one great prophet to another. The progress was so rapid that the time came when a wise man (who probably was considered quite a dangerous modernist, in his day) announced: "What doth the Lord require of thee but to deal justly, love mercy, and walk humbly with thy God?" This was revolutionary, in the face of all the shriving ceremonies, burnt offerings, and elaborate machinery of worship which the Lord had previously taken great stock in.

Every prophet's deliverances were good for his own time; but became quickly superceded by the advancing theories of his successors. They dealt with local problems, mostly, and were dated with the perplexities of the current social order. Every religious philosophy adduced by them, gleamed for an hour — and began to fade in the light of new predicaments.

Every ancient religious philosophy — however powerful and satisfying, to its initial devotees, gradually lost its grip. Inevitably, it just stepped down from one phase of influence to the next lower — a peculiar catabasis like that of radium. At first it was a religion: an inspiration; then a morality, an ethic;

then a liturgy, a ceremony; then a relic, a fossil: a museum-piece.

In the case of the gospel, there not only was no fading out of the philosophy of Jesus, but an increasing glow. He did not offer a gospel that was good for an era, or a localized area — a gospel which would presently become outmoded and obsolete. It was a cosmic evangel, with the flavor of eternity saturating it. . . . It was so far beyond the mere transient issues of the day and country, that the people who heard it hardly realized its implications.

About the best that most of the people could arrive at — when they heard Jesus speak — was to say that they were astonished at his doctrines. . . . The fourth gospel record states the case quite without exaggeration when it says: "The world knew him not. He was a light shining in the darkness, and the darkness comprehended him not. He came upon his own; and his own received him not."

The early church failed to evaluate the gospel except in its loyalty to Jesus' love, and its admiration for his sacrifice. Paul said he dared to know nothing further than Christ Crucified. . . . Adam had sinned and we were all lost. Christ had made it right and we were all saved — provided we accepted him as our Saviour. The budding church of Rome became interested in the dramatization of this plot, by which God had taken humanity back — for Jesus' sake —into the security of a long-abrogated love.

So far; so good. . . . But it was a very long time before men began even to *suspect* the possibilities of the gospel for reshaping the whole thought-life of the world. They continued to go to war for their respective beliefs — and even in comparatively recent times butchered men and women by the thousands for dissenting to whatever body of thought and technique of ceremony happened to be current with the cult temporarily in the saddle.

Now — the nations are trying to maneuver themselves into the position where they may make the adventure of experimenting — for the first time — with the primary injunction of a gospel nineteen hundred years old!

Also — for the first time — the wise men are considering seriously a more equitable distribution of human privileges than has ever been thought of before.

Also — the whole program of social rehabilitation is being viewed — for the first time — in a mood that sounds curiously like the mind of Jesus. We have, for example, agreed that one of the tenets of the gospel demanded the relief of distress: feed the hungry; clothe the naked; and still more lately we have gone in for the ministry to the *sick* — and there is a faint glimmer of interest in the imprisoned. Did it ever strike you oddly that Jesus talked of the sick and the imprisoned as of the same category? Not meaning that the sick were of the same sort as the imprisoned; but meaning that the imprisoned were *sick* — and should be treated as such. We are in the first phase of a social program that believes this to be true.

Let me repeat: while every other prophetic deliverance, in the ages past, has sufficed only for a term of years, and has been supplanted by other, better, more timely beliefs and admonitions, the gospel of Jesus has not only stood the test of time — but has fresh revelations for each age, as men — propelled by the strength they have had from it — grow mentally and spiritually to the stature where they can understand the more exacting and hitherto baffling features of it.

Which now gets us back to the place where we started. Man found himself, originally, at war with the earth, and restless in his environment. He despised himself for it, and thought God was angry. The fact is that man was *intended* to live down and ignore the laws of the jungle. The primary legislation of the forest and field was *self-defense*. The primary law of the gospel is *self-sacrifice*. Whosoever shall lose his life for the Gospel's sake, the same shall save it.

When we use the word "gospel," let us not think of it as a compendium of maxims spoken for the crowds of country folk who gathered on Galilean hill slopes, in the Augustan era . . . Let us think of it rather as a body of thought which grows more and more luminous as the human race proceeds to put it into active operation.

I do not know of any other approach to the Gospel of Christ which contains more elements of satisfaction. Let us leave off our dismal reproaches of the social order that it has been so slow to make this gospel effective . . . We have been thinking of it too much as a system of laws which nobody obeyed to the full. Let us think of it rather as a lofty ideal, toward whose magnetic radiance humanity *must turn* — whether it wills it or no — for salvation.

"And I, if I be lifted up," said Jesus, "will *draw* all men unto me."

Instead of torturing ourselves with remorses over the world's failure to make more out of the Christian Faith — let us thank God that we have come as far as we have — and pledge ourselves that we, in our own time, and according to our several abilities, will try to practice as much of it as the circumstances of our lives permit, looking unto Jesus, the Author and the Finisher of our Faith, who, for the joy that was set before him, endured the cross, and is seated at the throne of God.

Montreal
May 28, 1933

christianity — the cult of adventure

EIGHT THOUSAND Christian representatives of sixty-five nations are convened in this city to discuss more adequate methods of calling the world's attention to the saving gospel of Jesus Christ. Immeasurable possibilities for progress reside in the counsel and encouragement of such a conclave. Were it to resolve upon nothing of definite advancement, in matters of religious pedagogy, and confine its endeavors to mutual cheer and inspiration, the convention would be well worth while. Just the enterprise of mobilizing these dynamic Christian forces, that they may see their own strength, is of incalculable value.

When the thirsty and disheartened Elijah, lying prone, under the juniper tree, laments that his nation has quite abandoned its faith, it is a complete renewal of life for him to be informed that there are four thousand who have not yet bowed to Baal.

And should the impatient Christian, who suspects — from the general indifference he sees about him on the streets and in the papers, to life and law and light and love — that the religious motivation of our time has become enfeebled, he may recharge his courage and optimism by observing the enthusiasm of these hopeful couriers of the faith, gathered here from every state and nation, unitedly declaring their belief that the kingdom is coming when God's will for the earth shall be accomplished with something of the harmony and confidence with which it is done in Heaven.

All forward-looking leaders of organized Christianity, today, are agreed that the cultus of the Nazarene Teacher must be made adaptable to the demands of our new age. If it should be remarked that they vary, considerably, in their notions about the exact methods to be pursued, that diversity of opinion is not to be viewed with alarm. Perhaps there is no occasion for the standardization of methods.

One of the distinguishing features of Christianity is its capacity to serve various temperaments, moods, racial demands, and the exigencies of acute problems. Mary and Martha do not ask Christianity to heal them of disease. All that they want is assurance that Lazarus, their brother, still lives. Peter hasn't an ache or a pain; but wants to be relieved of his doubts. "Lord; help mine unbelief." Thomas wants to see the map of the way to Heaven, and the nail-prints in the Master's hands. Philip wants his theology straightened out. John and James want reserved seats in glory. The Samaritan woman wants to know how and where to worship. The Syrophoenician woman wants something for her daughter. The centurion wants something for his servant.

You can't standardize Christianity; and try to make it do the same thing for everybody. Not everybody wants the same thing. But, of this we may be sure: whatever it is that we want Christianity to do for us, it has the power to do it if we make the proper connections with it, and bombard it, in faith believing, until we achieve our desire.

The Cultus of Galilee has always possessed an extraordinary capacity for making itself accessible and easily understood. When it descended the stairs from the upper room, on the day of Pentecost, and scattered, on the streets of Jerusalem, to tell the story of its hero and its faith to the polyglot representatives of every nation in the East, some thought it a miracle, and maybe it was; but the event required no better explanation than the fact that the tongue of world-wide fellowship and altruism is a universal language which anybody can speak fluently without the aid of a lexicon.

Wherever missionaries of the cross have gone, throughout the world, they have contrived to make themselves intelligible; for the simple reason that they are dealing with a cosmic principle.

Sometimes we have become slightly confused in our attempts to interpret Christianity, mistaking the container for the thing contained; attempting to persuade other people to adopt our occidental habits, customs, dress, and conventionalities as if they were integral features of the Galilean Cultus.

The fact that Jesus wore his hair to his shoulders, and never had on a pair of stockings, and did not eat with a fork, and slept out-of-doors, needs be of no further significance to me than that a man could live like that, in Palestine of the Augustan era, and be living a normal, natural life. He couldn't do that in America, in the twentieth century, and be normal.

One of the first obligations of the Christian, who hopes to be of some influence and helpfulness to his own generation, is to consider himself a part of it. He cannot do much as a mere bystander, obviously belonging to some other age, either in his mood or mental attitude.

Christianity seeks a reproduction of the Christ-Spirit. And that spirit can be easily translated into the speech, conduct, and ambitions of every citizen of this earth, regardless of his background or his outlook. And if Christianity were ever left utterly without words to express itself, it could still make its way by the universal gesture of the outstretched hand — "Come. Come all ye that labor and are heavy-laden. Come!"

This cosmic appeal is not the only distinctive feature of Christianity. Another important attribute of this world-wide lure to the loftier spiritual altitudes is the ease with which it measures its duties to new occasions.

Oh, I am aware that there are certain set rubrics and ceremonies and sacramental modes and inflexible dogmas, which, in many Christian organizations, have long since gone to crystal, and belong properly to the inorganic kingdom of cold rocks and fossilforms, from which all life and energy have departed; but the real spirit of Christ is not to be confused with these venerable relics of the ecclesiastical tools and weapons of our pious forebears.

The living spirit of the Galilean Teacher is progressively adaptable to the needs of each new generation. If, in any way, we fail to interpret that energy to the adequate solution of new demands, it is not the fault of the energy, but of the interpretation.

Let it be ever kept in memory that the greatest obstacle Jesus encountered in his ministry of world-friendship, was the backward drag and sullen snarl of an obsolete church that had no message for its own generation; that met at the Wailing-place to lament its departed spirit; that dated its glory in the pluperfect tense; and regarded with suspicion any messenger of hope, outside the embattled walls of its ruined citadel.

Jesus would have won thousands of active, avowed, open followers to his cause, had these timid people not been reluctant about having their names scratched off the parish-roster of the synagogues, and the bodies of their dead refused burial in the village cemetery.

When Jesus of Nazareth went to his death, it was at the instance of and under the indictment of the established, proud and haughty, ivy-covered, smug and self-sufficient, walled and moated religion of the most religious people on the earth. And were he to appear again, in visual presence, to meet the mood and measure to the demands of the time in which we live, I daresay the greatest hindrance to his ministry would not lie with the vast, needy, greedy, shepherdless multitude, but would come from the self-contained ranks of a mechanical orthodoxy, vain of its cold creeds and its tall spires; but almost impotent in the face of the most dynamic pressure since the dawn of civilization.

It will be well for us, who rejoice in the capacity of Christ's gospel to deal with the world geographically, to remember also that it is quite as ably prepared to deal with the world chronologically. We know it can leap eight thousand miles of sea, and bring new hope and harmony to a previously unmapped area; but we have yet to demonstrate whether the gospel — in our hands — can bridge a brief decade of eventful years and bring a new motive and a better morality to this unprecedented era. We have given it its chance to demonstrate what it can do in terms of nautical knots, but we have been reluctant to make the adventure of interpreting it in terms of different days.

Christ's Gospel had one thing to say to the men of the fourth century, and another word for the tenth century, and another word for the sixteenth century. It is no small part of our business to see that it gets its full chance to speak commandingly to this twentieth century, in terms that the twentieth century can understand. Shall it be forced to remain a venerable classic, in an age that does all its thinking in a mood pragmatic? Shall it spend all its time in fervent recitations of its ancient parchments, in a time when men's sole inquiry of an energy is: "Will it work?"

Now, many well-intentioned people not only fail to see the importance of this, but doubt the wisdom of emphasizing it. They are committed to an everlasting gospel — and their idea of an everlasting gospel is a cultus that operates exactly the same way, as to method and phraseology, in July 1928, and July 1628, and July 328. Their idea of wooing, with the Gospel of Christ, this hectic, frantic, mentally-stampeded generation, is to pass resolutions refusing to let it do this-that-or-the-other thing which, in their opinion, tends toward moral disintegration. They think the salvation of society is to come by making war on its pleasures; denouncing its pastimes; railing at its recreations; anathematizing its blunders; and driving it into sour exasperation with its inhibitions and restraints.

It was by that process that the tiresome old temple in Jerusalem sought to make the public pious — by rules: what you could and couldn't do on the Sabbath; what you might eat on certain days; what kind of people you might ask to your house.

Jesus himself was always falling afoul of these laws, and was dubbed a Sabbath-breaker, glutton, wine-bibber.

The old church tried to save people's souls by interfering with the public's habits, and regarding it with a testy paternalism.

It's the wrong technique.

If you would like to see how startlingly out of keeping it is with the program of Jesus, just try to picture the Master, addressing a great congregation gathered on the public plaza in the city of Jericho, saying:

"Now, immediately after the benediction the ushers will circulate a petition among you which you are all urged to sign, calling for the removal of Zacchaeus as the tax collector of this district. You are all aware that Zacchaeus is a crook, and has been robbing you. It is not enough that he has sold himself to our enemy. He is a grafter, on top of that.

"Then there are several other little petitions we want you to sign. Certain people in this town are in the habit of dancing on the Sabbath. We want that stopped. As for ourselves, we don't dance at all. And we don't want anybody else to do so. Especially not on the Sabbath.

"Then there are the races, and the games. We don't like them, and we won't have anybody else liking them if we can help it. We hope you will be particularly keen to sign the petition against boxing. We never saw a boxing match, and have no notion how one is conducted, but it looks rough and vulgar, and we're going to stop it.

"Simon Peter is in charge of this matter, and is circulating the petition. See him. Peter has some strong convictions against boxing. Says it's brutal. When he wants to chastise anybody, he uses an old rusty sword.

"Now, don't get away without signing all these resolutions and petitions, especially this one about the removal of Zacchaeus. He's a bad influence."

No: Christ had a formula for dealing with Zacchaeus — with mean, crooked little Zacchaeus, up in a tree, scowling at the gospel. "Make haste and come down, Zacchaeus. I am (no, not making *war* on you) — I am *dining* with you." Whether Zacchaeus is going to continue being a grafter and a thief, with sneers for the gospel of Christ, or restore fourfold what he has stolen, and give half his income to charity, depends on the mood and gesture of the man who offers him a chance to find redemption.

Many good people resent the modern reappraisal of the Christian religion — stoutly asserting that it needs no change of mode. That it is the faith once and for all delivered to the saints; that it was good enough for our fathers and mothers, and is still good enough for us. What they seem to be leaving out of reckoning is the fact that a reappraisal of the technique of applying Christian thought to life does not mean that there is, or has been, anything wrong with essential Christianity.

When Sir Humphrey Davy improved upon Alessandro Volta's battery, it did not mean that there has been anything wrong with *electricity*. When Watt built a better engine than Savery's, it did not mean that there had been anything the matter with *steam*. And when Corliss came along with an engine that put Watt's in the museum alongside Savery's, it did not mean that Corliss considered Watt and Savery a pair of numbskulls, for the engine he made was structurally the same as theirs, with a better functioning of the power they had used. He complimented them, when he took what they had started and went on with it toward perfection. It was the same steam, all the time; the same steam that had wobbled the lid of Abraham's kettle, slung over the campfire in Canaan, thirty-five centuries ago.

All we want now is more flexibility of method, in applying Christianity — the same Christianity of the Apostolic age, and the Nicene age, and the Crusade age, and the Reformation age — to this pragmatic mood of the twentieth century. Our public is as sincerely inquisitive about spiritual culture as any public that graced the stage of human activity. But it must not be approached with a snarl and a growl and an indictment and an armful of sour and silly petitions to regulate its habits.

That was not the Jesus-way. He looked with compassion upon the multitude, and it came to him for counsel and courage. He looked with alarm and disappointment at crystallized religion, and it came to him with a crown of thorns and a cross.

Remember — you who would follow Jesus — it was not the publicans and sinners, the Sabbath-breakers, and the dancers, the gamblers and gladiators, the pickpockets and prostitutes who drove the nails into his entreating hands, but an incense-swinging, psalm-singing, law-cluttered, long-faced religion!

The approach to organized Christianity today is not unlike the tourist's visit to the Grand Canyon. Some people believe that the Grand Canyon was set down there, in that remarkable fashion, on the second day of Creation — according to the belief of the ancient Jews — and some believe that the Grand Canyon was engraved by the erosive wash of the Colorado River, over a million-year period — according to the guess of modern geology; but nobody knows much about it, one way or the other, and however it got there, there it is; and you can take it or leave it, very much as it stands.

Many thousands of people go to see it, annually; and it is well worth the bother. Some of you, who are here from the East, and other foreign parts, will have seen it on your trip. And you had better: for, if you do not, when you arrive home, the people will say:

"You stopped at the Grand Canyon, of course."

And then they will say: "What! You didn't stop at the Canyon? Well of all things! You might as well have stayed home!"

So, to insure against a disaster like that, you will either have stopped at the Canyon on the way out here, or you expect to do so on the way back.

People go there for a wide variety of reasons; some for the reason I have just indicated.

Some go because others in the party go; and they go along for company.

Some go because they have heard that the Canyon is a mile deep, and they want the sensation of looking straight down, for a mile; and the sensation of saying: "A whole mile: well, what do you know about that?"

Some go down into the Canyon. When Major Powell did it, in 1869, it was one of the most daring adventures ever attempted by the reckless. It can be done now without much risk.

Some go down because, having been able to exclaim, on the rim, looking down: "What? a *mile?*" will be able, in the valley below, looking up, to say: the same thing.

Some walk down, and are thus able to remember how they got there, for many days thereafter.

Some go down on burros — which is no small task, either — not only for the burros, but the burroed.

But nobody, so far as I am informed, ever visits the Grand Canyon, or fails to visit it, or goes down into it, or stays up out of it, either because he believes that it was put there by the definite act of the Jewish Jehovah on a certain Tuesday, five thousand nine hundred and thirty-two years ago, or was gradually washed there by the Colorado River.

Everybody gets his own thrill out of it, each in his own way. One man sees the awful grandeur of the unsurpassed panorama of noble rock-forms. Another is attracted chiefly by the changing colors and impressive cloud shadows. Another thinks of the awful possibilities of falling into it. Another is intent upon squinting out its details through a telescope.

One man wants only to stand still on the rim and be let alone. Another wants to go careening along the edge of it, for miles, in a bus, to see if, perchance, it looks different from somewhere else; which it does not.

Everybody, upon first sight of it, inquires of his neighbor, who had already arrived, and may be presumed to have a sort of proprietary right to it — the right of the earlier arrival — "How do you suppose it got there?"

And the other man replies, brusquely, "Erosion."

Presently, the earlier arrival, having had his fill of it, walks away and a fresh recruit comes up. He says to the man *he* finds there: "How do you suppose this happened?"

And our man, remembering what he has just heard, replies: "Erosion."

He gets it off as if he was mentally reserving the word "fool." He would like to say: "Erosion, Fool! Where have you been all your life? Don't you know erosion when you see it? Or don't you know anything?"

All of which sounds very like the stock answer many people have on hand for the mystery of our world's developing life. "How do you suppose this-that-or-some-other thing happened to be?" inquires some inquisitive soul. And the other man says, "Evolution."

He himself had asked the same question, a little while before, and someone had replied: "Evolution." So he says it. It sounds easy. Very simple, indeed. And the more simple the man, the more simply he says it. If he knows nothing about it, at all, he says, "Evolution, you Fool." If he knows a little about it, he says, rather hesitatingly, "Evolution — I guess." And if he has studied the matter pretty well through to as far as they go, he says: "I'm afraid I don't know much about it."

But, whether it be erosion due to the swift current of the Colorado or a specific act of Jehovah, that produced the Canyon, there it is, and you get out of it just about what you take to it, in the way of inquisitiveness, information, idealism, aesthetic appreciation, and temperamental disposition.

When you arrive home, however, and are reporting on your tour, you are likely to encounter some brother who says to you: "Did you visit the Canyon?" You are happy to say that you did.

"Do you believe that it was made on the second day of Creation, according to the first page of Genesis? Or are you one of these here Erosionists?"

You reply that you don't pretend to know much about it, but if a man has to register as an erosionist, in order to believe that the Grand Canyon was the product of erosion — why, you suppose you are indeed one of these here now erosionists.

He says: "Humph! Then you had no right to be there, at all. Your mental attitude is all wrong."

Presently, he says, "Did you go down into it?" And you reply, "No: I thought I could take in all the beauty I expected of it, from the rim."

And he says: "Humph! You don't know anything about it, if you didn't go down into it. *I* went down into it. The way to go — the *only* way to go — is over the Bright Angel Trail, on a *mule*. *That's* the way to go. That's the way *I* went. That's the *only* way to go. I belong to the Bright Angel Society, and our motto is 'Go on a Mule.'

"Furthermore, you have to go clear to the river. It isn't enough to go within a hundred yards of it, and look at it. You have to climb down to the water and puddle your feet in it. All other hope of knowing anything about the Grand Canyon is vain.

"Here, my friend," he says, "is the correct method. In other words — *my* method."

First, you go up there from Williams, Arizona, understanding that the Canyon was put there on a certain definite day, by a certain definite act.

Second, you go to the office of the Bright Angel trail, and hire a mule.

You ride down to the river. You puddle your feet in the river. No, it isn't sufficient to dip your handkerchief into the water, and mop your face with it. You've got to *put your feet into it.*

And when you come up, you want to resolve that you will blow and brag, all the rest of your life — like I do — about the infallible technique you pursued; and sneer at everybody else who failed to do it the same way.

That's the way to come to the Canyon.

Now, you and I are living in a time when that particular kind of nonsense is outlawed — and if it still occurs to us that there is only one way to come to Jesus, and that one way is the particular way that happened to be vogue in our little meeting-house of our little sect, in our little town, that happened to appeal to our temperament, training, and mental gearing, we are blocking the road between Christ and this generation.

This age of ours is taking less and less interest, every minute, in the old conventionalized, crystallized forms of religion; and is eager for a glimpse of the Galilean Cultus as an agency of Power and Beauty.

We will be finding out, at the behest of this new generation, that essential Christianity, far from building high walls of dogma and ritual and ceremony around the inquiring mind, to keep it on the old reservation, and make it toe the chalk line of tradition, is primarily a liberating energy that encourages pioneering, and invites the valorous to daring adventure.

The new emphasis will deal chiefly with such Christly recommendations as "Ask, and it shall be given. Seek, and ye shall find. Knock, and it shall be opened unto you."

It will put a higher premium upon the Christly principle of laying siege to life, for the delivery of its important secrets. It will stop detaining the truth-seeker, and urge him to go as far as he likes, or can, toward a searching out of the mysteries of our world.

The trouble with us, in the churches, has been our timidity to accept Christ as a pioneer and adventurer. We like to weep over the pictures of him as a helpless babe in his mother's arms, and as a bleeding corpse on his sacrificial cross. We like to think of him at the moments of his experience when the world had him at a decided disadvantage. We sing about his grief, his pain, his sorrow, his misery. It is so much easier, that way, than to contemplate him prescribing for the vast welter of perplexed humanity, of which we, ourselves, are a part.

We like him in a stained window, standing on a cloud-bank, with his eyes aloft, a sheaf of white lilies in his arms. We find it makes us uncomfortable to think of him as a pioneer! An adventurer! A world-leader!

You need not weep for him! He asks no sympathy, no pity, no tears! He wants courageous followers! Disciples; not pallbearers!

It's high time we accepted him on these terms. Much of our piety, which has taken the form of pride in the antiquities of religious forms and dogmas, is nothing but intellectual indolence, on the one hand, and timidity, on the other.

Pioneering is risky business. It is a lot easier to stand up and recite the Apostles' Creed, than to deduce, from experience, the imperative summons of Christ to nobility of life. It isn't going to take me anywhere to believe in God the Father Almighty,

Maker of Heaven and Earth, unless I sustain some personal relation to Him, as His child, which gives me constant access to His power.

Unless I live the comradely, courageous, high-minded, sympathetic life that was presented in its perfection by our Christ, it is neither here nor there whether I mumble something about his having been born of a Virgin, and having suffered under Pontius Pilate.

And if I do contrive to order my days and my ways by the counsel of that divine comradeship — that majestic courage — that healing sympathy — I don't care to have anybody informing me what I may or must believe about the biology of his birth, the mathematics of his martyrdom, or the geology of his opened tomb.

The new Christian emphasis will increasingly ignore these minor irrelevancies, and stake its faith upon the essential facts of a life singularly radiant and dynamic.

For a long time, whenever some pioneer has tried to devise a technique for bringing spiritual culture to the interested attention of our new age, somebody has said:

"Yes: but lookee here what the Prophet says, in the fourteenth verse of the thirty-seventh chapter."

Oh! but this oncoming age is going to stop all that, and give itself to a sincere inquiry into a way of life adaptable for this century!

What is this gospel doing for you? Is it developing your personality, and empowering you with larger capacity for making and keeping friends? Does it help you to do honest business more successfully? Does it make your home harmonious? Does it make you a better companion at the breakfast table? Does it make your automobile safer for pedestrians on the street? Does it open your purse to the call of poverty? Does it make you humble with your opinions?

Does it inspire you to see more beauty in art and nature and the hearts of common men and women? Does it make you passionately eager to put something into the world that will square, at least in part, for what you are taking out of it? Does it move you to a genuine interest in the welfare of other people, no matter how far apart they may be from you, in code and manners, belief and morals, aims and hopes?

Does it enable you to understand how all things do work together for good, in sunshine and shadow, in joy and pain, in calm serene and stress and storm, to them that love God?

If it does this, it is a power.

If it does it for you, you are a power.

Accept Christ as a pioneer, and his gospel as an adventure, and find your liberty in him; for if Christ set you free, you are free, indeed.

First Congregational Church
Los Angeles
July 15, 1928

Give us length and strength of days — if it be Thy will — that we may further and better invest ourselves in that which enriches and ennobles the experience of ourselves and those who may look to us for assistance and encouragement.

fIVE yEARS Of AKRON

IT HAS ALWAYS BEEN a notion of mine that the function of a church service is worship and instruction in spiritual culture. And, pursuant to that belief, I have tried to keep out of my pulpit all the little, episodal matters which have no direct bearing upon the main issues of this office.

It is practically impossible, however, to ignore or minify the fact that this service, today, invites the intrusion of a personal note into what I have to say, inasmuch as my ministry in this church terminates within the hour. So, I propose to talk to you, rather intimately and informally, in these closing moments — not so much in the capacity of a preacher addressing his congregation, as a personal friend in a heart-to-heart with comrades.

When I accepted this pulpit, in September of 1921, Akron was in the midst of a heavy and disconcerting economic stress. The town had experienced, for some years, a unique prosperity. Almost everybody's scale of living and spending had risen out of all usual bounds; and now the bubble of success had burst, with a loud report. Everybody felt poor. The unemployed tramped the streets, looking for work. Industry was in the grip of a paralysis for which there was no relief in sight.

And, at that hour of utter bewilderment, this church — confronted with a program calling for an expansion quite in excess of any previous demand — cheerfully and unanimously hooked about ten thousand dollars on to its customary budget, and gave its new preacher full liberty to promote methods which, he believed, would recruit a large congregation, and give the institution the fullest oportunity to do its work effectively.

I mention this first, among my memories of these five years in Akron, because it was, in my opinion, about as fine an example of good sportsmanship, courage, and adventure as I have ever seen; and that is saying a good deal — for my whole life, boy and man, has been lived in the church. I know churches, through and through. I know about what the average church will do, in a given circumstance.

This is not an average church. It is not customary with churches — when facing a time of stress — to solve their problems of poverty by adding thirty-three and a third per cent to their expenses.

Whatever debate I had with myself, over the call you gave me, was settled when I learned how cheerfully you had consented to launch forth on the new and expensive program of action — at a moment when everything else in town was bent on severe retrenchments. I thought I would like to be connected with an institution like that; and came, hopeful of your full co-operation.

I was not disappointed. From the first hour of my ministry, here, there was a consistent and continuous effort, on the part of the church, to make it possible for me to do my work. Naturally, my direct dealings with the church, as an organization, were had through the Boards of Deacons and Trustees. I wish to go on record with my appreciation of the ardent and generous support these Boards have given me, from the first hour of my ministry, on through to this last one.

I have never asked for anything that they refused to give me — or debated with me — or seemed in any way reluctant to offer me. More often, they not only acceded to my wishes, but *ex*ceeded them. I could not have wished for any closer co-operation, or any more loyal and liberal support than I have had from all the official bodies which have charge over the business and technique of the church.

And doubtless this fine spirit of co-operation, on their part, was made possible for them because they knew the loyal and generous and sportsmanly heart of the congregation. A board cannot promise much to the preacher if it is uncertain about the sort of backing it will have from the membership.

Only this past week we have staged what the officers of the American Board declare to have been the most successful convention of its long history; a distinction due to the wise and energetic work of the committees, backed by the wholehearted support of the efficient Women's Association, which offered hospitality and service; and the business and professional men of the church who so generously financed the undertaking. I am deeply in your debt for the way you all stood by, and helped to make that convention a notable event.

Financially, the church has gone through these five years — with constantly increasing expenses and demands — unterrified. It has had plenty of money to work with, and the congregation has furnished that money unhesitatingly. Many times I have come to you, direct, for pretty large favors, involving the expenditure of funds. You have never refused a single request. Many times I have known of rather serious needs which could only be handled with sizable funds — and have approached individuals, known to be in a position to give aid; and have always got everything I asked for. In this respect, my ministry here has been a constant joy and delight.

Believing that the place of inspirational worship in our nonconformist churches has been neglected, I asked you to co-operate with me in the promotion of a more inspiring service. You gave me full liberty to work out my ideas. Together we solved the problem of the church's music. I do not know of a more effective service than is rendered here, on Sundays; or of a choir more capable of continuing to offer a masterly interpretation of sacred music. This church is a place where people can worship God, and commune with their own souls. And that is saying a good deal in these days.

In the next place: when I arrived here, in the fall of 1921, I began at once to preach a gospel slightly different from the orthodox interpretation to which the church had been accustomed through all its previous years. This was in no sense a reflection upon the teaching and preaching of my predecessors. Twenty years ago, I, too, would have preached (and *did* preach) the traditional dogmatics common to nonconformist churches of our sort.

But I came to you from an experience of about ten years, spent upon the campuses of two great universities, where I daily faced the new problem of a readjustment in religious thought, to make it consonant with the more recent disclosures of the philosophical and scientific world.

Let me repeat — lest I be misunderstood — that the new gospel I came here to preach was in no way an implied criticism of the teaching offered by my predecessors. For the problem of readjustment in our thought was really a new problem, necessitated by fresh facts to which very few people had full access, only a little while ago.

One might have predicted a general uprising, on the part of the congregation, against a type of homily so far afield from the standard pulpit technique. But there was no uprising. Barring an occasional instance when somebody grew a bit restless under the bombardment of theories which had seemed fundamental to correct religious thinking, the whole church listened respectfully to the new heresies — not necessarily believing them, or accepting them at face value — but willing to hear them, and draw its own conclusions:

Which was, really, all I *wanted* you to do.

You can bear it in mind that I have never asked you to think exactly as I think, about these matters of religious belief; but only to *think*. *What* you thought was not of so great importance, in my opinion, as that you should have access to all the facts that *I* had access to; and, after that I was entirely willing that you should come to your own conclusions without too much gratuitous assistance from *my* quarter. It has been a marvel to me, always, to see the way you rallied to this call for a respectful contemplation of what must have been — for a great many of you — an entirely different hypothesis upon which to base religious thinking.

Through these days, here, I have had a few experiences with people who did not agree with me — experiences I shall not forget, to the end of my days.

One man, facing up to an emergency no less than a fatal disease, which ticked off his days rapidly, without diminishing — in the slightest degree — his mental vitality, walked up to the very exit door of life, confident in his belief in the old hypothesis — yet welcoming me into his presence, three or four times a week, to discuss the great imperatives of life and duty and eternity — in which we *were* in full agreement. I shall always think of him as one of the most knightly and valorous souls I ever knew.

Another man, who couldn't accept the new hypotheses — insofar as they affected religious thinking — and has doubtless been troubled, a little, over the general effect of the new gospel on the faith of our generation, nevertheless supported me — in every measure — as wholeheartedly as if there were no differences between us, in respect to our beliefs; and, one Sunday, when I had laid about with a pretty careless flail, at some of the doctrines which he cherished, he came down here to the chancel — after the service — smiled, reached out a warm and cordial hand — and said, "Well, good morning, anyhow."

I would like to see that remark posted up, conspicuously, on a big banner, to be suspended over the stage in our great ecclesiastical conventions, where so much rancor arises in the course of debates on metaphysical matters.

"Well, good morning, anyhow."

I don't believe that this particular man and I are much nearer together, as to our beliefs, than we were five years ago. He still thinks he's right; and, maybe he is. He's so right about everything else, he may be right about this, too. Be that as it may — I go away with the satisfaction that I haven't a better friend in town, and I want him to know that my regard for him couldn't be higher if he accepted every wild guess of Modernism.

A couple of weeks ago, when we dedicated the new antiphonal organ, the chairman of the Board of Deacons told you of two registers, in the organ, which were exactly alike, except that one set of pipes was tuned a wee bit sharp. The two registers are always played together — and the slight difference makes for a peculiar harmony not to be arrived at except through this apparent dissonance. Mr. Sherman said it was a Congregational organ, in that respect; and he was quite right.

What we want, in Congregationalism, is just enough variation, in our beliefs, to make for the larger harmony. We have had it here. We have discovered that as individuals we can think our own thoughts, deduce our own creeds, and differ as we like, without pounding each other over the head with any alleged infallible doctrines.

So; as I leave you, it is with a feeling of considerable satisfaction that I have been able to enjoy a complete pulpit liberty. Nobody, on the boards or in the membership of the church, has ever come to me with the request that I soft-pedal any of my views. Now and again, somebody has raised his voice in protest that I was doing too much whacking away at the old myths

— a criticism I presume was pretty well grounded in facts. I had it to do, and may have *over*done it, at times. Occasionally, I was a bit ruthless, and hit harder than I meant to. A man cleaning off a piece of timber where he hopes to build a house may inadvertently chop down a few trees he might better have kept for shade. I think I could improve on the technique a little, if I had it to do again.

In the next place: I have had much more liberty here, than preachers ordinarily have, to perform extra-parochial duties. I have been out of town a great deal, lecturing before organizations of all sorts. I presume there has been a little restlessness on the part of people who construe the preacher's ministry as an engagement to deal exclusively with the limited group comprising his congregation; but if there has been much sentiment to that effect it never gained enough momentum to be disturbing.

I felt that such activities were in the nature of missionary work. It gave me a chance to come before variously-sized companies of business and professional men with what I considered an important gospel of service and tolerance and broad-mindedness, which would spread the influence of this church more practically than through any other process I could think of. It was as if you were lending me to platforms where I could accomplish, through the week, the same sort of result I was trying to arrive at, here, on Sundays. I have appreciated these opportunities you have given me to do this kind of work — and I believe it has been one of the most useful features of the program you so cheerfully consented to, when I came.

In the next place: you have given me every possible comfort and convenience to make my life — and that of my household — pleasant. When we found the parsonage a bit too exciting, in its close proximity to the East Market Street Jazz-garden, you moved us over into Sunset View. You gave me extended vacations, in summer. You voluntarily increased my wages, without a suggestion by myself that such action was desired. In these past few days we have been delighted and touched over the many courtesies, gifts, and various evidences of a friendship running deep and strong.

It has been a good place to work. And I go away with the sensation of never having wanted anything that you would not give me. That is a pretty broad and sweeping statement for a preacher to make — after five years in a town — and the statement has the additional advantage that it is not only pleasant, but *true.*

In a little while, you will be doing the same thing for *another* man. Just at the moment, you do not know who he is, and, consequently, cannot be expected to stand ready with your full loyalty and support to hand to this purely hypothetical preacher, not yet located. And — at this hour — I am human enough not to be too sorry that you have not already begun the process of transferring your affection to somebody else.

But I know enough about you — from the dealings I have had with you — to be assured that your hearts are spacious enough to hold me in friendship when the days come that you are to give your loyalty and affection to my successor. I shall not deem it a compliment to my ministry if you should be tardy or reluctant to give the next minister the best you've got. You will want him to have his chance to succeed — and he can have that chance only by way of your co-operation, confidence, and full support.

I have a pretty warm spot in my heart for that man — whoever he is; and I am in a mood of anxiety about him, just as I am anxious about *myself.* For, at this moment, I am quite able to put myself, mentally, in his shoes. I am beginning another pastorate, in a few days — in a church where I follow a man who — for the past nine years — has enjoyed the warmest sort of love and loyalty on the part of his people. They were very sorry to let him go. They pressed him to stay; and assured him that nobody would ever be able to take his place in their esteem. True; they would have to get another minister, and the new man would probably go through the motions of doing his work in the church; but it would never be the same again.

I am that new minister. I expect to find them still in mourning for their loss of my dear friend, Dr. Carl Patton. But the very last thing he said to them, before he left, was an expression of his hope that they would be good to me, because he wanted me to have a successful ministry in the church he had loved so well.

Please remember this — as among the last things I shall say to *you* — as your minister — Clear the way for the new man. Let him have his head, and do his work in his own way. If he can't pull his load in the same sort of harness that I wore, let him get his *own* harness. There's very little standardization in our craft. I may solve most of my problems with a mallet, and the next man may solve his, even much better, with molasses.

I want you to understand that these occasional tearings-up of all one's comradely relationships — necessitated in my profession — are no fun. Perhaps you can estimate the seriousness of it if you — mentally — put yourself in our place, and reflect on what it would mean to you, who, over a long course of years, have relied upon a group of tried and true friends to be at your elbow, and within a few minutes' drive of your house — if, now, at middle-age, you were required, by the nature of your work, to leave the whole outfit of them and go into the midst of strangers.

Keep these things in mind, when your new minister comes. Remember that he has torn himself loose from people he loved — to come to *you.* Take him in, and make him and his family one of you, on the same basis of comradeship with which you made life so joyous and pleasant, here, for me and mine.

As I look back over my ministry in this town, in the reminiscent mood of one about to depart, I find that it has been, in some respects, a rather tempestuous career. It happened, in the course of events, that I have had to espouse several causes, here, which occasionally put me in the minority. I suspect that, at times, I have been quite vigorously despised by many people on account of the candor with which I assailed certain tendencies in this city.

I knew that it was far from pleasant to you when, over a period of months, you saw me vilified and excoriated in the "people's columns" of the local papers, and occasionally railed at, in contemptuous fashion, editorially; because I was against a pauperizing soldier bonus, or the quackery of chiroprackery, or the insidious influence of the Ku Klux Klan, or the impertinences of the "blue law" type of ecclesiastic, with which this city has been so plentifully endowed. Nor did I relish these attacks, myself. The mere fact that I never attempted to reply to them did not mean that my vocabulary was deficient in the phrases of warm reprisal — or that I was too thick-skinned to care what anybody said or thought.

I never told you, through those days, how I felt about these attacks — and I am not going to the bother of telling you NOW; but you may be assured that it was not an experience I particularly enjoyed.

It pleases me, today, to observe that the College of Chiroprackery has been closed up; and to have seen the Klan limping toward the limbo of a well-earned oblivion.

But, while there has been an occasional sprightly tilt with such things, I can remember with enough pleasure to drown all such rasping recollections — that the city has been extraordinarily good to me. I have been given every possible chance to render public service; have been given positions which automatically carried an influence with them; have had the closest sort of friendship with the men and women who operate our philanthropies, and have oversight of our municipal welfare.

If my service, in a public way, has not been as valuable as i, should have been, it is not the fault of the city's elders and betters. I have never lived in a city where I was accorded more courtesy, more preferment, or a larger chance to offer what little I had to give. Indeed, so prompt was my acceptance into the town, as a citizen, and so close has been the comradeship I have had with its leaders, that these five years, while seemingly short, in terms of the calendar, have been packed so full that I feel I have lived here a long time. In very truth, a preacher — if he is given a chance — can do quite a bit in the course of five years.

I do not feel that I am racing away, impetuously, from a ministry that had just begun —— and was nicely started. I do not believe in long pastorates; that is — not for me. I know of many ministers who have built themselves into the life of a community, and have stayed in one place through the length of their professional careers — and with much credit to themselves, and increasingly important service to their cities. But these are, I think, exceptional cases.

For the rank and file of us preachers, our message is limited as to its repertoire. The average minister has a restricted group of ideas, which are, to him, of supreme importance. No matter what theme he announces, or what text he takes, he is pretty sure to wind up on one of his pet hobbies. And after he has said the equivalent of the same thing — over and over — Sunday after Sunday — to substantially the same group of people, for five years, it may be presumed that they know everything he knows; and it is in the interest of all parties concerned that he move out, and let somebody else come in who may present the elemental imperatives of religion from a fresh angle.

You know, now, everything I have to tell you. I could stay here ten years more and say it all over again; but I have told you what my ideas are, on the subject of spiritual culture, so many times that you will have no difficulty remembering such of them as have met your acquiescence or stimulated your own thinking.

In this closing moment, I want to review the salient points of this general creed which I have tried to command to your attention.

I have not felt bound by any of the old dogmatics — either as to their form or essence — and have tried to unshackle you from them.

I have attempted to present an idea of Deity which portrays Him as a conscious kinetic energy, speaking to the world through all the media of His creation; not a parochial Jehovah, or Zeus, or Apollo, especially concerned with the welfare of any particular class of people, at any particular time in history — but a Universal Father of all mankind.

And, because I have so believed, I have made no effort to disguise my opinion that every alleged quotation of God's voice, reported in holy books (ours or any other's) which reveals Him as a parochial God, or engaged in any thought or action not consonant with the thoughts and acts of a cosmic and universal God — is no more to be believed or credited, because written several thousand years ago, by some pious shepherd, than if it were to have been written, yesterday afternoon, on some preacher's typewriter.

I have taught that the Bible is a library of impressions which certain men have had concerning Deity, and their relation to Him. I have not believed these men to have been invariably inspired or supernally endowed with wisdom from on high.

I have taught that Livingstone knew more about God than Jeremiah; that Pasteur had discovered more divine secrets than Joshua; that Faraday had been at closer grips with the Creator than Solomon; that Phillips Brooks knew as much about the real spirit of Christ as did Paul of Tarsus. I have tried to get religion into the present tense. I have wanted you to hear and see God at work in contemporaneous life.

You will remember that I have attempted to preach the gospel of a Jesus who presents an ideal portrait of perfect living. I have not hypothecated his divinity on any biological miracle which — instead of distinguishing him — would merely assign him to a place alongside the populous list of saviours whose origins were thought to have been had through miraculous generation. I have not requested you to believe — as actual, veridical facts — the traditional nativity stories. I have preached that he offered himself as our example — and, to be an example for us humans, he would — one thinks — have to live under much the same conditions which surround *us*.

You have been given full liberty to believe as much or as little as you liked about the magical and mystical element in his recorded career.

If you wanted to believe that he turned water into wine — actually — and thought better of him, as a worker of such magic — that was your right, and I hoped you found him greater and more lovable, in your esteem, for having done this strange thing. If you wanted to believe that this was just a poet's way of singing that Jesus' personality was so altogether lovely and healing and comforting and comradely — that when he came to their table, it was as if the water in their cups had turned to wine — if you wanted to believe that, I saw no reason why you shouldn't.

If you wanted to believe that he quieted the winds and waves on Galilee, I wanted you to do so — and find your Christ a peace-inspiring power thereby. If you preferred to believe that the magic words he spoke were addressed rather to the troubled hearts of these fishermen — so potently that they became, under his command, greater than their *fears,* I wanted you to think *that!*

But I did insist that the Galilean gospel — the Inasmuch declaration, the Golden Rule, the whole Sermon on the Mount — deserved your full attention and attempted practice.

I have not encouraged you to worry over all the implications involved in the ancient doctrine of the atonement. I couldn't see how as great a God as God would inevitably have to be, to create and operate the universe, would get himself entangled in a situation demanding that His son be killed in order that His own integrity might be conserved. I felt that a God so short-sighted as to get Himself into a fix like that would be hardly stable enough to see us through to the end of the trip.

I have told you that this conventional view of the atonement — in which the death of Christ became necessary to justify the parole of Adam — was unwarranted because there was no adequate basis for the *Adam* story. My grandfather believed in that Adam story. He also believed that the horse-chestnut, which he carried in his pocket, would keep off rheumatism. He was a good man, too. But he included, in his creed, a lot of things I cannot possibly believe; just as I probably include in my creed some matters which, in 1986, will be pretty generally disputed, or revised, or understood in better terms.

I have never asked your faith to attend to any business that your intellect could handle more easily.

I have asked you to believe in Jesus as a son of God, and to remember that YOU are *another;* that Jesus was in constant contact with the divine spirit — and that we might be, too, if we would. I have warrant for that belief in the recorded statements of Christ — substantiated by the valorous and self-obliterating lives of people who — even imperfectly and afar off — have tried to follow in his footsteps.

You will remember it of me that I was always pleading for tolerance; that my right to have an opinion reached only to the point of my denying some other man the right to a different opinion.

I have talked considerably about the value of Christian sportsmanship. I saw no good in churches that quarrel — either within their own ranks, or with others outside their gates. I proclaimed that whatever spirit it was that made people mean, and critical, and captious, and fault-finding, and petulant — you could be sure it was not the *Holy* Spirit; that if their lives were haunted with the shades of outworn fears, and inexcusable ignorances, and moldy superstitions — you could be sure their grisly ghost was not the Holy Ghost.

I have taught you that religion and science must be at one — if God is God.

I have taught you that the elemental principles of the new biology either must fit in with the elemental principles of Christian faith — or we lose the coming generation from the ranks of the church.

I have taught that humanity is on the way up, by the grace of God, toward some exalted destiny.

You have been encouraged by me to believe in evolution — not the kind of evolutionary theory which the untutored think resolves itself into a mere question of whether, or not, our ancestors were simians; but a theory of evolution which describes a vast physical, mental, moral, and spiritual pilgrimage through the ages — increasingly marking man's rise — on the stepping-stones of his dead self — to higher things; a hope and quest he still pursues without much more certainty of his ultimate goal than John conceived when, out of the mystical faith that distinguished his radiant soul, he wrote: "Beloved, we are the children of God. It doth not yet appear what we shall become; but we know that when we shall see Him, and know Him as he is, we shall be found to be like Him."

I have told you that we can add length to our earthly days through altruistic service; that whatever may be the nature of our future life, we know enough about this life to be assured that men do not quickly die and leave no trace who, in the quest of the Christian ideal, have contributed something of their hope and faith and work to the generation in which they had lived.

I have taught you that belief in a life beyond this world is consistent with orderly thought on the present values and duties of our earthly day; that it is inconceivable God would so endow us with this eternal hope, and disappoint us in the end with *death*.

These things have summarized my creed. I have tried to make them clear to you. Doubtless I have failed, sometimes, to get them to you; but that was not because they were hard to believe, but only because they were blunderingly stated.

I go away with deep affection for you; an affection too strong to be woven into the flimsy fabric of mere words, on the loom of inadequate speech.

And I pray that God's blessing may be with you, every one, through all the coming years.

Akron
October 31, 1926

Teach us, we pray Thee, that beauty of holiness that transcends all earthly grandeur; and that nobility of service far beyond all earthly laws.

part two

sidelights on abraham

WHAT I SHALL BE SAYING, this morning, concerns the first definitely recorded human quest for the spirit of one divine, unseen, omnipotent, communicable Ruler of the Universe.

The name of the pioneer who ventured upon this momentous experiment was Abraham.

The approximate date of his great inquiry places him, in time, as much earlier, as we are later, than the beginning of the Christian era. The scene of the story is Asia Minor, with a brief excursion into North Africa. Its prologue deals sketchily with Abraham's background in ancient Chaldea. Thence it moves across the Syrian Desert, halting at an oasis called Haran, and brings him, after much wandering and many stirring events, to anchor in that little strip of country made forever sacred, later, by the footprints of our Lord.

I presume that any informed Jew, Moslem, or Christian today could truthfully, and without bigotry, affirm of himself that he is an adherent of one of the three most vital and influential religions of the world; and, surely, it adds a unique interest to the desert sheik Abraham that each of these three supreme systems of religious thought harks back to him as the first spiritual pioneer, reverently calling him "The Father of the Faithful."

Perhaps it would be misleading were one to refer to the story of this celebrated patriarch as an epic poem, for that phrase has come to be just a polite and diplomatic way of saying that a tale, however meaningful and impressive, is legendary.

And, for that reason, I am reluctant to speak of the story of Abraham as a *poem*.

The ripest and most searching biblical criticism is practically unanimous in its acceptance of Abraham as a real character; as well proved and authentically placed in ancient history as any of the ancient Pharoahs, whose dramatic lives are fixed, everlastingly, in the inscriptions on Egypt's tombs; as definitely recognized in the graven annals of the remote Asian world as any Persian warrior or Babylonian king.

And yet, I find myself coming back to the thought that the story of Abraham must be read as one reads a poem; for it is impossible to evaluate these sonorous lines in Genesis, when one views them in the mood of common prose.

The eminently proper state of mind to cultivate, as a prefatory measure to studying this majestic figure, is a dreamy, mystical mood, in which one finds oneself standing before a suite of sublime portraits, dimmed with age, but luminous with the glow of an imperishable human longing, an eternal epic, done on priceless tapestries, the woof of which is the valorous adventure of one wise and saintly seer, now forty centuries in his tomb, but the warp of which is the wistful groping of the heart of man, from the first crimson streaks of civilization's dawn, to the fading purple of that vague and distant twilight when earthly Time shall be no more.

To view Abraham, emerging from Ur-Casdim of the Chaldees, in exactly the same mood with which we see Napoleon emerging from the Isle of Corsica; or, to trace, with a blue pencil, on the map of Asia, the migration of Abraham, across the Syrian sands, in the same mood as one follows Alexander the Great, out of Macedon, and across Persia, is not to grip the Abraham motif, at all.

For we are dealing, here, with a really tremendous spiritual quest and a rewarding spiritual discovery, to which all the incidents of Abraham's career — however stirring, must become subordinate.

And, unless one does make the mental approach I have indicated, one is apt to affix warped and false values to certain phases of this ancient narrative.

The reader sees the great patriarch engaged in diplomatic traffic with a powerful Pharaoh, and is disposed to think that this is, indeed, a high spot in Abraham's life; which it is not.

One sees him again, with a handful of armed retainers, waging sudden and successful battle with two powerful desert tribes, vanquishing their kings, and subduing them to lasting servitude, and thinks this a notable event; which it is not.

The true picture of Abraham holds him sharply in focus as a God-seeker, pledged to establish a nation whose dominant desire is for spiritual guidance, pitched to the exalted theme of Monotheism. It is in that mood we face our task.

And now that we know what our task is, we will do well to inquire how Abraham became possessed of his belief that, to find God, he must change his own address. The story of this important migration, out of Chaldea, has only come into its vivid colors in the past few years. Archeological research, in the long-buried city of Ur-Casdim, has recently shown it to have been a great center of metropolitan interests, and fed by commercial arteries spreading far to the outside world.

Dedicated to the worship of the Moon, Ur-Casdim was known as the Moon City of Chaldea. And there, in wealth and honor, dwelt one Terah, influential successor to a long line of notable names.

What impulse may have led the powerful Terah to close out his holdings in Chaldea, equip a great caravan, summon his family and servants about him, and move out of it all, is not stated.

We find him shortly, encamped on a little oasis which he named for a lost child, Haran.

Perhaps Terah thinks he is only resting on this fertile island of that vast sea of Syrian sand; but the days lengthen into months. The tent stakes are driven deeper. Children are born on the oasis of Haran, and grow to adolescence with the thought that the world is a mere forty acres of grass and grain bounded by yellow dunes shimmering under a tropic sun.

With what drab disinterest the family of Terah may have endured this narrow life, we do not know. But, whatever the natural grief of the little colony, when the mysterious old Terah folded his robe about him, and died, one presumes there was a feeling of general relief. Now, they could go back to the gay confusions and diversified interests of Ur-Casdim. Abraham, the son, heir, and now head of the house, had discharged his filial obligation to the utmost of love's demand. And when, that night, they buried the body of the weary old man, who had set out to seek a new country, and had settled on this little plat of vegetation, it may be guessed that there were light hearts beating under the conventional sackcloth of bereavement, and smiles lurking behind the ashes with which their brows were smeared.

And, in that night, Abraham dreamed a dream. The vision that had struggled for recognition in the mind of old Terah now demanded toll of Abraham.

While not meaning to tarry overlong at this early phase of the story, we will not grasp the Abraham mood unless we understand his reasons for making his decision. His father, Terah, was the symbol of a complete disaster due to the half-way performance of a great trust.

Dissatisfied with the empty pomp and artificial pleasure of Chaldea, Terah had resolved to cut loose from it all and seek sanctuary for his family in a far country.

But, on the little oasis, where he stopped to rest his camels, the vision paled. And what had been regarded a night's encampment, became his home.

There is something very pathetic about the loss of a great ideal.

Perhaps *you* may be able to revert, in memory, to some of the earlier aspirations of your eager youth, and can recall the slow evaporation of the longing to do, to be, to have, that which you now know you shall not do, or be, or have.

One thing is sure for Terah, if he wants to live purposefully and with even a bare chance of happiness, either he must stay back in Ur-Casdim, among his neighbors, however unprofitable their society, and low their aims, or, cutting loose from Ur-Casdim, he must go on until he finds the broad valleys of his dreams.

The world is fairly well-stocked with unhappy people who have let go of such pleasures as Ur-Casdim can provide, and have had just enough pioneering spirit to get themselves out as far as little Haran, where they pitch a tent, dig a well, plant a crop, and build a storehouse, always promising themselves that, one of these days, we will patch the harness, load the camels, and move toward the big thing that had lured them out.

One of the constant marvels of spiritual psychology is that halfway performance of human quests for heart's ease.

How many people in our own time turn determinedly away from the rackety joys of Ur-Casdim, to seek spiritual freedom, and fail to find it.

What a host of Christians renounce the colorful pleasures of gaiety and inhibit their conduct with lengthy rules and regulations against doing this, that, or the other which the general public finds pleasurable, and then, instead of moving on to the possession of spiritual realities adequate to compensate them for their sacrifices, *stop*, midway between the surrendered pleasures of Chaldea and the promised joys of *Canaan*, to live narrow lives of feeble purpose and small contentment.

What a vast, unhappy colony of them sit moody and petulant on their skimpy little sand-bound islands — quarrelsome, meddlesome, querulous, critical, sour and sullen — vainglorious that they are out of Chaldea, but spiritually poor and ragged because they haven't enough courage and grace to move on into the fertile land where the heart responds to the blue sky of simple trust — that all things work together for good to them that love God — and the cool springs of such generous kindness as insures life's joy.

Indeed, this is the kind of religion that seems to make some people mean. Anybody who knows, by experience and observation, the secret of this queer spiritual state, understands that there is a type of religion that only succeeds in making life very unlovely and hard and bleak. It takes great pride in its capacity to turn its back upon everything that has to do with the bright lights of Ur-Casdim, boasts of its renunciations, has a very low opinion of anybody who consents to remain in Ur-Casdim, treks out as far as Haran, and slays its camels for their pelts and builds a shelter and squats there forever in the sand, narrow-minded, irascible, ungenerous, wretched.

Now Abraham can decide, in the face of his father Terah's gloomy disaster, which way he will go. He can return to the world, the flesh, and the devil at Ur-Casdim (which is not without its shining rewards and brave show of pleasure) or, he can press onward toward some greater goal; but, being a wise man, *he will no longer stay in Haran.*

So, the next morning, after the funeral of Terah, when the order came to pull up stakes, and equip the camels, everybody was on tiptoe.

Genesis does not offer a journalistic report of the discussion which went on, that early morning, but we don't need it. Anybody can guess what Lot's seventeen-year-old boy said to his father, as he tightened the cinches on his pet camel. *He* was for going back to Ur-Casdim!

And while his father had little to say, in the face of the uncertainty of Uncle Abraham's decision, it is likely that Lot was
very eager to see which direction the caravan would take. He,
too, was ready to give up the quest for a dream country. It had
been a long time, now, since Lot had had a civilized ration of
filet mignon and French-fried potatoes, to the tune of whatever
Ur-Casdim offered in the way of syncopation.

I assume that Lot wanted to go back because, later, when
offered his choice of locations in Canaan he pitched his tent in
the suburbs of Sodom, which, from all reports, was not much
of an improvement on Ur-Casdim.

Abraham came out of his tent and anounced that they were
headed west, to seek the Promised Land. It was a very dramatic
moment. It was also an epochal moment in world history; for it
was the first effective step toward the making of that nation
into whose rich soil sink the roots of that spiritual organism in
which our own faith is nourished.

I doubt if we, who have mostly taken our monotheistic religion for granted, I doubt if we are qualified to understand what
a feat of spiritual pioneering a man had to risk, forty centuries
ago, in relaxing his hold upon all the gods of his fathers, which
were quite as thoroughly in command of men's imaginations as
The Absolute is in command of ours, and stake his life's happiness and the welfare of his tribe upon his unproved belief that
one unseen God would speak to him if conditions were made
right.

In the mind of Abraham, for conditions to be right, he must
migrate. Which introduces the very natural question, today, To
what extent is my feeble religious aspiration due to environment?
Were I to move out of all the distractions which cloud my way
to a clear and complete appreciation of the Divine Urge, might
I realize something of spiritual blessedness of this exile who became the Father of the Faithful?

We will find Abraham not only taking all his problems along, but accumulating some new ones. Abraham was not migrating to ease his burden, but to find strength to bear it. . . .

In Abraham we find that type of longing which is so bent upon achieving the Promised Land that it is barely conscious of what it is leaving in Chaldea — or of its exact *reasons* for leaving.

And from this point, onward, we will find great heroes of the faith going to their tasks, not because they were eager to leave what life had built around them, in friendships and property, but signalled from some beacon quite remote from their customary path.

It is a delightful advance in the spiritual evolution of mankind which shifts the motive of the wretched Adam, fleeing from the delectable Eden because his God was there; and Cain, tearing through the briers to escape the sight of his father's face; to Abraham, going out, not knowing whither he went, but assured that he would find the grace and peace of God at his journey's end.

From now on, you shall find them, not driven forth in remorse, but setting out in hope, not fugitives, but adventurers, and a valorous crew they are, too, Moses, lured from his sheep-trail by the bright flare of a burning bush; Joshua, led out of camp by an angel in glittering mail; Gideon, summoned from his threshing floor to become the general of Israel's armies.

Tradition has said that Abraham's father was a maker of images in Ur-Casdim. Were that true, Abraham was booked to be of that guild. Perhaps he had already fashioned, with cunning skill, the most beautiful gods his imagination could conceive.

It may be his very dissatisfaction with the results of his own hands, as he attempted to objectify the God he knew, was beating against the bars of his own soul, led him out to inquire for his soul's divine author.

Perchance with some such prayer upon his lips as Arthur Guiterman puts into the mind of the Idol-Maker, when, kneeling before the rough marble — mallet and chisel in hand — he says:

> *Great God whom I shall carve from this gray stone*
> *Wherein thou liest, hid to all but me,*
> *Grant thou that when my art hath made thee known*
> *And others bow, I shall not worship thee.*
> *But, as I pray thee now, then let me pray*
> *Some greater god, — like thee to be conceived*
> *Within my soul, — for strength to turn away*
> *From his new altar, when, that task achieved,*
> *He, too, stands manifest. Yea, let me not yearn*
> *From dream to grander dream! Let me not rest*
> *Content at any goal! Still bid me spurn*
> *Each transient triumph on the Eternal Quest,*
> *Abjuring godlings whom my hand hath made*
> *For Deity, revealed, but unportrayed!*

One of the majestic features of Abraham's story is its inherent fidelity to the truth about life. Let no one imagine that the questing patriarch is to find, at the rainbow's end, a blissful immunity from pain and anxiety, as a reward for his adventure.

Every manner of trial is laid upon him to test his faith in this unseen deity who had beckoned him forth, with a spectral hand, to found a nation of God-seekers.

There is the problem of an heir, for he is childless. Sarah, the beautiful and barren, urges him to enter into a morganatic alliance with a woman of the desert, that he might thus provide himself with posterity.

But no sooner does he effect this relationship than Sarah, to his infinite delight, promises to furnish the heir herself.

So, now, Abraham has two sons. Family life, in the tent of Abraham, becomes decidedly complicated. It is obvious there will not be room for them all. No tent was ever stitched together that would be quite large enough to house two women like Sarah and Hagar, and, since Sarah unquestionably took precedence, Hagar must go. Which marks the beginning of the most stirring story of the ancient world, a story which is not yet completed.

Hagar and her boy went forth into the open country, vagabonds.

In that boy's veins coursed two sets of the most interesting chromosomes ever mixed in human life; the hot, passionate, impetuous, savage blood of Hagar, the dusky woman of the desert, and the resourceful blood of a philosopher and seer.

Young Ishmael resolved to avenge his mother. In the years that followed, whenever the budding nation of Israel adopted some statesmanly policy of government, Ishmael patterned it for his desert host.

When Israel announced that out of their tribe of Judah would one day arise a Messiah, Ishmael announced that a great chieftain would at length emerge from his tribe Kedar.

As the generations passed, every time Israel turned a sharp corner, there stood Ishmael, waiting for him with a weapon. And I suppose that history holds no more dramatic tale than the constant age-long grapple between the descendants of the two sons of the old patriarch.

Indeed, so long was that struggle that at certain strategic hours it broke forth like a long-slumbering volcano.

Jesus, of the tribe of Judah, arises in the fullness of time, to be the great champion of Israel's spirit-claims.

Nor is the Jesus-culture more than recognized by the world, and seated on the throne of an empire, than there springs up another young man in the east who, in the sacred book he writes for his followers, announces that he is proud to be able to trace his lineage back by direct succession, to the tribe of Kedar.

And when all the Christian world made pilgrimages to little Bethlehem to kneel before the shrine where its Saviour was born, that other young man built a temple at Mecca, and in the temple there was a holy place, which every Moslem wherever he may be, today, hopes, before he dies, to visit and adore; that holy place is the traditional site of Hagar's well.

Nor are the spiritual sons of Ishmael and Israel done with each other yet: for the day is approaching when that ancient feud will ask for settlement, and the world will decide between the soul-supremacy of the camel driver of Mecca and the carpenter of Nazareth.

So, you see, Abraham really was an eventful figure in the history of the world's religions. And as one sees him, at the head of his long caravan, slowly swaying to the rythmic tread of his desert ship en route to a new endeavor, and propelled by a new ideal, one must be aware that this wraith-like procession moving majestically across the sands of Syria, is the actual beginning of that everlasting search for the absolute.

Abraham is a symbol of the great quest of the soul for its source.

Forever he will stand as the sign of a great adventure at the behest of a tremendous dream.

His successors still pursue his quest for clearer knowledge of The One God, who speaks to such as will attend His words.

Abraham is the Father of all who believe in the reality of a divine urge, and are willing, by faith, to seek that which they cannot see; cannot explain; cannot understand; but cannot do without.

Abraham is the father of the dreamers who leave all and venture to place their trust in the guidance of God. No disappointment can do them in. No loss can shake their hope. No task is too weary; no test too severe.

He whom a dream hath possessed knoweth no more of doubting,
For mist and the blowing of winds and the mouthing of words he
scorns;

Not the sinuous speech of schools he hears, but a knightly shouting,
And never comes darkness down, but he greeteth a million morns.

He whom a dream hath possessed knoweth no more of roaming;
All roads and the flowing of waves and the speediest flight he knows;
But wherever his feet are set, his soul is forever homing;
And, going, he comes; and coming, he heareth a call — and goes.

First Congregational Church
Los Angeles
September 25, 1927

OUR FATHER:
Be very near to each one of us — in the hushed stillness of our hearts — as we quest Thy spirit there, with a sincere wistfulness.

Make us conscious of Thy presence there. Teach us anew the glory of Thy love — the riches of Thy grace:

And help us to walk in the glow of that supreme possession — while life shall last — and into the world beyond:

Through Christ our Lord,
AMEN.

to nineveh via joppa

PERSONS UNLIKELY to become interested in Jonah are hereby warned that this is a dull tale.

Latterly, Jonah has been given a wide berth; not because he is in a sense a nautical character but because he is accused of being too picturesque to be practical. Do let us be practical! If anybody should dream a dream, get him to a madhouse with all possible haste.

Two grizzled old savages, the mole-eyed literalist maintaining that the very vowel-points in the Hebrew text are inspired, and the pulseless dogmatist pouring the blood of Golgotha into a test tube and holding it over a Bunsen flame to see what sort of precipitate it will throw down, who are forever on the point of rending each other asunder, and are always failing of it to the disappointment of most of us, have battered away at each other over Jonah's head until one feels uncomfortable at the mere mention of this prophet's name. Thus we have missed a sight of one of the most dramatic stories and heroic characters in the whole of the Old Testament.

Perhaps the most you know about Jonah you learned as a wee tot in the Sunday School. You were sitting in the Primary Class, dressed up very fussily and uncomfortably. Your dear teacher exhibited before your admiring and awe-stricken gaze an enormous, monstrous, garish-hued chromo on an easel representing a boat in a dreadful storm.

An old man with a white beard, an absurd little cap with a tassel and a long black robe, was diving head first into the tempestuous sea, while at the rail was lined up a company of pirates who took no pains to disguise their approval of his aquatic performance; if, indeed, they had not assisted materially in his rendition of it.

A great fish with anticipatory jaws rose to his cue — a terrible, horrible scene. It was so ghastly, in truth, that you dreamed about it that night; dreamed that you were Jonah and that they were trying to push you overboard; and so earnestly did you remonstrate that you kicked the cover all off, necessitating your mother to provide you with two drinks of water and a peppermint drop before you consented to return to your berth.

Jonah is worth a better picture than this.

Whenever any young man appears on the stage in the Old Testament, they invariably start him off as the "son" of somebody. Joshua comes into print early in his life as the "son of Nun." Saul, a mere lad, hiding from the old prophet who wished to ordain him, is called the "son of Kish." David, shepherd-minstrel, is known as the "son of Jesse." And Jonah, an aristocratic young Jew, is introduced as the "son of Amittai."

About this time, the Lord required a man for a special commission demanding bravery, energy, tact, oratory, and a magnetic presence. He picked Jonah for the part. Now, if you would joke about a man whom God would select from a whole cityful of brains and energy and resourcefulness, as the fit man for a special task, do have your fun. But see a doctor.

Having picked his man, the Lord came to Jonah, probably in a dream, and explained to the young man that he was to go to Nineveh, the oldest, richest and wickedest city on the face of the earth, and stand on the most prominent corner, and shout that Nineveh had but forty days remaining in which to repent before an earthquake or something a hundred times worse would blow their ancient and disreputable municipality to perdition.

Of course, you would have said, "Very well; just as soon as I can pack my grip and say farewell to the family!"

But Jonah was more conservative. There were two things Jonah could do with this dream of his. He could tell his wife, at the breakfast table, that he had had a very bad night of it; that he fancied the Lord had told him to go to Nineveh — Nineveh, of all places — and preach on the street corner; that he was not anxious to see a physician lest his malady be diagnosed as paresis. Or, he could go out by himself and wrestle over this vision until he had arrived at a decision to obey or not obey.

When he selected the second course, he is entitled to some respect in that he knew a vision when he saw one.

There are plenty of people, modernly, who have so far left behind them the fog of mysticism, that no intuitional impression ever bothers them. Far from believing in a divine call to a special task, they must have every duty blocked out for them in the most crude, crass, tangible way before they will lay hold upon it — and then they rarely touch it with anything more friendly than a check-book.

Old Scrooge has a bad night and finds new joy in the morning by practicing his lesson. Our fathers of old held converse with God, if, haply, he might be calling them into special service. But we have been so emancipated from the bondage of the inspirational that there is hardly a mystic or a dreamer left to us; and when we do find one, we generally refer to him as a blithering old idiot. And, more's the pity, our deductions, however brutal, are mostly correct. Dreams are not often necessary, nowadays. Our revelation is complete. If no reformer or faddist should invent a single new piece of machinery for evangelical purposes, we could easily rescue the world with resources already at hand. What we require now is not more apparatus but more operators.

But what I wish to emphasize by Jonah's belief in his dream

is that this man lived close enough to the divine to recognize God's voice and identify it from any other voice. He did not think this dream was due to impaired digestion or neurasthenia. He knew God had spoken and that this dream of preaching in Nineveh was a genuine summons.

As he stood there tugging at his chin and looking away out into nowhere, he could almost see the merrymakers of Nineveh stop and listen, laughingly, to his melancholy whine, "Yet forty days! Yet forty days; and Nineveh shall be overthrown!" He could almost hear them shout, "Ho, ho! What bawls the Jew about forty days? Forty days, indeed! Ha, ha! Pity for the chap! By the stone-headed, clay-footed gods of my father, this weather *is* hot! Plenty of addlepates this time of the year! Nay; but this man is not mad; he is just drunk! Here, Israelite, take this and buy thyself enough more to soothe thy nerves, and ours!"

Jonah saw and heard it all as plainly as if he were already on the ground. The Lord had made a mistake. There was no doubt about the reality of the message, but the Lord had delivered it to the wrong party.

Of course, Jonah had always thought of himself as the neighbors had thought of him — a young man of parts! He read the scriptures with a fine intonation. He conducted the tabernacle service, when his course was on duty, with an impressiveness and dignity which served to differentiate him from the common herd of priests. In this kind of liturgical business, he was supreme. But what the Lord could have meant by picking him out for that errand to Nineveh, Jonah was at a loss to understand. There were any number of men who could attend to this so much more gracefully and effectually than himself. How recent, you say, is this story! Yes; it reads as though clipped from last week's church paper.

People who had wanted to carry the drum and wave the

flag and wear the bell when there was something of a spectacular character on hand, have all taken to cover when a job like this at Nineveh was proposed, and have begun to recite, piously, "Blessed are the meek, for they shall inherit the earth!" For their benefit, the Beatitude should have read, "Blessed are the fatigued, for they shall be exempt from work!"

Herein is a strange thing! Here is a man who will make no effort to deny that he is an influential political leader; boasts that he can deliver, in original packages, so many hundreds of votes before ten o'clock on election morning, who when asked to say ten words in behalf of Jesus Christ to a group of working-men, rolls up his eyes and says he never made a speech in his life worth the hearing and that he is quite certain anybody else could do this better than poor he.

Here is Mrs. Ethico-culture, fresh from a long-winded address on "How to Keep the Aesthetic from Boiling Over" (she might have known the only safe remedy was to turn off the gas), who, when requested to corral a few of her godless neighbors and interest them in Christian work, says, "Oh, I just couldn't, don't you know! Some people have a taste for public work; but I — well, I just couldn't — and that's the end of it!" And so it is! She couldn't, and that's the end of it!

Here is a great city going to smash because Jonah, the preacher, robed, mitered, phylacteried, garnished and harnessed with all manner of holy millinery, who sang so beautifully and chanted so sonorously at the synagogue, feels that he either is not worthy or able or righteous or famous enough to stand on the corner in Nineveh and shout, "Forty days! Yet forty days!"

At this point, Jonah started to run. A coward, then? No; however unusual his course in starting off violently and running all the way to Joppa, it testifies to his heroic inability to stand there any longer and contemplate the situation. He knew that if he debated this matter further, the good in him would probably pick up the bad in him and hurl the whole of him into this hateful task. So he ran. I am glad he ran. I would infinitely prefer seeing a man run away from a decision for fear of deciding to do an unpleasant duty, than to stand there, stupidly wondering what he had eaten last night that had failed of proper assimilation. And if Jonah had never, in his life, gotten within a hundred miles of Nineveh, I should still think more of him for running away from the heroic instincts of his own heart, than of the sodden, stupid rascal who sits in church and watches a great demand paraded before his very eyes, with only a casual, "Why, how very remarkable!"

Arriving in Joppa, Jonah went directly to the office of a Mediterranean transportation company and booked himself for Tarshish; not because he had friends or business in Tarshish; but because he had been informed that the first boat out was headed for that port.

Then, having paid his fare, he descended immediately to his cabin and went to sleep.

If this book of Jonah is, as the sages suggest, the invention of some rank outsider, we will at least be permitted to guess that this latter had enjoyed a wide experience with religious people. After being prevailed upon to "come into the church," many a man decides that since there are no good reasons why he should not "come in," and two or three pressing reasons — such as his wife, his mother-in-law and the preacher — why he should "come in," "comes in," and pays his fare and goes to sleep.

I have known of cases where a church-ship had every berth full; and nothing short of a wreck or a mutiny among the crew could persuade them to come up on deck. Let there be a storm, and they will be the first to pile on the life rafts and howl for safety belts. But let there be a mutiny! Here it is that the sleeper ever rises to a sense of the occasion's importance. Nothing so appeals to him as the impressiveness and utility of a row.

But Jonah slept. He felt secure. God had many interests in Jerusalem; but he would hardly reach out this far into the Mediterranean. Jonah had several things to learn about the length of that arm that moved the stars.

Now, there arose a great storm out of a clear sky. The sailors knew there was something unusual about the storm for it had waived all the customary program of storms.

Every man, as is customary in a time of crisis, began to call upon his god, and as there were almost as many religions as people on board, it must have been an interesting prayer meeting. And while they cried, each to his favorite deity, the sailors began tossing the cargo over the rail as was the custom of ancient mariners. Whenever a storm came up, everything that was loose at both ends went overboard. But neither prayers nor work availed. A council was called. One religion represented on board had not yet been heard from. The captain, determined to avail himself of the services of all the gods he could influence, rushed to Jonah's cabin, and knocked him out with the roar, "What meanest thou, sleeper? Arise, call on thy God that we perish not!"

But Jonah was not on speaking terms with his God and scouted the efficacy of a prayer addressed to a Deity he had hoped to leave behind.

I have heard some very sick people trying to get acquainted with God on short notice, when all the use they had priorly made of his name was by way of filling up the waste places in a desolate and poverty-ridden vocabulary. It is a pitiful and gruesome sight. I have always disliked to be a party to a transaction in which some sordid fellow discourses volubly to the Lord about his love for him when he had been moved to do it by a just fear of the devil and the undertaker.

The sailors gathered about Jonah. The Jew was known everywhere as an expert religionist. Religion was his "chief concern." Surely his God ought to be able to rise to this emergency.

"Tell us, we pray thee," they entreated, "why is this evil come upon us?" And Jonah told his strange story. He left nothing out. He said that he was trying to escape from his God and that the storm was clearly a divine judgment.

"But what shall we do?" they queried, anxiously, for the sea was rolling higher with each thunder-peal.

"Take me up," replied the fugitive, "and cast me into the sea; for I know that for my sake is this tempest come!"

It was a bold, brave speech, so spoken like a hero that they all said they would take one more turn at the oars and at least show this man's God that they had a good boat and strong arms. But no boat was ever sufficiently sea-worthy to float if God had planned otherwise. Then they all forgot their various gods and began to pray to Jonah's God — strange business! Men do not worry much about dogmatics in time of storm. They prayed to Jonah's God to deliver them and the storm boomed a mocking accompaniment to their frenzied supplications. At length, the captain, in despair, approached Jonah again and said, "Now, if you are certain that the only thing that will save our lives is to pitch you overboard, why, hard as it is to do, over you go!" A score of reluctant, but strong arms followed the command, and over he went.

The storm ceased.

I have frequently wondered why some people in the churches, who surely cannot fail of seeing that they are storm centers and the cause of all manner of tribulation to the other passengers, have not the courage and grace to say, "If I am the fault of all this disturbance, do pitch me out!" Whereupon all the people should lend a willing hand and accept his magnanimous offer; after which there would probably be a calm. There should not be too dead a calm, however, for such a state of the weather is generally as unsafe as a storm.

Now, there was a great fish, perhaps a whale, swallowed Jonah — with much more ease and grace than the critics have swallowed this narrative — and raced off with him toward Nineveh. Herein is a miracle. Whenever you are able to explain a miracle, you may assure yourself that you have not been dealing with a miracle, at all, but with a prosaic and common fact.

If I wished to find something in this story to cavil at, I should set to wondering how the fish happened to land Jonah so near Nineveh, whose only waterway was the Tigris River which had no outlet into the Mediterranean. There was only one way in which the fish could get into the Tigris River and that was by passing through the Suez Canal.

In any event, Jonah spent seventy-two hours in the fish and during that time he decided to go where the Lord wanted him to go and to be what the Lord wanted him to be.

There was a three days' journey awaiting him after the fish had disgorged Jonah, which nicely explains the difficulties of making port.

Down on the avenue, Jonah began. He felt sure they would laugh at him; and the Jew was too thin-skinned to enjoy scorn.

But to his great surprise the people took him seriously. They held great meetings. The Chamber of Commerce and all the social, political and commercial interests of Nineveh became aroused. The mayor ordered a fast. Animals were clad in sackcloth. Not a wheel turned. Business was paralyzed. The only man in the city who seemed self-possessed was Jonah — late of a sailing vessel bound for Tarshish.

Every morning, he appeared on the corner. "Thirty-eight days, twenty-six days, thirteen days" — and Nineveh would be destroyed.

At length, he had doled out his thirty-nine days. Tomorrow would end all. Nineveh had become saintly. Prayers ascended from all quarters. The police had nothing to do. The jails were empty.

About this time, Jonah should have begun to be sorrowful over the doom which threatened a city so repentant. But Jonah was going to have his pound of flesh. The Jew was strong on Law. The "quality of his mercy" was strained to transparency.

The fast was a real fast — not a mere substitution of fish for beefsteak once a week. Nineveh was a closely shuttered city from which no sound or traffic arose to drown the noise of weeping and wailing. The weird chant of Jonah, echoed now by a thousand aching throats, amounted to the actual voice of God, foretelling doom.

The prophet had now come to the end of his ministry. According to the schedule handed him, tomorrow would be a great day in Nineveh. The inhabitants were in a grand state of terror. They were ready to do anything, say anything, be anything that he suggested. Now, he would retire on his hard-earned laurels and let Heaven do the rest.

Not caring to be too close to the base of operations on the morrow, Jonah retired a little distance from the city where he had constructed a booth, and there he decided to wait for the crash.

I would not do Jonah the probable injustice of intimating that he was happy or that he strained his ears and tensed his muscles for this dreadful disaster with any feeling of glee, but I do not think he was as sorry as a prophet ought to be to see a city destroyed. When I recall the anguished cry of the Saviour of this world as he looked upon Jerusalem and contemplated her sad end, I find it in striking contrast to the picture of Jonah as he sits before his improvised shelter with his elbows on his knees and his chin in his hands, waiting for the first mutterings of an earthquake.

At first, Jonas felt very sure the event would occur early in the morning. God would not wait a minute longer than necessary. But the forenoon passed uneventfully. Jonah then decided it would probably occur at high noon; but it didn't. He then concluded it would be at night. To be sure, it would be much more dreadful at night. So Jonah sat out there and waited and listened.

Early in the morning of the forty-first day, the hum of traffic arose. Nineveh had gone about her accustomed business with a great sigh of relief. Jonah told the Lord that he had been forever disgraced. Nobody would ever believe him again. He thought more of his reputation as a prophet than of the one hundred and twenty thousand people in Nineveh. And then God showed him, by a miraculous vine which came up in a night to shelter him, and died again, leaving the prophet disheartened, that if a gourd vine of twenty-four hours' standing could so bereave a man by its death, what would a Creator feel for a great city full of children.

Thus ended the ministry of Jonah in Nineveh. I do not know that the city continued long in a state of righteousness. Perhaps not. Some very badly frightened people have gotten over their repentance before the surgeon has taken the stitches out.

The great lesson which cost Jonah so much inconvenience and humiliation was that occasionally a situation demands that some man must cast himself unreservedly into the breach and become a martyr to a crisis. He learned that sometimes a man must give up all that he is and all that he has and be grossly misunderstood and actually become the laughingstock of his age and race, in order that some great idea, for which the world was unprepared, might be planted safely and securely.

However all this may have turned out for Nineveh, it had undoubtedly given a brand-new character to the seagoing Jew.

One of his early sermons

the collapse of jericho as viewed from the inside

AT A DISTANCE, it looked like an ingenious quadrangle of dry mud. A huge, battlemented, sealed-up square of sun-baked mud. It was the city of Jericho.

It was Jericho slowly crumbling, parching and cracking into little wavy lines of open fissures under the pitiless glare of southern Judea sunshine.

It was mud-built Jericho on the border of the Promised Land.

Some say it was an historic city; some say it was a legendary city; but, whether it was a real city or a mythical city, Jericho was a city of sun-baked mud, at the south extreme of the Promised Land, and to re-enter that land, the Israelites must contend with it.

Some say that the siege of Jericho was a truth; some say it was a sample of early Hebrew folktale; but whether fact or fancy, the Israelites are trying to get back into their Promised Land, and to do so, they must lay siege to Jericho.

I want to tell you this remarkable story. There is plenty of room for speculation as to the situation on the *out*side, in that siege. But I shall not be greatly concerned about that. My interest is attracted mainly by what may have happened on the *in*side.

But before we go *in*, let us make sure we are acquainted with the predicament of the people who were *out*.

Very briefly: The Israelites, after five hundred years in

slavery under the Egyptian Pharaohs, have been led out of their bondage by Moses. Moses was eighty. This emancipatory act was his *magnum opus.* All his life he had been marking time, tending sheep, listening for celestial orders, and treading the narrow mountain paths of Midian, waiting for the strategic hour when it would be wise and effective to strike for liberty.

The hour arrived. He descended into the valley. He organized the Hebrews. He led them out, en route to their Promised Land. He had been waiting all his life to perform this one great service of emancipation so they could go back into their Promised Land. But he was eighty, and he had spent all his ingenuity on this one great liberating deed. He was powerful enough to lead them *out,* but he had no resources left sufficient to cope with the problems of leading them *in.*

He makes a very acceptable prototype of the radical leader who, sensing a need of reform, has the capacity to direct a movement whereby people are led out of their enslavement to superstition, bad customs, weak and unjust laws, inadequate religion — with a goal in sight for them — but hasn't the ability to take them on into anything better.

Moses could unbind the people and lead them into a wilderness, but that was as far as he could go.

So, the Israelites, only a little better off than they were in bondage, wandered, aimlessly, impatiently, petulantly, half-starved, ragged, sick, with their hopes dashed and their morale shattered, for forty long, drab, bleak, uneventful years.

And Moses died. And the angels buried him, no man knew where, and Israel wept for a day; and inquired: "What now?"

A new leader was appointed: one Joshua, the son of Nun — an energetic, intrepid, resourceful fellow with an uncanny sense of good psychology, and a vast need of it, for his problem was to take his people back into the Promised Land by his wits; seeing he had no weapons.

The road ahead was carefully reconnoitered; reports made;

secret counsels held; a plan resolved upon.

The first obstacle to be met was the walled city of Jericho. They marched toward it, under strict orders from Joshua that no matter how apparently indefensible or absurd were the measures to be employed, absolute obedience was necessary.

They went into camp, one late afternoon, within hailing distance, but out of arrow-reach of the armed city of Jericho.

Next morning, they maneuvered into marching formation, and silently tramped around the city, keeping an equal distance from its walls. Not a word was spoken. Not an order was given. Not a drumbeat, nor the squeal of a fife; not a look toward the city. Neither of pity, fear, curiosity, or threat. It was as if the city were not there. The great assembly, in close-formed ranks, marched silently, around Jericho.

Bristling with spears, and ugly with creaking catapults, the swarming walls of Jericho watched in amazement this strange procession. Jeered, catcalled, laughed; but the procession moved steadily on; and all was silence in the ranks, save for the monotonous scrape of heavy leathern sandals on the ground.

I'm not saying it was an easy task for the marchers. In that great, mute unseeing throng of passionate pilgrims, there were thousands of strong men with hot hearts and eager courage, who would gladly have broken ranks to avenge the insults hurled at their tatterdemalion crew by the well-fed, well-armed, self-confident men of Jericho. But each man trusted his leader, and trudged doggedly on, with his eyes fixed on the back of the man in the rank ahead of him.

An imaginative bard, of our own time, wonders if each man may not have evolved his own unsung marching song — wonders if the sullen resentment of the marcher, tortured by the ribald laughter of prosperous Jericho, may not have settled into a rhythmic hymn of hate, tuned to the steady rasp of scraping sandals:

Jericho: Jericho;
Round and round the walls I go
Where they watch with scornful eyes,
Where the captained bastions rise;
Heel and toe; heel and toe;
Round and round the walls I go.

Jericho: Jericho;
Round and round the walls I go;
There the golden ones of earth,
Regal in their lordly mirth:
Heel and toe; heel and toe;
Round and round the walls I go.

Jericho: Jericho;
Round the walls of Jericho:
Past the haughty golden gate,
Where the emperor in state
Smiles to see our ragged show
Round and round his city go.
Heel and toe; heel and toe;
Round the walls of Jericho!"

At four o'clock that afternoon, the Israelites had completed
their journey and put back into camp; silently munched some
frugal rations; doused the lights; went to bed. Slept.

Next morning; up early; religious ceremony; fell into line;
and marched all day, around Jericho. Not a word; not a look
toward the city. At four o'clock, wound up in camp; ate supper;
put out the lights; turned in. And that was the second day.

Next day, the same. And the next, and the next; and it was
now the morning of the seventh day. Up at the first pink
streaks of dawn, and marching at double-quick. The rhythmic
beat of the hymn of hate drummed now in the temples of the
passionate marcher at allegro, with the tempo rising hotly to-

ward *maestoso* — racing now into lurid *stretto* — pounding, deafening:

> *Heel and toe; heel and toe;*
> *Round the walls of Jericho;*
> *I will blow a thundrous note*
> *From my brazen bugle's throat,*
> *Till the burning sand will know,*
> *And the thorn and thistle grow*
> *O'er the walls of Jericho —*
> *The leveled walls of Jericho:*
> *The ruined walls of Jericho.*
> *Jericho: Jericho: Jericho.*

Seven times round, at ever accelerated pace.

There was a crisp, crackling, shrill order shouted! It was the first sound that had been uttered for seven days. The great concourse halted, glued in its tracks, and stood, en tableau. The priests lifted their trumpets to their lips, and stood, statuesque, waiting for the signal. The word was given. The priests blew one long, shrill, screaming blast; the people raised a mighty shout. And Jericho fell!

Of course, if we were having anything further to do with what had happened on the outside, plenty of things might be said. Things of profit. There might be something said about the remarkable fact that nobody wrecked the whole scheme by attempting to supervene his own opinions. There hadn't been one moment, in those seven days, when some little pigmy of a man might not have ruined the whole campaign with an impetuous word, or a heady outbreak of an inflamed ego.

All that was necessary to wreck the movement was for some impertinent little man to pull out an impudent little leather slingshot from his silly little belt, and whirl it around his empty little head, and fire an impotent little pebble toward his revilers on the walls.

That would have done up the whole program, and the Israel-ites could have gone back to the woods to eat bark and berries. All that was needed to do up the scheme was for some impatient fellow, who knew too much to follow and not enough to lead, to break ranks and go galloping up to his captain to say that he and five other fools had had enough of this and were they going to be allowed to do anything, or were they not; that's what he wanted to know.

The program was constantly at the mercy of any crank, any boaster, any egotist, any bumptious yokel with a pigeon-brain and a big biceps.

But, strangely, they all kept their heads, held their tongues, obeyed orders, minded their own business, and Jericho fell.

We might be further moved to reflect that the thing that tortured Jericho to the wind-up was not the final blast of noise, but the uncanny week of *silence*. Casually viewed, silence may be thought a mere negative condition; mere absence of sound; mere nothing. Critically surveyed, silence is a powerful dy-namic.

A latter-day poet has called the roll of the impressive silences in his dramatic lines:

> *There is the silence of a great hatred,*
> *And the silence of a great love,*
> *And the silence of an embittered friendship.*
> *There is the silence of a spiritual crisis,*
> *Through which your soul, exquisitely tortured,*
> *Comes with visions not to be uttered*
> *Into a realm of higher life.*
> *There is the silence of defeat.*
> *There is the silence of those unjustly punished;*
>
> . . . .
>
> *There is the vast silence that covers*
> *Broken nations and vanquished leaders.*
> *There is the silence of Lincoln,*

Thinking of the poverty of his youth.
And the silence of Napoleon
After Waterloo.

. . . .   •   •   •

And there is the silence of the dead.
If we who are in life cannot speak
Of profound experiences,
Why do you marvel that the dead
Do not tell you of death?
Their silence shall be interpreted
As we approach them.

Silence for seven days; then a mighty, piercing blast, a thunderous roar of exultation from the besiegers, and Jericho collapsed.

Now, the rest of the story that I mean to tell you is not in the Bible. You may be deeply perplexed whether the story I have told you, as viewed from the outside, of Jericho, is fact or fancy. But no such problem need destroy your peace from now on. I *know* the rest of the story is wrought out of a man's imagination; for I did it myself.

If you want to believe that the Almighty God set one social group of His children into such a state of mind that they campaigned against another social group of His children, and then commanded them to go into that ruined city and kill every living thing, old men and women, babies in arms, sick people in the beds, sheep and oxen, and little children's pets, battering and smashing and maiming and slaying until there was nobody left but a brazen prostitute whose establishment was saved because she had traitorously given out some information, previously, to the spies — if you would like to think this might be true, take such comfort in it as may be indicated. But the rest of the story, I can promise you, is sheer invention.

This, then, is what happened on the *in*side:

It was on a late afternoon; in the sumptuous palace of the emperor of the city of Jericho. The emperor sat playing chess with the prime minister in a heavy silence punctuated only by the rhythmic swish of peacock-feather fans, wherewith a dozen sweating Nubian slaves stirred, for their ineffable master, a wisp of muggy breeze, and diverted the attention of the royal flies.

The captain of the guard, parting the portieres, stood at attention — but received none — for full fifteen minutes, when the emperor, with a lazy chuckle, moved an ivory piece, muttered a single guttural, and the prime minister, smiling foolishly, bowed and shifting his gaze slowly toward the door said, "Well, what?"

"A large number of Hebrews, my lord — a very large number, probably all the Hebrews in the world — are encamping five hundred yards south of the golden gate."

"Humm!" said the emperor. "Strange. Armed?"

"Apparently not, your Majesty."

"Humm!" said the emperor. "Strange. We will go and look. Are the gates all shut?"

"Yes, my lord."

"And fast bolted?"

"Yes, my lord."

"Then keep them shut. Nobody goes out and nobody comes in. That clear to you?"

" 'Tis well, my lord."

They went to the tower over the golden gate and looked; looked a long time, and laughed, boisterously.

The word spread throughout the city, and everybody who might presumably have any business on top of the southern wall was, that late afternoon, on top of it. The army was called out, and squirted a little more oil into the tension-springs of the catapults; counted their arrows; unlimbered their bows; examined the pyramids of rocks piled at intervals on the broad surface of the wall.

And the whole city was very merry, that night, and much wine was drunk.

But the army was ordered to remain on top of the walls, ready for whatever might come to pass, though it was evident that their ragged, emaciated, weaponless mob of thorn-torn beggars were as powerless as they were numerous.

The emperor spent a merry evening but did not sleep very well, and arose in the morning groggy and perplexed.

He went early to his seat over the golden gate and watched the Israelites' morning sacrifice, and the blue smoke that arose in a tall, slender pillar from their rude altar.

He watched them fall in line, and his heart beat a bit quicker as they moved forward, obviously confident of what they were going to do. He wondered what that was. He wished he knew. He asked everybody in his royal household, and they all said that they wished *they* knew. If they did, they would tell him.

The marching continued. The Hebrews came no closer, but they kept marching on, until they had displayed their full numerical power.

The heavily armed soldiers of Jericho massed their strength at the successive salients of the walls, as the silent besiegers moved along.

And, late afternoon, the baffling pageant was over and the Israelites trailed back to their camp.

Obviously the strategy was a reconnoiter. The whole nation of Israel — declared the emperor of Jericho — had been fetched out for instructions as to specific duties and adventures in the attack they proposed to make.

Probably the onslaught would be made that night. The word was passed that nobody in Jericho was to go to bed that night.

The army was to remain, in full fighting strength, on top the walls, and the civilians were to be up and in their clothes, ready to make whatever defense they might, of their own homes.

Certain optimists in the cabinet protested that the emperor was taking the matter too seriously; but he replied that these people had no weapons.

"That's just it. No weapons. If they had weapons, they would probably be weak weapons, stuff twisted out of the trees of the forest, and tied together with thongs. If they had weapons, we could meet them. We are sure of *our* weapons.

"But you see, they are not proposing to fight us with weapons. They have something else in mind. And whatever that something else is, they have confidence in it. They might turn out two dozen fools, with a wild scheme. But out there are many thousands of people, a whole nation, confident that what they are planning to do is practical. And, the supreme danger that we are in, is that we don't know what that plan is. It's a new kind of battle. And our weapons are not built for it.

"When they come, with such complete unanimous confidence in their own strategy, it means they know exactly what they can do to us. Did you observe, this afternoon, how, when the soldiers jeered, and taunted them, they marched on without a change of expression? Not a word: no bravado; no threats. I tell you they have something."

Next morning, the army on the walls had to be prodded to activity. Sitting out all night in the desert chill, nursing their spears, had not improved their spirits.

The march of the Israelites was again in full swing. Oh, the maddening, baffling, terrible silence of that grim host of empty-handed vultures, trailing ominously over yesterday's path, drawing a tragic line of fate around the doomed city.

The laughter on the walls was raucous and shrill today, but it came in spasmodic spurts of hysteria. The merchants in the city nervously attempted to pursue their usual duties; but customers did not come to buy — just to wonder and whisper and ask questions which nobody answered.

And that night, no one slept again.

And the next day, the army was unable to eat, for worry and watching and the general neural drain of anxiety; but, orders had come that every hour that passed added to the certainty that the attack was imminent; so, that night, with redoubled vigilance, they manned the parapets and sat, with aching eyes peering into the gloom that overhung the encampment, and waited for the dawn.

And there wasn't a moment of that week when the army of Jericho, by opening the gates, and rushing out armed for battle, could not have driven their uncanny enemy into the nethermost tangles of the wilderness.

But the trouble was, these besiegers had no weapons. That meant that the ordinary processes of giving battle were of no use. Jericho must sit and watch and wait and worry.

Late Thursday afternoon, the Jerichoans began to take to their beds. The more sensitive had quite some time ago gone entirely off their heads and were raving maniacs, requiring the services of three strong men apiece to keep them from running amuck.

The slightly better balanced of the neurotics were racing about from house to house, waving their arms and inquiring, futilely, "What are we going to do?" Nobody had any appetite; nobody could sleep; the strain was rapidly winding them up tight; taut; tense. The nerves of the steadiest were tied in hard knots, and a mere touch of a man's elbow would set one off into a shrill screech of pain.

So, by Saturday, Jericho was all set to collapse. That morning, early, a listless, crumpled army watched the Israelites moving at double-quick. It drove its persecuted muscles to obey its painful nerves, and roused to the everlasting business of following along the wall, clutching spears in cold hands that shook as with palsy.

Faster and faster, the marchers moved. So fast, that the army was bewildered and dizzy with the effort to keep abreast, on the walls. Once around; twice; three; four; five; six; seven!! Jericho was all keyed now to the breaking point. Nothing remained to happen but the final catastrophe. There was a piercing blast, and weary, nerve-frazzled, care-worn, fear-harried Jericho collapsed.

A stirring picture of the inside of many a human life.

There are movements going on, outside, which it does not understand. It has rigged certain little weapons wherewith to meet certain conventional campaigns of attack, but a great many of the perplexing conditions, outside, are not to be met with the old weapons.

At this moment, as never before in the world's history, the life of the individual is beleaguered with a host of mysterious enemies whose tactics he knows he is not prepared to deal with. He is like the beleaguered city on the border of Judea.

The wise and bloody old book of Joshua says: "Now Jericho was shut up tight; none went out; and none came in." Many a scared life is like that. Shut up tight. Nothing comes out of it. Nothing goes into it. The portcullis is down and the drawbridge is up. Many a modern man is like that. He fears the foes outside.

The economists are out there, marching around his doomed civilization, with nothing but empty bags in their hands, symbolic of the impending threat held over the social order that soon it will have eaten all its food, and, unable to keep pace with the demand, must starve.

"But what are we to do about it?" shouts the besieged. And nobody answers, for nobody knows.

The sociologists are out there, marching with their arms full of pamphlets, crammed with statistics — The rising tide of color against the white race. The impending innundation of Anglo-Saxon civilization by the Slav, the Mongolian. The approach of a holy war, staged by the Musselman — holding the balance of power as to numbers; and insuperably fierce and ruthless as to temper. "But what can we do?" desperately queries the besieged; and there is no reply.

The eugenists are out there, portentous of an over-crowded world in which the morons will vote fifty-one per cent of the stock.

The nationalists are out there, pledged to excite his fear of foreign invasions; aliens, coming with empty hands, and lustful of our possessions, doing up our national spirit; riddling the national pride; menacing the national fellowship — and what can we do?

The whole world becoming indifferent to the mutual rights of citizens, and what can we do? Agnosticism rampant, and the old religious sentiment breaking down; and what can we do?

Now just sit and worry, and read the bulletins of the alarmists, and perspire, and tremble and lose your appetite — wondering what is going to happen in your world, and if enough people can be persuaded to do that, presently the thing *will happen.* That is the psychology of panic. Panic feeds the people's fears on *dread of that which they do not understand.*

What the individual, today, needs to take note of is: first, he is self-contained, if he wants to be. He can get out in the open and meet his enemies. Or he can stay inside and trust to the strength of his city. But to worry and wait is a program that inevitably heads toward collapse.

Most people who fail in this life do so through a gradual surrender to the obstacles and threats which they cannot understand. They are done up by their doubts and fears. They use their supply of nervous energy in worrying about things they either are powerless to deal with, things which, for the most part, do not concern them — or haven't the good sense to meet them in the open — on the level. All the mental and spiritual verve they might be projecting into constructive tasks, they squander in helpless, fruitless anxiety. They cross innumerable bridges before they get to them; they die of epidemics which haven't yet struck their town; they lose their incomes through depreciation of stocks which haven't yet occurred. Every worry is capitalized; every anxiety is taken to bed with them; every bitter word, every sneer, every disappointment — they keep all these ghosts a-dangling, each on its own separate string, to make their lives a jumble of misgivings, doubts, and chagrins.

Now, if, for any reason, you are living in Jericho, beleaguered, afraid, distraught, anxious, fear-ridden — consider your own resources. For *he that hath rule of his own soul is better than he that keepeth the city.*

It is exactly at this point of human weakness that the gospel of Christ comes with its most healing and invigorating ministry: Be not anxious. . . . Take no troubled thought for tomorrow. . . . You cannot add a cubit to your stature . . . but not even a sparrow falls to the ground without divine notice. . . . Let not your heart be troubled. . . . Your heavenly Father is prepared to give good things to them that ask Him. . . . Take my yoke upon you; learn of me; my yoke is easy. My burden is light. Ask what ye will. . . . Seek and ye shall find. Knock and the door will open. . . . For God sent not His son into the world to condemn the world, but that the world, by him, might be saved. . . . Fear not. It is your Father's good pleasure to give you the kingdom.

Great; impressive; wonderful; epoch-making days — the days in which we live. Our lives beset with new perplexities, unknown potentialities, unprecedented problems, moving in swift and baffling procession about the old protecting walls of a former day's manners, mores, laws. Moving steadily, indifferent to our anxiety, disdainful of our old weapons; our old creeds; our proud gates and thick battlements. But *wonderful* days. *Epic* days.

What are we to do with them; how meet them; how use them; how grow great and strong and joyous in them? Surely not by fears or doubts or forebodings. It takes Galilean poise to be steady and keep one's head in such a time. But it is a great era!

How may we hold these days of wonderment and bind them into unity and purpose, as with a thong, ere, like a fleeting dream, they pass along, into the waste of vast events forespent?

How may we keep what the great powers have sent — the prayers fulfilled, more beautiful and strong than any thought could fashion into song, of all the rarest harmonies inblent?

Oh, for that calm serene of those who, in certain other epic days, when fear was rampant, all about, knew in whom they had believed, and were persuaded that he was able!

That he was able!

Still to be persuaded that he is able to keep that which has been committed unto him.

Oh, that steadied life of those who, trusting, mount up on wings as eagles; who run unwearied; who walk, unfainting; who know how to *wait* on the Lord.

I have seen [wrote Wordsworth] a curious child, who dwelt upon a tract of inland ground, applying to his ear the convolutions of a smooth-lipped shell; to which, in silence hushed, his very soul listened intently; and his countenance brightened with joy, for from within were heard murmurings, whereby the monitor expressed mysterious union with its native sea. Even such a shell the universe itself is to the ear of faith; and there are times when to you it doth impart authentic tidings of invisible things; of ebb and flow, and ever-during power, and central peace — subsisting at the heart of endless agitation.

First Congregational Church
Los Angeles
May 20, 1928

OUR FATHER:

We wait in Thy presence, conscious of our failures to trust ourselves in Thy hands.

We have not taken Thee at Thy word, nor have we patiently tested the value of our faith.

Give us a new spirit of courage. Help us to confirm our professed beliefs . . . May we live exultantly — above the menace of fear — safe in the confidence of the Eternal Goodness; through Jesus Christ, our Lord,

AMEN.

CROSS COUNTRY WITH A NEW IDEA

Behold — a Sower went forth to sow. — Matthew 13:3

THE SPIRIT of Christ is tramping through the world — compassion in his heart for the shepherdless millions.

He trudges through China, Poland, Russia, Armenia, India. The wounds of his body bleed afresh for the sorrows and anxieties of his world.

The Spirit of Christ is restless; but eternally undismayed.

He is the Sower — who has gone forth to sow. He carries the living germs of an *idea* that has the power to make the world over into a garden. And wherever this seed is given a chance to grow, it brings forth flowers and fruits.

The big problem is to give the seed a chance. The Sower guarantees that the seed will be sown. He does not guarantee that it will grow, except in a friendly soil, and under proper conditions.

One afternoon, on the seashore in Galilee, Jesus conducted a heart clinic which must ever stand as the ultimate word *in defining the capacities of human souls.* As was usual with him, he used an impromptu story to make his meaning clear.

Most of the people to whom he spoke, that day, were farmers and gardeners. So Jesus talked about *hearts* in terms of soil — and his *new ideal* in terms of seed.

"A Sower went forth to sow — and as he sowed, some seed fell on the highway."

Oh — that highway! That hard-pounded thoroughfare!

Sometimes, late in the night, when sleep is tardy, instead of counting imaginary sheep, jumping over a fence — which, for some reason, never did *me* any good, no matter how many sheep kept coming — I close my eyes and permit myself to be dizzied by great crowds of hurrying people.

Now I am standing on a corner in Munich — near the Rathaus — crowds — I can see them, hurrying to the day's work. Now I am standing on a corner in Naples — more crowds.

I skip about in fancy, from city to city — letting the rushing crowds bewilder me.

Now I am at the edge of the sweeping current of humanity on Champs Elysées — now on the Strand — now on Fifth Avenue — now on Michigan Boulevard — now on St. Catherine —

Now I am letting myself be milled about in great stations — Paddington, St. Lazare, Grand Central, Windsor —

Oh, these *highways* —

What a diversity of interests travel over them! What an ocean of major and minor tragedies sweep over them! Not just once in awhile; but ever and always — by day and by night.

Jesus said some hearts were like the world's highways. So much has gone over them; such a volume of traffic; such a constant pounding, *that the seed of the Great Ideal really had no chance*, at all.

And if that was true enough to remark on — in the comparative quiet of an apathetic little province, two thousand years ago — it is worth a word today.

For the Life of the Spirit has a hard struggle on the highways — in the congested cities — where, for so many, many thousands, there is all too little chance for quiet moments — for undisturbed attention to the still, small voice; where the rasp of steel flange against steel rails, and the rat-a-tat-tat of rivet hammers, and the grind of gears hurl the weight of their raucous racket against us, until, for sheer self-preservation, we erect neural defenses against them — and literally *wall ourselves in.*

How many thousands of people, these days, have just been tramped on, and walked over and ridden over — and over — by the crushing loads of economic burdens, and an assortment of little tragedies — until The Great Ideal can't get through to where they are. High time we Christians prayed:

> *Oh Master — from the mountain-side,*
> *Make haste to heal these hearts of pain;*
> *Among these restless throngs abide;*
> *O tread the city's streets again.*

More and more my sympathy and understanding go out to these people with hearts like pavements. For the most part, they're just like anybody else — down in the inside of them — but the crust is too thick for the Great Blessing to reach to the soil.

Down inside — somewhere — very, very deep, there are longings for the beautiful things of the spirit.

In the late autumn, when the birds are migrating, even creatures *born* within a cage feel the strange urge to go — and flutter their useless wings — and beat themselves clumsily against the bars. And — sometimes — the Highway Hearts experience this impulse to seek liberty. But — what with the poverty, and the noise, and the miscellaneous dreads — dread of accident, dread of sickness, dread of births to come and deaths not paid for — they could not live, they think, but for this hard, thick, impenetrable pavement over their hearts. And the Great Ideal can't get through.

If — just once — it could get through — *what* a transformation would occur — for a living plant abhors a wall, and there's nothing quite so bad for a pavement as a growing tree. If —

instead of covering their hearts with this thick macadam of indifference, and sullen cynicism, these harassed millions would simply lay themselves bare to the healing rays of faith and hope, and let the Great Ideal in to have its way with them, one of the most tragic problems of our present life would speedily be solved.

I do not mean that it would promptly put beautiful pictures on everybody's walls, and soft rugs on their floors, and an abundance of food into their kitchens; I do not mean that it would immediately work miracles in easing them of their responsibilities. But if that Great Ideal were let through to them, it would soon begin to hang beautiful pictures on the battered and discolored walls of many a hitherto ugly mind; and mellow rasping voices that shriek infuriating discontents; and transform what little they have into agencies of sweetness and peace.

Jesus said some hearts are like highways — and while, in many cases, we cannot too seriously blame them — in all cases, we cannot too deeply pity them.

"And some seed fell upon stony places where they had not much earth; and forthwith they sprang up, and when the sun was high, they were scorched — and because they had no root — they withered away."

Not long ago I took occasion to refer you to a new book by Mr. Lippmann, in which he invoices some of the tendencies of our time. And, concerning lives that are too shallow to grow anything with enough root to sustain it, he has this to say:

> *North Americans, more than any other people, have lost their association with the old landmarks. They have crossed an ocean; they have spread themselves across a new continent. There are few of them living in their grandfather's house.*

*There are few of them who have not moved at least once,
since childhood and — even if they have stayed where they
were born — the old landmarks themselves have been carted
away to make room for progress.*

*Many of them have moved up out of their class — not only
out of their class but out of their culture — leaving their old
folks behind, thus breaking the continuity of life. For faith
grows well only as it is passed along from parents to their children, amid surroundings that bear witness to a deep permanence
in the order of their world.*

*It is true, no doubt, that in these great physical and psychical
migrations, the household gods — or their equivalent — are
carefully packed and put in with the rest of the luggage, and
then unpacked and set up in new places.*

*But what is taken along is at best only that which could be
sawed off level with the ground.*

The roots remain in the old soil.

Unquestionably, there is some point to this reflection of Mr.
Lippmann's in accounting for the shallowness of our present
life. There has been so little time for the accumulation of a soil
— in this new western world — deep enough to sustain enduring and valuable traditions, so important to the growth of the
spirit.

But what Jesus meant by thin soil was the heart that all-too-
quickly responds to every impulse, and as quickly lets these
impulses go. The Great Ideal is tossed into a heart like that —
and wins an immediate hospitality! — and then, withers!

Sometimes I have wondered if, in our interpretation of Christ's
gospel, we preachers are not tempted to present it too, too sentimentally — thus taking the risk of having it *accepted* only
sentimentally — and, the consequent risk of having it wither.

I know there is something very tender about the picture of
Jesus as a little baby in his mother's arms — for all the world

loves a baby — and no baby has ever enlisted quite so much sentimental interest as the Holy Child of Bethlehem. But I doubt if there is very much to sustain a hard-pressed faith in the experience of a man, engaged in the rough-and-tumble of competitive life — to be offered through the sentimental appeal of the Nativity.

I know there is something very tender about the picture of Jesus on his cross — and of all the heroes who have died for the sake of high principles that picture will remain incomparable. But still — it does not represent the gospel in its application to the actual daily requirements of the ordinary man. To his mind it is a beautiful and ennobling sentiment — but a sentiment.

His problem is not whether he shall be dragged through the streets, at the end of a rope, and nailed, lashed and bleeding to a cross. So far as his own affairs are concerned, that is a sentiment — and only a sentiment. HIS problem is not nearly so *serious* (he is willing to grant you) but it is entirely *different.* For him there will never be given a chance to walk up and settle the claims that Destiny makes on him, through any decisive, dramatic act. At times he thinks he might even welcome some catastrophic Calvary — and have done with it all. He hears the story of the cross and says:

> *I could bear grief, if it were only thorough;*
> *If it were sharp and brief,*
> *And measured to my strongest mesh of armor.*

> *But pressure — like the pressure of a snowfall*
> *Upon a fall of snow;*
> *Because it seems unworthy of a rapier —*

> *Too slight a foe*
> *Betrays me, as I sit and brood at evening*
> *For happiness half won:*

> *I am undone by sifting, snowflake pressure,*
> *Thus am I undone.*

A Persian poet wrote:

> *It was not in the open battle*
> *We threw away our swords.*
> *It was in the darkness, waiting,*
> *By the waters of the fords.*

And sometimes I think we would do better — in our presentation of the gospel — if we left off, for a little while, our eulogy of it as a thing that came in, with a burst of celestial song and a blaze of celestial starlight — and reached its climax in a heartrending tragedy — and just talk about what it will do to and for ordinary people, who are not deciding whether to go out the Via Dolorosa to execution, but are wanting some good formula for helping them remember that there are sixteen ounces in a pound — when the competitor across the street has tinkered with his scales — for helping people to chasten their hair-trigger tempers; and empty their minds of desires for revenge; and cleanse them of their lusts, their greeds, their envies, their scramble to outdo their neighbors.

But — no matter how the seed is sown, some of it meets a prompt disaster when it falls into shallow ground.

How often people — suddenly struck with the beauty and possibilities of the gospel, take it into their lives and have a go at it *for a few days*. They accept it as a sentiment — and it grows luxuriantly, as a sentiment, and presently, it just withers away for lack of depth of soil.

"And some seed fell into thorny ground, and the thorns sprang up and choked them" — the cares of this world — prosperities — choked them.

There are a great many people, today, who have once known the joy and power of possessing that Bright Ideal in their lives. But there were too many wild things growing in the garden of their hearts to give the ideal a chance.

And exactly as a long run of irksome poverty and hardship is apt to turn a heart into *a hard pavement* — so is a steady prosperity likely to turn a heart into a bramble-patch.

You can see them — anxious people, hurrying from one novelty to another — on a constant hunt for pleasure — almost anything to distract their minds — people who have in them the potentialities for doing some great service — if only the ideal had not been choked out — smothered out.

Oh — I know they pretend that life is filled with interest — and you would think, from the amount of time and money they spend in amusing themselves that they were satisfied with what destiny is handing them — but, in such few quiet moments as they have, they can't help knowing that they were meant for better things.

Mostly, they brave it out, with heads high. They have their moments of remorse — but — it is time to gallop off to the next sensation — and the penitent mood passes.

One disillusioned little flapper — who had a lot of talent, naturally, scribbles these lines:

> *Thistles there are, and thwarted thyme,*
> *And a lonely tree and a looted lime,*
> *And ragweed running everywhere:*
> *But I shall say I do not care.*
>
> *In this small chaos, I shall learn*
> *To wear a cloak of unconcern —*
> *And jauntily pin red pimpernel*
> *With a nagging thorn to my lapel.*

Only — forgive me if I pause
And wipe two tears with spiders' gauze —
For the sake of spring and flowering pear —
Not that I care — not that I care.

But — they care.

And as the doors of life close, softly, one by one, on opportunities for achieving something — they care more and more.

There comes a time in every life when *anticipation* must step aside to make way for *remembrance*. And *then* they *care*.

"And some seed" — fortunately — "fell into fertile soil."

It was not all of the same grade of soil, to be sure. Some soil had had but little attention; maybe it was about worn out with growing all manner of crops before the important seed fell in.

Some people wait until they've used up nearly all their nitrogen on other vegetation, before they start in on a demonstration of the gospel — and their yield really can't be as large as if they brought to it all the vitality and enthusiasm of youth.

Indeed, many a man has begun to boast — in his sere and yellow days — of what the gospel is doing to keep him from sinning — when perhaps most of his problems have been outlawed by nature, rather than solved by Grace.

But — there are all kinds of soil in which the Great Ideal will grow — *somehow.*

In some lives, the gospel grows just strong enough to keep people from cheating. That is good — so far as it goes — and ever so much better than if it hadn't taken root, at all.

In some soil — the gospel will grow until it is strong enough to keep people from mistreating the neighbors — but not quite strong enough to keep them from being mean and snappish and surly at *home.*

In some soil — the gospel develops until it makes people decent and kind — but not quite strong enough to rid them of their worries and their fears.

But — in some hearts — it just becomes a deep-rooted, everlasting, ever-living organism: that dominates the whole life. No trial can batter these hearts down; no calamity can do them in; no pressure can wear them out.

And — upon them rests a great responsibility. They must let the world into the secret. They must try — somehow — to share their joy. And they do — mostly — just by their example.

So — to them —

> *Go make thy garden fair as thou canst,*
> *Thou workest never alone:*
> *Perhaps he whose plot is next to thine,*
> *Will see it — and mend his own.*

Montreal
January 26, 1930

Grant that we may so live that in our hearts Thy kingdom may come and Thy will be done on earth as it is in heaven.

Desert Bread

It is a very pleasant testimony to the earnestness and comradeship of the Protestant churches of this city that this series of community Lenten meetings has been provided.

I have accepted, with pleasure, your invitation to come here on this occasion, and I hope I shall have brought to you some inspiration — so that I may not be too heavily in your debt for the inspiration you are giving me through your obvious interest in this preservation of the Lenten tradition.

In view of the fact that this is the first of these events for the season, perhaps it may not be amiss if we refresh our minds concerning the institution of Lent.

Early in the history of the Christian Church, it was felt that the people would be advantaged by observing a season of self-examination to commemorate the forty days which the Master spent in the Jeshimon Desert — before beginning the ministry which was to open a new and better way into the Kingdom.

The Lenten period was happily timed to begin just as the recurrent mystery of swelling buds — the overtures of returning birds — the accelerated movement of the streams — and the resurgence of all Nature urged man's restless spirit to similar feats of recovery.

Every man finds himself — at the first, faint, tremulous throbbing of Spring — strangely stirred to join all the rest of God's creation in this concerted desire to achieve newness of life.

Like the river — tortured with a longing to cast aside its crumbling mantles of ice, and proceed in the sunshine toward the sea — and the forest, impatient to unfold its tenacious shroud and stretch out demanding fingers toward the sky — the human heart pulses with an instinctive urge to be free of its frustrations.

With zealous fidelity, the church made the most of the Lenten idea — occasionally investing it with added rubrics and regulations — as the centuries passed — but always preserving its essential values.

During the confusions and bewilderments incident to the reappraisal of Christianity, beginning in the early sixteenth century, Lent was practically discarded by the Nonconformist churches. It is only lately that persons of our temperament and religious training have endeavored to recover this important feature of our Christian legacy.

Unquestionably, the season will mean more to us if we put into effect some practical sacrifices in the interest of our own self-discipline — remembering, however, that no amount of fish added to our menu, or beef deleted therefrom, will improve Christian courage or prompt Christian hope unless these little renunciations serve merely as tokens of our sincerity in wishing to emphasize the claims of the spirit, by restricting our indulgence of the body.

Now — I fancy you are expecting me to approach this Lenten issue by repeating the redundant platitude that we are all in vaster need of self-examination than any people who ever lived, seeing that this is a pleasure-mad age in which only a small minority take time to observe the inner workings of their lives.

Quite to the contrary — one is safe in saying that there never has been a time when so many people were engaged in self-quest. Nor has there ever been a time when so many devices were offered to make such a pursuit interesting and rewarding.

Our forefathers talked a very great deal about the soul — mostly in terms of the soul's ultimate salvation. Today — we do not speak quite so frequently about the soul. We are bent on saving and improving the personality, which, in the opinion of most people, comes to much the same thing.

And that, of course, is true in the sense that the soul is the inner vital urge which comes to flower and fruit in the personality — in the sense that all we can possibly know about each others' souls is discoverable only through our personalities.

But soul and personality are not the same thing — any more than an acorn and an oak tree are the same.

Doubtless the forester can do a fine service to the young oak by spraying it with disinfectants and clearing away the tangle of neighboring brambles which cramps its growth — but the really fundamental fact about the oak tree's life resides in the acorn.

We have spent so much time lately, spraying the personality and chopping down adjacent growths that might cloud its sunshine, that we have overlooked the importance of the soul.

I do not wish to be misunderstood as speaking contemptuously of these modern psychological excursions into our basic thought-life, with a view to straightening out the knots and tangles which account for much of our unsuccess in dealing with our problems. Without doubt, many deeply embedded phantoms and phobias, which have menaced the peace of their victims, have been adroitly and scientifically relieved by being traced back to their cause, and chased out into the sunshine where they may be recognized for exactly what they are. And it is probable that as such research proceeds (if it is not made ridiculous by the zeal of the uninformed and the commercialism of the charlatans) we may expect more and more liberation of thwarted personalities by this process.

As for the bulk of the counsel we are receiving, however, on the subject of personality development, the will-doctors are treating the symptoms rather than the disease. They are reducing the fever with ice packs, in default of locating the focal point of infection.

One of the most important features of a powerful life is courage. The personality-expert, therefore, suggests techniques whereby you may register courage in your posture, gesture, tone, and general demeanor — promising you that if you will adopt these practices, you can impress others with your self-containment — presumably to the end that you may make friends more quickly, sell what you have to sell more easily, and dominate whatever situation would otherwise make you timid and diffident.

But how much more promising and practical if one were offered an adequate reason for disposing of one's fears. When Jesus counseled men to be of courage, he did not tell them to cultivate the gestures, postures, and inflections that might denote an inner valor. He showed them how their lives were every way related to the Life of God, who had no occasion to be fearful of anything that He had made — or any combination of circumstances arising out of forces which he controlled. Jesus postulated human courage upon human-devine harmony.

You cannot rub courage into a man from the outside with "personality" improvements — any more than you can rub arthritis out of a man with liniment. You may set up a temporary counterirritant that will distract his attention from his disability, but that is all. The treatment gives no promise of permanent aid. You can apply an electrode to the sciatic nerve of a dead frog, so that he will kick a few times, in a very lifelike manner — but the dead frog, in the long run, is a lost cause.

You cannot make a man permanently hopeful by inviting him to join in singing "Pack up your Troubles in your Old Kit Bag and Smile" — nor does it help him to foot up the month's business in black ink by singing "Happy Days Are Here Again . . ." We have relied too heavily on these brief intoxicants to furnish our optimism.

To the achievement of hope, a man must become assured that he is living in a universe that is entirely solvent and time-worthy — in the hands of a God to whose own interest it is that the universe shall preserve its integrity. He must lay hold upon the conviction that the Divine urge, of which he is conscious, is an organic part of the Life of God — and that when any one of these Divine sparks, in human creatures, smoulders to extinction — for sheer neglect — God's power in the universe is impeded by just that much.

It is entirely logical — and by no means sacrilegious — to believe that if the entire projection of God's Spirit, into the countless power units of the human race, were rendered of no account, through humanity's wholesale unwillingness to accept and use that energy — the very Life of God Himself would be imperiled.

Now — it is this problem — the everlasting problem of being in harmonious relation with a Spiritual Father — and, at the same time, properly adjusted to a material Universe — that must be solved — not through attempted modifications of the outward-showing personality, but in the very plexus of the Soul. It was this problem — the problem of the scorn — thrusting powerful clutching fingers into the black, ugly ground, at the same time it stretched forth an open, eager, imploring hand toward the clean, blue sky — that Jesus faced in the forty days which we commemorate in Lent.

The story of Jesus' dilemmas — traditionally referred to as his "temptations" — in the course of that self-quest, is well known to you. The records say that Jesus was forty days in the Jeshimon Desert — but they do not say that he went there to stay for forty days.

Conscious of an urgent desire to do something for his fellow-countrymen — to make their lives more livable — Jesus decided to go out by himself and examine the resources of his own spirit, in an effort to discover how this mission might best be fulfilled.

Of course, it is the customary thing with us to view the life of Jesus as if it were planned — down to the last minutia of detail — before his birth . . . to watch him enacting the great drama that had been written for him "before the world was" . . . to observe him obediently pursuing a program, which he had no right to change, in the slightest particular.

I think we will find the career of Jesus much more inspiring if we set him free of all such restraints. He has a great commission; but is, as are we, permitted to execute that commission according to his own ideas. His temptations concerned issues of a very practical nature. They concerned matters of technique, relating to his Vocation. He possessed an ideal that would unquestionably save the world — if the world would accept it. The process for communicating that ideal to the world was not yet determined. His great ministry had not yet begun.

If there is any doubt in your mind about the uncertainty in Jesus' mind — at that period of his life — as to the proper methods for saving the souls of men, it may interest you to note how undecided he was — a little later — as he sat on the pinnacle of the temple, and wondered whether to win public attention by a spectacular leap from that height — and thus demonstrate his spiritual reliance on God's care — or descend the Temple stairs, a step at a time, and go out into the country to talk quietly to individuals about the terms of personal power.

Jesus was in the desert forty days — but when he went there, he had no hard-and-fast plans . . . His kinsman John — the Hermit — had lived out there for eighteen years. He had been hungry, out there, too; but, when he was hungry, he had eaten locusts and wild honey.

Eventually, he had come back to civilization to preach the

kind of gospel that might be expected from a man who had lived alone in a desert for eighteen years — eating locusts and wild honey . . . It was a bitter, brittle, savage religion, whose symbols were the ax and the flail; whose only message was a threat; whose only promise was catastrophe.

But — Jesus had seen John in action; had heard him preach; was convinced of his essential honesty; had joined his church, in fact; along with sundry thousands of his fellow countrymen.

Men who went out into the desert to examine themselves, spiritually, were accustomed to long periods of lonely hardship. I think it is beyond all question that John was of the Essenic party — in his lineage, and his temperament — and the Essenes were deeply impressed by the mystical . . . Many of the more zealous of them espoused the monastic life — and were known as Nazarites. John was a Nazarite.

Thus influenced — it is quite consistent that Jesus should have gone to the desert for a sojourn. It is evident from what happened there that Jesus was satisfied to be alone in the Jeshimon. He had left the world behind him — the raucous cries of the greedy market-place — the piteous pleas of beggars and lepers and all who, for fault of theirs or someone's, were finding life difficult.

Out there, the air was clean and invigorating. The star-lit nights were enchanting. The sky was friendly, and God was very near. It delighted him to be free of that world clamor — and all the pains and shames and shams and hates and lusts that that clamor expressed. It would be pleasant to say out in this peaceful place — and never have to go back to the sordidness and artificiality of what was so glibly called "civilization."

Is it not entirely believable that in Jesus' opinion, at the hour of his arrival in the desert, the real way for a man to get a clear — unbiased, properly focussed view of his own soul was through a complete detachment of himself from a noisy worried world, where the claims of the body shouted defiantly into the sensitive ear of the spirit?

It was not long, however, until the young Galilean discovered that he had brought the gravest problem of the world along with him.

He began to be hungry.

He had presumed that this shrill, competitive, hungry world — that he had left behind him — was all awry; all out of focus; a world so confusing and disordered that a man would have to retire from it to examine his soul. Now, he is beginning to suspect that that was, after all, the real world — and that this lonesome desert — where he stood in peaceful communion with his God — was an unreal world.

Back there in the confusion of that complex social riddle, where, at every hand, one recoiled from the avarice of the rich and the inconsiderateness of the poor; from the sight of frustrated childhood and disgruntled senescence — that was the real world. Out here, where one was unrelated to that tangle of mixed motives and the tug of world-demands — this life out here was a mere mirage.

It gives us a very comradely feeling toward Jesus when we read of the circumstances that brought him acutely face-to-face with this fact. He began to be so hungry that the very stones at his feet — shimmering under the glare of the desert noon — resembled loaves of bread.

The records state that Jesus was tempted to exercise divine power in a work of transformation that would convert these stones into bread. The possibilities in the case are provocative of some interesting speculation.

Had Jesus attempted to perform this act, and had failed — for sheer misuse of his own divine energy — that would have been very disappointing. Had he tried it, and succeeded — that would have been a great tragedy . . . What irreparable damage would have resulted to his gospel, had he misspent the power given him for the performance of constructive service in behalf of the social order.

As for the practical lesson taught by Jesus' victory over his temptation — what have we? Is it that we should on no account yield to the temptation to turn stones into bread? . . . One suspects that the moral hazard, in our own case, is negligible. Is it Jesus' renunciation of heavenly assistance, at a distressful moment — that we are to observe? But no: To make that lesson logical, would it not demand that Jesus — having chosen between miraculous bread and starvation — must now stay out there in the desert, hungry and faint, until he has paid the price of his own courageous decision? The narrative says he went back at once to the city.

To discover the inner significance of this event — we have to get back to the Master's reasons for being out there in the desert, at all.

He had gone out to be by himself because the world bothered him. He couldn't think straight about his own inner life, with all these great world-problems shouting into his ears. He would get out where he would be spiritually unhampered by these confusions.

Tortured by hunger, Jesus realizes that he must either create bread — or return to society. If it is permissable for him to create bread, he can stay here indefinitely. To create bread would be clearly a profanation of his power. The logic of the case is that he must go back to his fellows.

It is evident, from his own experience, that an individual soul cannot even be examined — much less developed — apart from world contacts. It is clear to him, now, that he cannot realize his filial relation to God — in all its fullness — apart from a fraternal relation to the world.

The acorn cannot stretch forth its hands to the sky — wistful for the gift of sunshine and shower — unless it consents to sink its roots in the soil.

So — that was the problem — the dilemma of an idealist, whose sensitive spirit has been rasped by the cries of the world; whose personal inclination is to keep out of earshot of all that shouting and quarreling and sobbing; an idealist who would like to discover some process whereby an aspiring soul may keep clear of this defiling world — and live in the calm serene of an atmosphere unpolluted by this world-soil — and untroubled by these world conditions.

If he can stay out here in the Jeshimon, there will never be any clash or cries to upset the tranquillity of his communion with God . . . He will owe no man anything; no man will owe him. He will not have his ears assailed by the deceit of the market place, or the plaints of people who cry for material things they cannot have.

But not even the Son of God could develop a triumphant soul without taking the world into account. The very adversities and sorrows and ugliness and pains of the world furnished the chemistry of the soil in which his spirit must grow.

Who does not sometimes share the mood of Wordsworth? "The world is too much with us; late and soon, Getting and spending, we lay waste our powers" — or the indolent despair of Omar Khayyam, who wants to escape from a scheme of things he would — but cannot — shatter and rebuild to suit his heart's desire.

Who does not — especially when his heart reaches out — in Lenten wistfulness — for something beyond himself that makes for spiritual poise — long to detach himself from his encumbering problems — and put the whole world behind him — and give his spirit its first real chance for expansion?

Jesus tried to do that — and found it impossible.

Life properly lived was in the nature of a concerto in which neither the imploring plea of the questing soul — nor the answering assurance of the Super-soul — is complete without the full orchestral accompaniment of the social order.

Out in the desert — Jesus cannot sound in the depths of his own spirit because his view of it — alone — lacks the third dimension. It has the height and breadth — but it lacks perspective. So — he trudges back from the wilderness to take his place as a social unit in a great, dynamic organism — no part of which could live by itself alone.

He returns with an adequate message. He had discovered that a man could not live solely on ideals. He had tried it. He was returning to a civilization largely made up of people who had been trying to live solely on bread. He had been tempted to reach toward the sky — and keep himself clear of the soil. They clutched with greedy fingers at the soil — but failed to stretch forth a hand toward the sky. At that moment — Jesus was in greatest need of the world — even as his fellow creatures were in greatest need of God.

Returning — he looked with compassion upon the multitude. In a very real sense he belonged to these despairing people — and they to him. His soul was pushing roots into this common soil — into which his neighbors had deeply and blindly dug themselves — and in which they had come to place their whole reliance. He must urge them to stretch a hand to the sky.

Men must have bread — but they did not live by bread alone. The forces that would draw them up into full stature were the various intonations of the voice of God. Every word that proceeded from His mouth was significant in the expansion of their souls.

Had he not spoken in the beauty of the lilies of the field — in the confidence of the birds of the air?

"Show me your God," — the doubter cries . . .

I point him to the smiling skies, the woodland greens, the sylvan scenes. I show him winter's snow and frost — and ocean's waters tempest-tossed.

I show him hills rock-ribbed and strong — I bid him hear the thrush's song. I show him rivers, babbling streams; I show him youthful hopes and dreams.

I show him stars, the moon, the sun; I show him deeds of kindness done.

Man does not live by bread alone, but on these soul-expanding words which proceed from the mouth of God.

But who can hear them, in their full significance, unless they be shared?

I commend you to the story of this first temptation of Jesus — as you endeavor to make the most of this Lenten season in your own experience.

You cannot find God by yourself. You cannot examine your own heart, except as it is related to the whole social structure.

Who seeks for heaven, alone, to save his soul, may keep the path, but will not reach his goal;

While he who walks in love may wander far, but God will bring him where the blessed are.

Rediscover for us the paths to our own hearts.

Show us how to realize the gift of Thy divine Fatherhood — through a sincere recognition of our human brotherhood.

We ask it through Jesus Christ our Lord.

spiritual engineering

WHAT WILL a man give in exchange for his soul?

It was at one of the most stirring and strategic moments of his life that the young Man of Galilee issued this ten-word message. Today — the carpenter of Nazareth had come to the parting of the ways. His activities in behalf of humanity had excited the hostility of every order of society that looked askance upon a social gospel.

For ages — religion had concerned itself with making things easier for prosperous people with property. Invariably the prevailing religion was inseparable from the State. The king was its actual head; and the high priest was his creature; his servant; in short — his tool. That went for all the religions.

Now and again a high priest would grow restive under the thumb of the king — and stage a revolt. If the king sat precariously on his throne, and the priest was popular, religion might become temporarily free of court dictation — but not for long.

A new king would ascend the throne — a new high priest would be anointed. Religion would settle back, with a sigh of relief — into the snugness of the smugness of the old ways — and become again what it had been before: an instrument to keep the poor man resigned to his poverty.

Kings have always been required to defer to the sentiments of the propertied class. It has been part of their job to protect the property of the heavy taxpayers against the snarling desperation of the ragged and hungry masses. If religion would make the poor docile; if religion would file their fangs and mitten their claws — by all means, let us have religion. All the kings have been intensely religious — they have been God's anointed — they have been Pontifex Maximus — they have been Defenders of the Faith.

The ancient religion of the Jews was no exception to this general rule mentioned a moment ago. Even the Ten Commandments — so precious they were bound upon the foreheads of the priests, and chanted on the street corners by the pious — were composed by and ordained for men of property.

"Thus shall a man deport himself in regard to the Sabbath — for example: to wit: He shall remember the Sabbath Day to keep it Holy. On that seventh day of the week, he shall do no work: neither shall his servants work. Neither shall his beasts of burden be expected to pursue their usual tasks."

All of which was very fine for the man who *had* some work. Most people found it difficult to get work to do, on *any* of the seven days of the week. Most people had no servants to command — either to work or not to work. Most people had no beasts of burden. Most people were unable to advise the strangers within their gates how to conduct themselves on the Sabbath, because most people were too poor and friendless to extend hospitality.

True, the Commandments had recognized the other sort of humanity. They had admonished the poor man not to covet the possessions of his more fortunate neighbor. He was to rest content with what he had, if he had anything — or go without cheerfully, if he had nothing.

The majestic Decalogue had arrived at an impressive climax by calling the roll of the rich man's possessions which the poor man must not even *look at*, wistfully. Taking them by and large, the Ten Commandments were made from the viewpoint of — and for the particular use of — the man who had something.

Jesus of Nazareth had felt a call to preach a gospel to the brokenhearted, to offer good news to the poor, to open the eyes of the benighted, and to spread tidings of the coming of a season which the Lord could consider acceptable. This was highly revolutionary, thought the priests, who had ever truckled to whatever forces were in power. Any man was a dangerous disturber of the peace who would talk of extending larger liberties to the poor.

So, the priests — to a man — hated the young prophet of Galilee who had scored them thoroughly, both in public and private, in the second person and in the third. On the other hand, the small but radical revolutionary party, in Judea, had lost faith in Jesus because he had no sympathy with their program of violence and revenge. The pietists and ultra-conservatives had no use for him because he had ridiculed their futile hypocrisies, and compared them to whitewashed tombs — outwardly calm, clean, and fair — but inwardly quite the reverse.

He was too dangerous an influence with the masses to be left at large among the people — said the priests. He was too serene and noncombative to be a leader of the social revolution — said the radicals. He was too indifferent to the old traditions to suit the pietists. He was too spiritually minded to please the pragmatically ambitious. He had lost caste with them all. He was a man without a party.

The time had arrived when he could no longer continue his ministry on that basis. Either he must modify his program, or expect to be silenced. For a few days, on the coast near Tyre, he debates the next step. I do not think he was trying to decide whether to make concessions. He was debating the manner in which he could meet this rising tide of opposition. Should he make a last stand, and attempt to parry the blow by summoning all the influence of the people who already believed in him — or walk quietly and unresistingly into the trap?

It all depended upon one's view of life. What was a man's life worth? HIS life was as good as lost, if he went back to Jerusalem and continued his ministry. Could he afford to lose his life? That was the question.

There was plenty of work still to be done. Perhaps he would better try to save his life, if possible. But how does a man save his life? In this case — obviously by losing it.

So — Jesus surveyed the situation from every angle. His friends attempted to dissuade him from going back into the hands of his enemies. Peter said: "This must not be," and, instead of rewarding this blundering fisherman's solicitude with an affectionate smile, and a murmured, "You cannot understand, Peter. There is no other way," Jesus turned upon him, almost fiercely, and startled him by shouting: "Get thee behind me, Satan."

For, there were voices within the Galilean's heart which had been pleading, "This must not be. This must not be." Jesus had silenced these soul-voices, only to hear them break forth afresh on the lips of his friend, "This must not be."

As if unwilling to reopen the question, even to reason with his friendly adviser, Jesus denounces the thought: "Get thee away. Thou savorest of the things of men. Exactly so have other men tried to solve their difficult problems. It is not God's way. Get thee behind me!"

No — there was only one road out. There were times when a man had to save his life by losing it — however paradoxical that might sound. And this was one of those times. Compromise, concession, silence — anything that looked like dalliance with the new social program would amount to the loss of his soul — for his soul was steeped in this fresh plan of men's redemption.

"What would it profit a man," he exclaimed, "what would it profit a man to gain the whole world and lose his soul?"

Whereupon, there were plenty of questions ready relating to the soul. Just such questions as you have asked yourself, and others. And, in the midst of this discussion of the soul of man, the youthful prophet of Nazareth utters these words, which, I fear, have not been understood very well: "What will a man give in exchange for his soul?"

Of course — if Jesus had said, "What would a man *take* for his soul?" — the matter would be simplicity itself.

What would you take for *your* soul? Suppose some man of great possessions came to you, this morning, and said: "I should like to negotiate with you for your soul, my friend. I observe that you have taken reasonably good care of it. You still enjoy the blend of colors in the sunset; and a glimpse of the moon, through the treetops, gives you a curious stir, which you have never been able to analyze; and the climax of a symphony quickens your pulse; and the sob of a cello brings a tightening in your throat. Moreover, you have large capacity for friendship: a winning smile, a magnetic hand, a sympathetic voice. People turn to you, gladly, for cordiality.

"Now — you are conscious that your poverty is a distinct handicap to your ambitions. You love good pictures, but you haven't the means to see them. You love good music, but you haven't the time or the money to hear it. You love inspiring books, but your workaday duties keep you out of them. You love travel, but have neither the leisure nor the means to travel.

"Come — let us strike a bargain. You shall have the fortune — and I shall take your soul. You may have mine. True, it is a bit jaded, and has been through some rather trying experiences. But, you may have it, and welcome. I throw that into the bargain. Come — what do you say?"

Well — what *would* you say?

No — the Galilean does not mean that, this time. He very

plainly says: "What will a man *give*" — not *take* — "for his soul?"

Let us assume that you are in the business of building a soul. Let us be quite practical and call it a work of spiritual engineering. Let us assume that you have a rudimentary soul — somewhat like a piece of realty — with a good foundation already built for a house, and that you are now planning that house.

That is to be *your* soul.

How much are you willing to invest in it?

What will a man give — for his soul?

Is it just pure gift — or is it an achievement? Let us examine the evidences.

First of all — it may properly be held that the foundation of the human soul is inherited.

There is the soul of the race.

As the generations have passed, this racial soul has been gathering power until the child who is born today has built into him certain principles which make a very fair foundation for the support of the soul which he may erect thereon.

There is a soul of the nation which is also built, rudimentarily, into the child — and is his by right of birth. The taste for freedom shows up early in the soul that has sprung from a freedom-infatuated nation. The taste for physical supremacy reveals itself plainly in the soul that has emerged from a nation where force is God.

Biologists explain that once certain little animals of the forest which lie motionless on the ground, in time of trouble, blending with the colors of their environment — and the fleet-limbed animals which bound away, under high speed, when danger threatens — were of the same parent stock. Long ago, their respective ancestors had elected, in time of stress, either to sit tight, and depend upon their camouflage to see them through, or get up and dust. And, of those who elected to sit still, only those who sat very, very still were able to survive. Indeed, only those who resembled the leaves and fallen branches in which they crouched, survived — no matter how still they sat.

So, as the ages passed, they bred a race that looked so like their habitat that the resemblance is almost uncanny.

On the other hand, the animals that elected to run away, had to make very good time, or they were overhauled. In the course of time, they largely ran to legs, and became distinguished mostly for their exceptional transportation facilities.

In like manner — there have been bred national souls.

Russia develops one type of soul. Though just now it is rather difficult to define its peculiar attributes. Yet — with all the present Russian restlessness — you can pick out the Russian, and have no trouble explaining why he is as he is.

England breeds a certain national soul. France another. India — Japan — Egypt — all have their nationalistic souls.

And so on.

You may be sure that your little contribution to life is having its effect upon the evolution of the soul of America. It may be a trifle — but of trifles is this universe made up.

Again — there is the soul of the age — the spirit of the time — what the Germans call the *Zeitgeist*.

The child of today receives, at birth, the foundations of a soul that is influenced by the *times*. His spiritual processes are quite different when he is born in 1928 than they might have been were he born in 1776 — or 1603 — or 1517 — or 1492 — or 870 — or 320.

And, as he grows to manhood, certain facts which his great-grandfather had deemed of great importance will seem to him of only negligible consideration. Inversely — he will emulate the worthiness and significance of principles which his ancestors, four generations removed, hardly reflected upon, at all.

I do not mean incidental and ephemeral matters of culture,

customs, usages. It goes without saying that it should be true of *such* things. I mean that the soul of a given time is radically different from the soul of another time in respect to considerations of fundamental value. There will be a complete rephrasing of the process by which spiritual culture and salvation are to be had.

Sometimes, an age will go to the lengths of making an entire reappraisal of the conception of God, traduced for uncounted centuries. We are passing through such a phase *today*.

To sum up, then, the rudimentary soul — the foundations of the soul — derive from such forces as: first, the soul of the race; second, the soul of the nation; and third, the soul of the age.

Now — in the next place:

No sooner does the child become conscious of this possession of a rudimentary soul (yes, even long *before* he is aware of it) his bequeathed soul begins to be acted upon by forces which environ him, as an individual.

His young soul (I should better say his old soul, for the soul he has, at this period, is mostly a very ancient institution, sinking its roots away back into human history staggeringly remote) his soul, then, is in the grip of agencies which he may not choose.

His parents have a great deal to say about the manner in which he starts to build his individual soul upon these foundations which they had bequeathed to him, even as they had formerly received them as *their* legacy.

The flight of years may ultimately dim the influence of his mother, but he cannot live long enough, or badly enough to escape it all. Neither can he forget it, utterly, or sin it all away — and when he has reached the tip end of his resources, and is ready to declare his life a failure — if there is anything still left to him worth hanging on to, it is more than likely to be something his mother said to him, or did for him, at that age when he was plastic and impressionable.

Neither can he ever quite manage to outlive the menace of harmful forces which may, unfortunately, operate on him, through that period.

To have been brought up, through childhood, in a home atmosphere of fault-finding, back-biting, caustic criticism, undisciplined temper, know-it-all-ism, unfriendly gossip about the neighbors, the constant imputation of low motives to other people, sullen disregard of others' rights, studied irreverence, jeers and flings at that which is beautiful and right and high-minded, and gentle —

To have been reared in that kind of air makes it next to impossible for an individual to reshape his early attitude toward society.

To have been brought up in a home where Mother-always-knows-best and rules the roost, or where Father stages frantic fits of unbridled rage to which the family succumbs — not because they love him, for they can't and he won't let them — but because he carries the pocketbook and they must pretend to be patient with his abominable petulance and silly savagery, sheerly for economic means — *will stamp a child for all his days.*

Life is hardly long enough to permit of a process sufficient to cut out all the diseased tissues in his soul, grown there through contagion with such influences.

So — the first force that grips the rudimentary soul is the *home*.

In rapid succession, thereafter, follow the influence of the schoolteacher, the school fellows — the influence of the chum. Oh — the chum! How much he has to answer for in the day of judgment!

Then, comes the increasing liberation of the early bonds. New and more forces gather about the soul, in the making, and leave their impress.

Along will come some other soul, slightly more matured, and lead this growing personality off into curious ways. Sometimes toward the light of day. Sometimes along a path that has ruin for its destination.

Often and often, an apparently chance meeting of two souls will mean that both of them are to go up — and on — or down and out.

Bobby Burns said, as he watched a drunken fellow staggering along the street:

> *My heart melts at human wretchedness;*
> *And with sincere tho' unavailing sighs*
> *I view the helpless children of distress,*
> *Whom Vice, as usual, has turn'd o'er to Ruin.*
> *O but for kind, tho' ill-requited friends,*
> *I had been driven forth like you forlorn,*
> *The most detested, worthless wretch among you!"*

And, as a matter of fact, he did, and was, not very much later. And, if the exact truth be told, Bobby was drunk and pretty well started down the slide when he wrote these lines.

But, even *that* in no manner disproves his theory. It may be said to tighten up the evidence, a bit, I think.

So — to the building of a human soul, there is erected upon the foundational soul, bequeathed by nature, a superstructural soul, made up of environmental forces, many of which are quite beyond the individual's volition.

Now comes the period of furnishing and equipping and decorating and preserving this soul.

What will a man *give* to have a soul that suits him — that not only suits him, today, but will be a decidedly pleasant soul to have about when he is eighty.

In very truth, he must give something to achieve a soul that is really worth having. This is a law of life.

The athlete does not try to save his muscles. He must use them — spend them — give them — if he would be strong.

Just as the farmer must take his grain and throw it away, and cover it up with dirt, if he expects to reap a harvest.

The student does not develop his brain by refusing to use it. The artist does not develop his talent by leaving it to lie dormant.

This is a law of life that we have only in proportion as we give away.

So — to the building of a really valuable soul — a man must give much. His life must be a continuous expression of service. Its motion must be centrifugal — constantly giving off power, rather than centripetal — gathering and hoarding it.

Every day, a miracle is wrought in him by which he is able to divide and subdivide his spiritual wealth, and pass it along, by kindly word, and gracious deed, and, not infrequently, through quiet, self-effacing sacrifice.

All this sounds trite, and old, but this is the law of life. This is the way a soul is built. What will a man *give?*

Edgar Park writes in an essay entitled "A Trip Around My Soul":

> *I am nothing but the head resident in the home in which my ancestors happen to be living at the present time. I sometimes stroll into my soul to visit them. In the center, I find a noble band drawn up ready for the day's work. There stands the old crusader in his armor, the Puritan martyr, the Pilgrim adventurer, and the solid phalanx of noble knights and squires, honest yeomen and laborers. There they stand, and their eyes flash back at me as though to say: "Here we are, Master. Command us whither you will!"*
>
> *These stand in the central campus of my soul. But soon my eyes begin to roam around the darker corners. I see there more ancestors who have not fallen into line. Lurking in the shadows around the edges I begin to discern them all. The lazy ones leaning up against the walls looking idly on; the*

snobbish ones with upturned noses in a group apart; I see to my astonishment the savage with paint and hatred on his face; and far away in the shadows at the back I seem to see one hanging by his tail to the trees of the forest.

Then my work begins. I pass round the dark corners of my soul and bring these recreants forth and whip them into line. The lazy ones I haul forth by the back of the neck, squealing and whining, and I have been even known to go so far as Saint Paul and kick them into their places in the line. The brutish ones I set at the hardest labor. The snobs I jeer and ridicule until, for very shame, they have to join the ranks. The savage I fight and conquer, though often blood is drawn before the victory is mine.

At last with every ancestor at my back I give the order, Forward, march! and we start off together for the day's work, every man in the ranks and the very monkey behind dragging a load.

A queer little conceit — this. But one which might offer much help if practiced consistently.

Temptation comes to me to do an unworthy thing — to take an unfair advantage — to play the coward — and I say, spotting some sneaking ancestor, lurking in the dark of my soul:

"Ah — so it is you — you who were yellow, and ran away, when your comrades were in a tight pinch at Marston Moor — so it is *you* who would smear me with your ocher. We'll see about that. Forward! shoulder arms, march!"

Would you have a great soul?
How much will you give?
"What wilt thou?" — quoth God. "Pay for it — and take it."

First Congregational Church
Los Angeles
September 2, 1928

the tarsan—a reappraisal

I ATTENDED a club luncheon because my good friend and neighbor, Sellem, was to make the talk.

The chairman, evidently thinking he could do his modest guest a good turn by giving him a brilliant send-off, arose, after the pie, and said something like this:

"I have the great honor to present, at this time, one of our most distinguished citizens, Will I. Sellem, who is not only an uncannily successful merchant but a thorough student of economics. During the table-talk of the past half hour, Mr. Sellem's ready wit and ripe wisdom have convinced me that he is an experienced raconteur. He will now speak to us on 'Personality in Business,' a field in which a Pied Piper personality such as his should surely find itself happily at home. Gentlemen — Mr. Sellem!"

As a matter of fact, Bill Sellem, albeit a prosperous merchant, is not a finished yarn-spinner at all, and doesn't think he is. He knows next to nothing about economics, as viewed academically. Bill is an upright, solid, generous, congenial chap, with a substantial store of information about merchandising, amassed by experience. Had he been presented in that role, he would have made an interesting and helpful speech.

But, unable to make a quick recovery after this complimentary jab in the ribs, Bill began with a perspiring, stammering disavowal of the flowery fiction that had been predicated of him, lost his way to the first point he had hoped to make, became utterly stampeded, and produced one of the dullest and most disheveled speeches I ever heard, which is saying quite a lot. I fancy that Mr. Sellem will remember that introduction as one reveres the tailor who flattered one by making a dress-coat that was too big, all over, and obviously intended for somebody else.

We have now come to the season when Adult Bible Class teachers are preparing to lead pilgrimages over the hallowed trail blazed by the most eminent Christian missionary who ever lived. And if they will just have the good judgment to be honest and discriminating in their interpretation of the celebrated Tarsan's career, these teachers can make this a memorable tour for all who have the good fortune to accompany them.

You will find that it is very easy to miss the point, in studying the life of Paul. No other character immortalized in the Bible has been so unfortunately presented. The typical portrait of this great hero of the faith is quite out of focus. There is always the temptation to build up a myth about him, a myth that clouds the real picture. Remembering his passionate sincerity, we may suppose that this would be as distasteful to Paul as it was to Montaigne when a complimentary artist painted him without his warts, and thus made the portrait unrecognizable.

Of course, the first mistake you are likely to commit, in teaching these lessons, is to devote too much time to the map of Asia Minor. I'll concede that maps are interesting. Your class should be instructed how to trace the journeys of this gallant apostle. Show them, in five minutes, the sweep of that adventure, from Antioch to Cyprus, Iconium, Lystra, Derbe, and back again to Antioch. The map will help make the story real; but don't try to make the map do all the work. This is not primarily a class in Geography. Don't imagine that you have accomplished anything important if everybody in the class answers correctly in unison when you ask what city Paul was in when he wrote the second letter to the Corinthians, or what time of the year it was when his ship was wrecked at Malta.

But that is not the most brilliant mistake threatening you. If you are not conscientious and courageous enough to risk a wee bit of dissatisfaction on the part of a few people who cherish some preconceived notions about a mythical Paul, your class will be defrauded of a fascinatingly interesting story that it has a right to know.

Get it firmly into your consciousness that Paul was by no means another Jesus! Make no attempt to dodge this valorous man's weaknesses, or to offer frail and unconvincing explanations of his blunders. One of the most valuable facts in a study of Paul is the ruthless candor with which his biographer in the Acts of the Apostles exposes his mistakes, and the costly sincerity of Paul's confessions of weakness. If Paul knows, at this minute (one hopes he does not!), what a vast misunderstanding prevails about him, in the minds of Christians, he is too chagrined to enjoy Heaven as he properly deserves.

Make sure you know exactly what were his points of strength. Be equally informed about his points of weakness. In your first clear view of him, Paul is galloping up and down the Palestinian roads, making life frightful for the little groups that were meeting by stealth to encourage one another in their Christian faith. Then you come to that dramatic occasion, on the highway near Damascus, when it is revealed to him that he has been making a terrific blunder. From that hour, Paul is the fearless, tireless champion of the faith he had set out to destroy.

But keep this in mind: Paul's spectacular conversion changed his religious opinions, but it did not change his temperament. He threw himself into the new cause with all the ardent, twenty-four-hours-per-day, self-abandoning zeal that he had previously invested on the other side! I do not mean that he went about now persecuting and killing the anti-Christians, in the same heat and violence of temper that had distinguished his career until then. Having espoused a pacifistic cause, he was all done with weapons and warfare. But the same uncompromising energy possessed him.

Naturally, this pleases us. There is nothing we like more than courage. You can have a very good time stirring your class with the story of Paul, skating on pretty thin diplomatic ice when he defended himself before Felix and Agrippa, in the course of which adventure he presented these self-satisfied officials with an X-ray picture of their own insides that was a great deal more honest than handsome. You should take pains to show your class the lonely courage of this great Christian when he confronted the silversmiths at Ephesus. Don't let your people miss Paul's audacious bravery and indefatigable zeal!

Make sure that you, yourself, adequately appreciate the amazing character of Paul's faith. His unquestioning belief in the ability of Christ to sustain him and see him through any and every crisis, is absolutely unexampled in the long story of Christian fidelity through the ages. One of the most conspicuous features of that faith is its optimism. Everything was going to turn out all right. Paul in chains, sitting on the damp floor of a dungeon, writing a cheerful letter admonishing his friends to keep up their courage, and reporting that he was contented and happy, is a noble and salutary sight to present to aspiring Christians — especially in view of the fact that so many good people have a notion that sighs and whines and tears are among the precious fruits of faith.

Paul never pitied himself. Be sure they get that! He never despaired. While he waited for the executioner, he wrote that he had fought a good fight, had kept the faith, and was en route to a crown!

But be careful to let them see, also, the temptations that are bound to assail a person of Paul's temperament. He is so zealous, he is apt to be impatient with people who can't keep up with him. He doesn't like to take the time, from his busy, tempestuous life, to sit down with someone who disagrees, and quietly talk it through in a placid temper.

Do not try to make a flattering picture of that event when Paul stampeded the Jewish synagogues in Corinth, made a blustery speech, grew hotly indignant when it was not pleasantly received, stormed out of the place shouting he would have nothing more to do with them, and opened a rival church, next door. Don't try to reconcile this impetuous outburst of zeal with the plainly stated wishes of Jesus for the spread of the gospel. Jesus would never have done anything of the kind!

In short — be fair with Paul; and, to be fair with him, you must present him as he was. Nobody could ever understand the Tarsan's defects of method any better than he understood them himself. There was always a big war going on inside him.

Be careful, too, that you do not yield to the common temptation to justify all of Paul's attempts to be doctrinal. At many points, the Christianity taught by the Tarsan is a different cultus, entirely, than the Christianity taught by the Master. These errors are to be accounted for on the grounds of passionate zeal, and, for that reason, are easily forgiven him; but don't try to teach your class that they were not errors.

Paul was rather proud of his ability as a philosopher and logician. When he started out with an argument, he bestrode it and rode it until it dropped of sheer fatigue. The all-embracing salvation offered through Christ is made to include not only the soul but the body. Not content with letting it go at that, Paul explains how physical resurrection takes place — an entirely new item in the program of salvation which Jesus had not known about. The absolute power of God was so far-reaching that He knew — and indeed decreed — which human souls were to be saved and which were to be lost before it was put up to them that they were expected to choose whether to accept or reject this great salvation. One thing was sure: God was going to see that justice was done: He was not going to be flouted; He was coming, pretty soon, almost any day now, in judgment. It was an easy step from that position to the belief that the end of the world was imminent! Paul confidently believed that the final wind-up would occur during his own lifetime.

Don't try to show the class that Paul was invariably correct in his opinions, or in the technique by which he promoted his opinions. It is not a part of your task to make a minor deity of Paul, or to set him alongside Jesus in the regard of Christian believers. Picture him exactly as he was, and the story will be inspiring. There will be a few people to whom this honest appraisal of Paul will be offensive. Nothing will content them but to deify Paul and make his every word as authoritative as the words of the Christ. You will discover, however, that the large majority of your class will welcome this re-invoice of the noble Tarsan, because whatever little they lose of veneration for him as an infallible teacher, they will more than gain by finding him to be a comrade in the great adventure of Christian faith.

St. James United Church
Montreal

Incline us toward the beautiful things of life. Give us keener zest for the discovery and adaptation of the forces that lift burdens from men's shoulders. Increase our zeal to make the world a fairer abode for all mankind.

GALLIO — A PORTRAIT OF THE LARGER INDIFFERENCE

And as Paul opened his mouth to speak, Gallio said unto the Jews: 'If there were a question of wrong done, or a criminal action, it would be reasonable for me to bear with you; but if it be a matter of words and names and your synagogue laws, look ye to it; for I will be no judge of such matters.' For Gallio cared for none of these things. — Acts 18: 14-17 excerpts

So DELIGHTFULLY engaging to the student of Christianity's early development in the hands of the resourceful and intrepid Tarsan, Paul, is the eventful story of this missionary's career, that what he did, and what he said, has the effect of driving into almost total eclipse the life and thoughts of the individuals who play the minor roles in that drama which Luke offers in The Acts of the Apostles.

And, without meaning to subtract an iota from the commendable interest attaching to the heroic and faithful Paul, it is rather a pity that we have so concentrated our attention upon him that we have failed to see the really tremendous importance of certain characters whose lives, at strategic moments, connected so interestingly with his own.

Indeed, this failure to evaluate the personal qualities of some of these people (important contemporaries of Paul's) has disabled us from viewing the great missionary, himself, in the light of all the intriguing facts which — when known — add human interest and warmth to the figure of the great apostle.

It is with this thought in mind that I am prepared to offer

you the story of Gallio, the pro-consul of Achaia, distinguished for his carelessness in respect to any sectarian religion — and his indifference to all squabbles among fanatics.

In all the discourses I ever heard, on the subject of Paul's experience in Gallio's court, the judge might as well have been without a name or a story. What the preacher was always trying to get at was the bad time Paul was having in Corinth — persecuted by the Jews — and mobbed by a miscellaneous rabble on the streets — and haled to court where, before a probably fat and lazy Roman judge, the case was dismissed because the magistrate had no interest in religion. If Gallio was noticed at all, in the homily, it was only to deplore the fact that he was so indifferent to an important issue.

About all that the present-day Christian knows of Gallio, therefore, is the passing comment of the homilist who remarks that Gallio, like so many other people, unfortunately, was indifferent. He didn't care.

I bring you, then, the case of careless Gallio, today. I am not going to say much about Paul. For the moment, he is to be the minor character in the story. Instead of Paul's occupying the center of the stage, with all the actors merely tossing him cues for impressive speeches — Judge Gallio is to be the hero of the piece.

And, that being the task before us, I want you to take a walk about the city, first, and make sure you have all the scenery in its proper relationship, before you become acquainted with the biggest man in it — the ruler of it — the very life or death of it — who happened to be Marcus Annaeus Novatus Gallio.

If you carry in your mind a picture of Greece, you will not need to be told that this historic country is all but broken in two where the Gulf of Corinth and the Saronic Gulf lack but four miles of union. From the earliest times, little boats used to make a portage across the isthmus; and Julius Caesar did some digging there, in the hope of a serviceable ship canal. At widely spaced intervals the work has been resumed, and, at present, there is a small waterway which the big boats are afraid of, and rarely use.

But, largely because the city of Corinth was an easy clearing house between Eastern and Western commerce, it was always a coveted position, and, consequently, a frequent battleground of ambitious militarists, eager for possession of this territory, known to the navigators as the Bridge of the Sea; to the politicians as the Eye of Greece, and to the poets as the City of Two Great Waters.

In 150 B.C., at exactly the same time that Scipio was ruining the beauty and sacking the wealth of Carthage, another Roman, Mummius, destroyed the glorious old city of Corinth, which for many generations had been the most important mercantile and military stronghold of the Greeks — a municipality whose great prosperity had encouraged that leisure which promotes the arts and letters.

At that period, Rome was not only ruthless, in her drunken infatuation with her physical supremacy; but, not yet having achieved any interest in life beyond military and commercial advancement, despised all people who had concern for such silly and effeminate fripperies as sculpture and song and drama. Polybius writes that he himself saw Roman soldiers — during the sack of Corinth — playing checkers on the backs of priceless paintings, torn from marble galleries; and no one can calculate, today, what enormous losses — to the world of beauteous ideals — were sustained when Corinth, the lovely, fell under the barbaric broadaxe of Mummius.

But, no matter how badly a city may be dealt with, it cannot be ruined for all time if situated in a geographical position of command. So, upon the ashes of art galleries, and the crumbled remains of unreplaceable statuary, Rome began to build what rapidly became a boom town. It fairly sprang up in a night, like Singapore.

The Greek merchants, who had fled for their lives, were encouraged to return. Rome never had any objection to the prosperities of her provincials — greatly preferred that they should be wealthy and happy, indeed; for it was easier to get tribute money out of them if they had it to pay.

But when the Greeks came back, with nothing but their personal belongings — and had to start life anew — they were too hard-pressed with strictly economic perplexities to give any attention to arts and letters — so the Corinth of shady groves, gloriously landscaped by artists, and embellished with masterly statuary, was forever gone, to be replaced by a new and noisy Corinth, bent on making money, the easiest and quickest way.

And thus it came to pass that the city, when Paul visited it, was again at the height of prosperity — but, this time, not wealthy of mind or soul — but full of purse, rotund of figure, insolent of manner, and avaricious beyond the telling.

You will have observed of the New Testament that — while the four gospels are distinctly pastoral in tone, written in the open country — and mostly about country people — with a figure in the center of the action who calls himself the Good Shepherd, and has much to do with fishermen and vine-growers — the Letters of Paul resound with the grind of traffic, the tension and torsion of high-keyed life in great and wicked cities. Paul was essentially a metropolitan; and his admonition, consequently, is particularly useful to the city-dweller, because it comes from a man who knew the inner life of the larger metropolises of his day. And because great cities are all singularly alike, in their problems of poverty and vice; nerve strain and competition; with too much flamboyant luxury at the top and too much sullen discontent at the bottom — the Pauline Epistles are quite informative to urban people, everywhere, albeit a bit depressing.

The general average of humanity, in the world, wasn't nearly as wicked as the little cross sections of the social order that Paul knew in the slave slums of great port cities.

Paul spent a year and a half in Corinth, and, as you are aware, practically all of his preserved letters were written from there; a fact which (when we know what kind of place Corinth was) lights up certain rather dismaying comments of his concerning the rapacity of politics, the plight of the poor, and the keen activity of the world, the flesh, and the devil.

Not only was Corinth crowded with eager and predatory Italians, hopeful of easy fortune; and the returned Greek merchants, now more concerned about bread and butter than painting and philosophy; but the city was rapidly filling with Jews. Previous to the ruin of the splendid old city, Corinth had not encouraged Jewish immigration. But now that it was to be a commercial center, pure and simple, there was no reason why the Jews should be frowned upon. They came (it was an easy voyage back and forth to their beloved Jerusalem) and brought along all their bigotries, their racial customs, and their exasperating self-assertiveness.

Wherever Jew met Greek, there was a brawl. And the imposing synagogues — which began to clamor for attention — were noxious in the eyes of what was left of the old Corinthian stock. As for the Romans, they had consistently pursued the policy of letting their subjects worship anything, anywhere, anyhow. No religion was too ridiculous to be scorned, too preposterous to be disciplined, or too abominable to be stopped — so long as the people who believed in it were contented.

This, then, is a sketchy picture of the new Corinth — noisy and vulgar, claptrap and sordid, selfish and greedy — that Paul lived in, as part-time preacher of the Gospel, working as a sailmaker to pay expenses, and loving nothing better than a row with the Jews who hated him because he was a Christian, and the Greeks who despised him because he was a Jew — with occasional skirmishes with the Romans, who were annoyed because his disputes frequently blocked the traffic, and stirred up distracting controversies among potential customers.

But — you must know Gallio. I quite insist upon that. I want you to like Gallio; and I think you will, when you become acquainted.

Luke doesn't say much about him, but Tacitus and Pliny do. Paul knew practically nothing about him, I presume; but the greatest Romans of the period loved and admired him. For — in spite of the fact that the bulk of the Romans were crude, ill-mannered, rackety go-getters, infatuated with desire to strut before their neighbors, there was a little group of very fine souls, whose names are still alive — just because they were committed to high ideals.

Such a family was the house of Annaeus. What a brilliant group of relatives they were.

There was Annaeus Meia, the oldest brother, who became the most celebrated geographer of his day.

Annaeus Meia's son even outsped his father's fame, when as Lucan the poet, he handed his name to the field of everliving letters.

There was Lucius Annaeus Seneca, the immortal philosopher-essayist, the second brother.

And the younger brother of the Annaeus family was Marcus Novatus who, while in school (suddenly bereft of his father) was adopted as a son by Rome's most brilliant rhetorician, Gallio. Marcus Novatus took his foster father's name; and was ever afterward called Gallio.

We are induced to believe that here was one of the most lovable and interesting men one might ever hope to meet. Seneca dedicated a monumental set of his books to his brother Gallio, and — in the brief page of dedication — he pays the most tender tribute to the youth whose geniality, uprightness, love of justice,

and personal charm had so constantly made him beloved. ("Dul-
cis" is the word he uses — his "sweet" brother.)

I wish I might tell you a very great deal about the experiences
of these two brothers — Seneca and Gallio.

Very briefly: Seneca, disgusted with the hard, cold, rasping
greed and external glitter of rapacious Rome, became quite a
social radical — and was banished, for his public utterances, to
the Isle of Corsica.

Gallio grieved for his exiled brother until his health was shattered. He was sent, by his foster father, on a long voyage. He
toured the whole known world; seeking distraction from his
sorrow, mellowing into a broad-minded cosmopolitan, who had
seen enough of the world's hopes and fears, its programs and
perplexities, its sodden superstitions and tiresome sophistries, its
benighted bigotries and insolent intolerances, to have completely
graduated from the puny little ideas which inhabit the minds
of most persons who live with their noses to the grindstone, and
no vision of other tasks and ambitions than their own.

After a few years, Seneca was recalled from exile by the impertinent Agrippina, who desired him to come back and be the
tutor for her dear little boy. The little boy was a darling child
— and must be brought up with all the fine intellectual graces
of a gentleman; so Seneca was picked for his teacher.

The little boy was Nero. He may have been, as a little boy,
all that his mother thought. But he gave her a great deal of
anxiety before he finally had her assassinated.

We are informed that the first five years of Nero's reign were
distinguished by wisdom, justice, and the other solid virtues
which Seneca loved. But, when Seneca, discouraged with the
growing attitude of headiness, self-infatuation, and grandiose
paranoia of his epileptic sovereign, found that he must abandon
his own efforts to save Rome's soul, through Nero, the gentle
patriot committed suicide. Which act, by the way, was not
considered reprehensible at all by the intellectuals of that period.

If a man came to some impasse where he would be annoyed or humiliated or frustrated, he stepped out of life as easily as one's retiring from any other scene of disorder. Gave a party to his intimates; divided his personal trinkets; mixed a glass of poison — and was out-of-it.

(Nero's actual slide into complete moral ruin dated from the hour of Seneca's death.)

When Seneca abandoned life because Nero had so cruelly disappointed him, Gallio made some public comments on the sort of leadership that would hound to death the best brains of the empire — and Gallio was beheaded.

I have wanted to refresh your minds on all these things about Gallio before viewing him at the time of that story, in the Acts of the Apostles.

Seneca had just been recalled from Corsica, and is, apparently, in high favor at court. Undoubtedly owing to his influence, his brother Gallio gets the appointment as pro-consul of Achaia, with headquarters in Corinth. Gallio is combination mayor, chief magistrate, consul, superintendent of the port, revenue collector, and minister-extraordinary. Whatever Rome has to say to that part of Greece, she will say through Judge Gallio — and whatever back-talk is to come from Achaia must be returned through Gallio.

And how the gentle-spirited, world-minded, lovable Marcus Novatus Annaeus Gallio must have despised the burden of dealing with the selfish brawls of greedy classes, grabbing things out of one another's hands — can only be imagined.

According to custom, his pro-consular chair was carried about from one precinct to another; where it would be put down, a rug spread before it, guards stationed about it, and here was a court. The docket was read, of cases to be heard in that locality, and the Judge listened to every murmur of plaint.

On this particular day, a bad-tempered mob came lurching

into Judge Gallio's presence, dragging Paul on a rope, and shouting that he was breaking up their synagogue, teaching a form of worship flat against their belief. They proceeded to call the roll of his bad doctrines, and define his heresies; and when they were out of breath, Paul — gifted in forensic art, and abundantly well qualified to take care of his own interests in a debate — squared himself to reply.

He was all set to go, with a very deferential greeting like Most Honored and Worthy Gallio — but, for once, Paul did not get a chance to be heard.

Gallio wearily raised a hand, as he saw the prisoner tuning up for an address, and said:

"Jews: if this were a question of wrongdoing, or a criminal action, it would be reasonable for me to bear with you; but, if it be a matter of words and names and laws of the synagogue, look ye to it; for I will be no judge of such matters."

This delighted the Greeks, who stood by. Not that they had any special interest in Paul or Paul's religion; but they were glad to see the Jews get a drubbing; so, to show their appreciation, they jumped into the party, laid violent hands on the leader of the synagogue contingent, and pounded him vigorously. Gallio made no remonstrance.

Luke says: "Gallio cared for none of these things."

I don't wonder. I don't blame him. Nobody could fool Gallio. He had been about, quite a bit. The world was an open book. He knew what led people to quarrel and fight over religion: it was because they hadn't any. Gallio knew enough about the things of the spirit to understand that whenever religion gets to fighting in order to prove that it is the correct attitude for a man to have toward God, it only makes itself ridiculous.

Some of the commentators on the Acts of the Apostles say that Gallio was certainly a blasé and cold-blooded judge — to sit there and say nothing while a Greek rabble pounded a Jewish plaintiff, in a Roman court that could have sent the whole outfit of them to the galleys for life by the mere wave of a hand; that Gallio certainly didn't care much what happened in his tribunal. But I think that Gallio was just sitting there dispassionately contemplating the enormity of the insoluble ignorance of men who would excoriate one another, and assault one another, and rush to court, and bang people over the head — in an endeavor to show how much nearer God they were than their contemporaries.

Gallio cared for none of these things. . . . No; who could *expect* him to care?

Gallio was a gentleman. Gallio was a scholar. Gallio had the soul of an artist — and the mind of a philanthropist. All he wanted of the world was that every man might have a chance to live in as much peace and comfort and happiness as his station in the scheme of things permitted. To be honest; to be generous; to speak kindly of people; to give credit easily, and censure sparingly — that was the Gallio whom Seneca admired — Seneca who had been driven into exile for loving the people and hating the tyrants.

And had the brawlers from the synagogue come before Gallio to inquire whether it was better to love than to hate; whether it was better to forgive than to carry a grudge; whether it was better to be neighborly than to quarrel — I am sure the brother of Seneca and the uncle of Lucan would have had something to say. But if it was only another long-winded controversy over words and names and the relative superiority of ceremonies — Gallio was willing they should fight it out among themselves.

I like Gallio. He is of the salt of the earth. He would have loved the simplehearted Galilean, who dealt with the harmonious and elemental truths of life lived in the spirit.

To me, this great Roman stands as a type: a well-informed man of large affairs — who longs for the supremacy of the true, the good, the kindly and the beautiful — to whom Religion would be a distinct embellishment if it were interpreted as the quest of the soul for its relation to its Infinite Source.

But how often these high-powered Gallios are obliged to view religion as a mere debating ground for pedants — and how often they turn away from the church because of the inner ferment of captious and quarrelsome people who use it as a mere clearing house for their petulance and a forum for the airing of their pettiness.

Gallio cares for none of these things: why should he? Who wants him to? What merit could attach to him for pretending to take an interest in that manner of spiritual culture?

To my mind, one of the most tragic facts in modern life is the apparent incapacity of organized religious institutions to attract a larger number of the Gallio type of heart and mind. It is not that the Gallio sort of people are cold-blooded intellectuals, disdainful of the sentimental considerations involved in a proper reverence for The Infinite, or indifferent to the social needs of less privileged persons:

For, wherever the beauteous things of Nature are on display, we find them eager and enthused. They are true patriots in their desire for the peace and prosperity of their country. They are patrons of the arts; they encourage enduring literature; they give of their time and money to remedial programs of charities, corrections, and sensible reforms.

But, how perplexing it is to see the casualness with which they dismiss the responsibilities of church activities; candidly declaring (when pressed for a decision) that they do not care for such things.

Why don't they care? Is it because they are too little and mean to take interest in the unselfish altruism of Jesus — the great Head of the Christian Church? No; their general attitude toward society makes that charge untenable. Is it because their wide experience of life's larger activities and aims has made them mentally remote from the generality of people — and temperamentally enisled from the common problems of humanity? No, their vital interest in the rehabilitation of broken lives testifies that the trouble is not at this point.

Their difficulty is the same as Gallio's. What they would like to derive, from religious teaching and religious organizations, is a cultivation of the spirit-life. Nobody can fool them about the real imperatives of imperial living. They know what virtues are requisite to a man's spiritual exultation.

They know that to be spiritually efficient a man must have arrived at such magnanimity that (without conscious mental struggle) he can sincerely rejoice over people's good fortune; to be completely free of little jealousies, petty envies, and rasping covetousness. They know that to be spiritually sound, one must live in an altitude quite above the miasmic fog of back-biting, quarrelsomeness, and fault-finding.

They look to the church for direction in purging themselves of these devastating littlenesses, which make life hard and unlovely. And, too often, they discover, to their disappointment and dismay, that the churches are not only unequipped to offer help, in that field, by noble precept and shining example — but are frequently honeycombed with the particular kind of ferment and unrest which they have so earnestly desired to escape.

Unfortunately, not every preacher can prudently say these things because, if his own church is disharmonious, it looks as if he were scolding. But — no such trouble being at issue here at St. James, one needs not be reticent about calling a spade a spade!

The Gallios have found out enough about the world at large to know how easy life is to live for people who are consistently courteous; who practice gentility; ready with their sympathy; generous in their judgments; and calmly tolerant of other people's convictions.

They know that Jesus taught this type of high-mindedness, and lived it, every hour — including the last one, when, on his cross, he pardoned his torturers because they didn't know the enormity of their blunder. And, seeking to build into their own lives something of this splendid Christ-spirit of love and under-standing, they seek his Church — to find, not infrequently, that there is no more real love and understanding *there* than in the covetous market place, or the brawling secular forum.

The preachers have railed at Judge Gallio, because he didn't care. Why should he care? What allurement was there in this tempestuous racket that could possibly attract a man the size of Gallio?

One wishes that this noble Roman, when voyaging in the East, might have toured inland from Tyre, a day's journey, and sat, for an afternoon, on the beach of the Lake Gennesaret, in company with some old fisherman, who could have told him of a religion he would have loved, and a spirit-filled personality he would have been glad to follow.

One looks forward with hope and longing to a very definite renaissance of that religion — a faith that made men valorous, generous, confident, open-minded, open-handed. For, when that becomes Christianity's prime motive and exclusive errand, Gallio, and all his spiritual successors, will be glad to listen.

What we most need now, in this turbulent world, is the spirit of goodwill among all the people. Whatever hinders that blend-ing, conciliating, healing gospel of sympathy and understanding is — wittingly or unwittingly — at enmity with Christ, even though it may seem to be a very pious institution.

And whoever turns away indifferently from everything that makes for divisions and discords can be assured that, in-that-far at least, he is a friend and follower of The Nazarene.

Los Angeles
October 23, 1927

peter's denial

Did I not see thee in the garden with him? — St. John 18:26

PETER, the rock — Peter, the Christ-appointed head of the church — Peter, the adoring, impulsive disciple, had denied his Lord.

From time immemorial scoffers have railed at the seeming inconsistency in lauding the life of one, who in the hour of trial — in the crucial test — had disowned his Saviour. It has been difficult for the church to explain the disciple's conduct on this occasion, and reference to it from the pulpit is seldom made because it *is* an unpleasant affair. But the Bible is its own apology and no part of it should be withheld because it narrates something which seems humiliating. The practical man would say that if the Bible cannot support itself without hiding some of its inexplicable features, it should be abolished as a rule of faith: and the practical man is correct in his assertion.

It should not be our purpose to attempt an explanation for every biblical narrative, and to soften and palliate every inconsistency in Christ's early followers. It is an offense against man's reason, and really damages the cause of Christ. If the Christian religion cannot stand alone without any human veneering to cover the less beautiful parts of its structure, let it stand in all its gaunt ruggedness, and let the world behold wherein the structure is imperfect. *Christ,* himself, despised gloss, and tinsel, and whitened sepulchers, and asks for no human varnish of pretty words and apologetic phrases to be spread artistically over those parts of the great structure of religion which may seem imperfect to man, with his poor weak understanding.

This *structure* of religion is not unlike an old, massive church which has stood for ages as a symbol of peace and comfort to worshipers. Even the unbeliever cannot but admire its architecture, its sublime beauty. *It* has its lights and shadows. What if the giant oaks do cast a shadow through its great stained windows! What though the weeping cypress trees do gracefully bow in plaintive sadness before its very doors! What if the ivy and the lichen do tenderly fold their tiny arms about the tower, and the mold of ages all but obliterate the date of her erection from the cornerstone! — is it not all the more *beautiful*, and *sublime*, and adorable for *that?* And if some of the stones look gaunt and ragged, and unpolished, does that not show that they have been exposed to severe tests of wind and weather, and does not the exquisite beauty of the neighboring stones appear all the more glorious in contrast? And now should we scale the modern ladder of our own original ideas, and paint these ancient building stones with our poor gloss of man's invention?

Some modern theologians are trying to remodel our old church. They are seeking to tear away the ivy and the lichen from its walls, and to hew down the shady oaks that there may be no shadow — and the cypress that there may be no tender sorrow. They will paint the whole edifice with modern theorizing, and then, what will be left? Simply an absurd, old-fashioned building — robbed of all the embellishments of nature which made it a grand and stately legacy of the ages past, and humiliated by comparison with neighboring twentieth-century edifices. The grand old church of Christ is of the ages. It was built in an earlier day. Let us adore it! It has endured the chilling blasts and scorching heat of centuries. It is strong to protect us, for it was built by Christ.

Is it not indeed beautiful as it stands so old, so imposing? And as the rush and whirl of our active, busy, modern lives sweep past her stately walls, is she not still a protection — a strong fortress? And within her chancel the old organ which has pealed and echoed truth for centuries, need not be supplanted by modern orchestras, discoursing the light and flippant notes of popular opinion.

Peter, the hitherto invincible, had denied his Saviour. He, who had cried at the Last Supper "not my feet only, but also my hands and my head." He, who had been asked to tarry in the garden while his Master prepared for the bitter hour which was to redeem the world at a cost of the first and only sinless life. Peter — who would build a temple for the Master — he who had openly declared his knowledge that Christ was the Son of God — Peter, with an oath, had denied him, *thrice*.

And just in a passing thought, let us ask ourselves if a denial of Christ today is any less heinous in a follower of him than it was in a terrorized disciple. How free we are to condemn the weakness and cowardice of Christ's early followers. We are all impatience when we read of our Lord's crucifixion, and we ask, "Why could not the hundreds who had praised his name one week before have rushed into the midst of his murderers and rescued their Master?" And again we ask, "How could these men, who loved the Lord, stand about and see him cursed and reviled?" Ah well, Christ lives today and is present with us, and yet we, his acknowledged disciples, are often willing to stand and hear his name reviled. We even smile sometimes when some witticism of a friend is colored a little by the blood of our Saviour. And if we, who countenance such idle profaning of our Lord's name — if we are not just as surely standing about his cross, and smiling at his pain — the difference is yet to be explained.

'Tis sunset on Calvary! Hours ago the crowd of cruel ruffians departed — quarreling over the clothing, the very touch of whose woven hem had healed infirmities — departed, and wended their way toward the city, shouting and clamoring to keep down the morbid spirits of terror and remorse. Did you ever notice that when a *man is in the wrong*, and *knows it*, and *will not admit it*, he makes more noise than the man who is right, or the man who is wrong and admits it?

The company has long since disappeared, and now the sun sinks between the hills leaving a glorious blood-red streak across the western sky. And the stars, never more bright than in beautiful Palestine, twinkle as if all unconscious of the sorrow on Calvary. We shall not attempt to picture the great rough tree on the summit of Golgotha, as it stands dimly outlined against the darkening sky.

The crucifix is often thought of as a symbol of Roman Catholicism, and Catholics are often condemned in its frequent use, and although I would not have you holding continually before your eyes the image of that great tragedy, still, I wish that away down in the sacred treasure house of the memory, there might be a tiny crucifix. It might be so very small that you could just see the white form of the Dying Saviour against the little cross. And when men curse your Lord, or speak of him disrespectfully, or lightly drag his Name into the foreground of some jest — I wish that that tiny crucifix which is hidden away in memory's treasure house *might rise and expand* in your mind's eye till it obscured the vision of all else. I wish that it might appear with a cross more rough and nails more cruel and thorns more sharp than brush can paint or chisel carve. And hung thereon, a form more fair; a face more filled with plaintive sadness, furrowed o'er with streams of crimson blood more red than art is able to portray or words describe.

But to return to Golgotha at eventide. Two men with marks of Jewish aristocracy plainly written on their faces are toiling up the mountain and timidly approach the cross. They take the pierced body from the tree and bear it gently away, with tears and bitter sorrow. Are they the only Nicodemus, and Joseph of Arimathea of whom we know? Have we ever allowed Christ to be put to open shame, and reviled, and persecuted without remonstrance, and then when evening was come, and the crowd had cleared away, and all had become quiet — and you know what an effect the approaching night has on one's feelings — a sort of recapitulation of the day, that misty hour, when as the poet has said, "The day is done, and darkness falls from the wings of Night, as a feather is wafted downward from an eagle in his flight" — did we not then come close to the cross, and with bitter tears and agonizing remorse tenderly care for our Saviour?

Newell Dwight Hillis:
Sin may warp the soul out of line, but repentance will spring it back again to its normal place. He who has pondered long upon life's deepest problems knows that memory holds no dearer recollection than hours when the erring child moves from sin toward confession and forgiveness. Disobedient, the child fears the parents' disapproval. Dreading the discovery, it conceals the sin through deceit. Soon the sweetness of the stolen pleasure passes away. Remorse makes a dark cloud to overshadow the child. Each moment increases the gloom. And when darkness falls, and the prayers are said, and the mother's kiss leaves the child alone, with solitude comes increased sorrow. Because its first lie is a sin greater than it can bear, the child calls aloud, and flinging itself into the arms of the returning mother, in a wild, passionate abandon of tears, and sobs, pours forth the full story of its sin; and mingling its torrent with the parent's tears, is cleansed in that deep fountain named the mother's heart. What hour in life holds a happiness so deep and sweet as that hour of confession and forgiveness for the child, when it falls asleep, having recovered its simplicity? And men are but children grown tall and strong.

There are many types of remorse. There is the remorse of Judas, cowardly dog, who drops his blood-bought silver, and hastens to the forest to hang himself and rid the world of his worthless life. But the remorse of Peter turned its current of fiery self-indignation into a living stream of fervor for *work, hard work, dangerous work.*

And when *we* are filled with remorse until the very inmost fibers of our beings revolt against their own activity — and we crave death that we may be rid of life, yet fear it because we know what the future must surely hold for us, let us arise, and *work* — ever actively, never ceasingly, *work.* It will not hurt us. Few men die from overwork. Many die of worry and some of misplaced energy, but few from the effects of hard work, and triumphant indeed must be the end of that few.

Peter did not spend the balance of his days with eyes red from weeping, and mind shattered with worrying, but from the very day of Pentecost, Peter was simply irresistible in his extension of the gospel. Working, praying, preaching, teaching — looking not behind except to gather new impetus from the memory of his Master's life, but pressing forward continually, he became indeed the rock upon which the church was to find a firm foundation — safe and sure. And if Peter ever did look back to his act of perfidy it must have been in the spirit which inspired Tennyson to say, "I hold it truth with him who sings, To one clear harp in diverse tones, That men may rise on steppingstones, Of their dead selves to higher things!"

What this indefatigable servant of Christ passed through in his later years is largely conjecture. It is known, however, that when the time came for Peter again to choose between owning or denying his Lord, he was not questioned by a harmless maiden, but by officers of one of the most dastardly despots in the most cruel reign ever recorded in history, and Peter chose to *own* his Lord. And the death which Christ had predicted for him was administered brutally and accepted willingly. There is a legend, well founded on fact, that Peter requested that he be crucified head downward, deeming himself unworthy to die the death of the Saviour.

The world thinks little when an unbeliever scoffs at Christianity. The very attitude he assumes in the matter debars him from wielding any particular influence, for should he speak disrespectfully of Christ, the world says, "You cannot judge; you have never investigated the Christian religion. You cannot speak wisely on the subject." But when a believer — a professing Christian — denies his Master, the world pauses in its busy strife for just a moment, and asks again to make sure, "Are you not one of his?" And when he denies his Lord again, the world, as if disgusted at the man's own weakness of purpose, asks: "Did I not see thee in the garden with him?"

The busy, practical world hates a turn-coat. This cold, stern race of ours detests a traitor. The Christian cannot make himself smaller, even in the world's estimation, than by denying the holy cause he once espoused. The unbeliever may profess faith and embrace Christianity without proving traitorous to any cause. He is merely escaping from the prison house of sin. He has not been serving as a loyal, loving subject to the host of sin, but rather as a serf — a slave. For what man can be found who can truthfully say he loves the devil? So the sinner, escaping from the prison house of doubt and trouble, is not a traitor. But when a Christian deliberately surrenders and casts himself into the ranks of the enemy for protection, oh, what a traitor he is — and what protection he obtains. His very captors hate him for his cowardice, and scoff, and say, "You were wandering around outside the picket line without your armor on. Oh, what a soldier."

Do you remember the historical narrative of Benedict Arnold? And how he expected homage at the court of England, to whom he had sold his honor, and betrayed his country? And as he was shown through the corridors of the royal palace during an evening of court festivities, the nobles turned at his approach and were peculiarly interested in some other direction. Heartsick at such disfavor shown him when even a royal ovation could scarcely have lifted his spirits from remorse, he turned to an aged noble, whose name was always a symbol for valor, and with outstretched hand, introduced himself. The old General straightened up haughtily, ignored the proffered hand, and said, sternly, "I cannot take the hand of one who has sold his country."

Do you remember the narrative of another traitor of whom we have been speaking? How the angel said to the women at the tomb, that first bright Easter morning, "Go tell his Disciples, and Peter" — *and Peter* — for fear that he might no longer lay claim to the title disciple.

And thus the merciful Father pardons traitors to His cause. If it were not for His Infinite Goodness and Mercy, I fear the Hallowed Home above would indeed be a lonely place, and did God mete out the justice we deserve, it is to be feared that a traveler from this orb to Heaven would find himself alone with God. "Did I not see thee with him in the Garden?" Did I not hear thy songs of praise, and fervent prayers, and sincere exhortations? Did I not see thee at his Table? Did I not hear thee say that should all else forsake the Master, that thou, *thou* shouldest be faithful?

Is the world asking us such questions? Are we loyal to Christ, or are we strong in the morning, weak at noonday and repentant at twilight? We may save ourselves many hours of remorse by being always loyal and true.

And let us not forget that tiny crucifix which we are going to lock away in our memory's treasure house. And may it be the lodestar in the firmament of our lives.

Shining Brightly, on our pathway;
Guiding Truly, through our perils;
Welcoming Gladly, at the Throne!

Flat Rock, March 31, 1901
Monroeville, April 4, 1901
North Manchester, April 21, 1901
Marquardt, June 10, 1901
Antioch, July 30, 1901
Des Moines, July 13, 1902
North Manchester, November 22, 1902
Slater, July 20, 1902

May no sloth of ours, nor any despair, nor memory of past blunders, keep us away from the divine companionship.

the master's cup

I PRESUME that we all find our thoughts turning occasionally toward our childhood days and the dreams which made them so full of happiness. Some of these same cherished dreams are ever to remain indelibly stamped upon our memories.

Our fancy was pliable as wax in those days. The very toys with which we played were realities, and we took them much more seriously than our elders thought.

The tin soldiers composed a real army. There were bold and daring dashes into the enemy's country — not unattended with danger and peril of death. For others of us to whom the varying fortunes of war did not appeal, the dolls were living creatures who attended tea parties, mindful of all the conventionalities of which the youthful fancier was cognizant. And often illness came into the mimic family, and some have been known to die and be interred with due solemnity — while real tears coursed down the little cheeks of those who later were to know grief in all its fullness — the prototype of this queer play.

Ah, the irony of it all.

I know of a woman grown who, when a child, dressed her imitation children in bits of silk and satin given her by a friend employed in a casket manufactory.

And thus life and death — the real and the unreal — the

visionary and the plainly seen — go hand in hand and side by side.

The years passed slowly — very slowly. Each was a young eternity. And the tin soldiers and the dolls gave place to other things as visionary as they. We began to absorb ourselves in fairy books — in dream books. Did any printed page contain statements easily believed and quite in accord with our experiences — that page was dull. We concerned ourself about genii and the wonderful lamp of Aladdin. We didn't care for facts — we wanted fancies — and oh, the dreams we wove into illusive webs of which the warp was as stable as the rainbow and the woof as enduring as the dew.

We went with our fictitious heroes into strange battle with wild beasts and ogres which none had ever fought outside these books. We were courageous in those days — and though our little hearts beat very rapidly when danger seemed to threaten, we never quailed, and always came out victorious with the last page.

Chiefest among these adventures were those of feudal days, "the days of old when knights were bold and fairy tales were told."

Always fighting — always riding — always pursuing. It didn't make much difference to us then why we fought, or where we rode, or what we were pursuing.

True, it was mentioned occasionally when a knight took the oath, that he was pledged to search for and recover the Holy Grail — but we did not know what the Holy Grail was — nor care very much — for, as you remember, we considered no details or causes or principles. They were quite immaterial.

And the years passed — a little more swiftly — and we read now with more attention to motives and causes.

We pored over the volume of ancient history — and found the realities of the things which as idealities we had loved so

well. We read once more of those hazardous, perilous, pilgrimages in pursuit of the Holy Grail — and this time we must
pause and ascertain what was this Holy Grail — this Holy
Grail that had been running through our minds all through the
years like a fragment of some half-forgotten song.

'Twas the same old story of life and death — the real and the
unreal — going hand in hand and side by side —

Just as the little child had sung as she made doll clothes of
coffin linings — this Holy Grail — woven into our early dreams
of fighting and rescue, with all the glitter and gilding of our
resourceful fancy —

This Holy Grail was a thing no less sacred and holy and real
than the CUP from which Jesus Christ and his disciples drank
on the eve of the payment of the price.

To him who finds the study of ancient folk lore and symbolisms to his liking — the use of the word *cup*, in olden time,
would appeal with singular interest.

In the Eleventh Psalm it is said that "To the wicked snares
and tempests should be the portion of their cup."

In the Shepherd's Psalm, with its note of joy and gratitude
for God's blessings, the cadence draws to a rapidly accelerated
crescendo, in the words: "My cup runneth over."

Isaiah speaks of the cup of trembling and the cup of fury.

Much later one said in great agony: "If it be thy will, let
this cup pass from me."

I have striven vainly for some expression which would meet
the evident demand of this word *cup*. The best we may say
of it is that cup followed one of those peculiar rules of language
by which a word may mean either the container or the thing
contained. It might be translated heart, soul, emotion, sorrow,
or happiness.

Indeed, it was either so indefinable in its scope of application, or claimed so many possible meanings that even the sons of Zebedee knew not what it meant in their own tongue.

One would think that the mother of such men as James and John might deserve more than a mere impersonal designation — but so the biographer states it — Then came the mother of Zebedee's children with her two sons, worshipping him and desiring a certain thing of him. She wanted a request granted, and doubtless her prayer took such form as: "Lord, I desire that Thou wilt grant me a special blessing."

Oh, how often in our prayers we approach the mercy seat in just such a way: "Give us a blessing, Lord — a special blessing." Possibly it had not occurred to us just what this blessing should be, but God is all powerful, and all knowing — He would divine our need and measure the supply to the demand.

God wants us to be definite in our prayers.

"Grant me a blessing!" What do you mean? What blessing do you want? You would go to no human friend with any such vague request. Why plead so indifferently with God? What would you have? Is it some temporal pleasure — or release from the consequence of some sin?

"Grant me a blessing." "What blessing?" God asks us now, as Christ asked the mother of Zebedee's children: "What wilt thou?" He does not commit himself to fulfill *any* request that her caprice might suggest. He will promise nothing he does not expect to grant in fullest measure. It is all very well to ask for a certain thing: "But what wilt thou?"

And now the request is set forth — a most unusual request. "Grant that these, my two sons, may sit the one on thy right hand and the other on thy left, in Thy Kingdom."

Now, before we pass judgment on this woman — let us pause just one moment and give her credit for a few things. In the very first place, she had unbounded faith. In her mind, Christ was a king, and he possessed a kingdom. So much for her faith.

Furthermore, he held full sway there, insomuch that he might ordain the appointments and elect his favorites as he chooses. That much for her estimation of his power.

And then the strikingly human feature of the request was her manifest devotion to her sons. She did not ask this favor for herself. Indeed, when she had this opportunity of making a request with the assurance that any reasonable prayer would be heard — one might think she would be mindful of her own destiny — but not so — the uppermost thing in her mind was the eminence she would have accorded her sons —

The mother of Zebedee's children was ambitious.

She had seen how prominently her sons, John and James, appeared in this work of promulgating the gospel. And since they were zealous, she fancied the Master, himself, was showing favoritism to them. This would be the golden opportunity of making sure of their high standing in the spirit-world.

But she had placed herself in a most unfortunate position and must expect censure. In the first place, we question her courtesy in making such a request in the presence of those other loyal men who had left all and followed the Saviour. It was inordinately selfish — on the very face of it. She had misinterpreted the Christian principles. She had overlooked the constant teaching that the servant was to be greater than his master — and that he who was least should be greatest — and that the first should be last — and the last first. Ah, how she had misled herself!

Supremacy in God's sight did not belong to the people of Palestine, even though they knew the Son of God through personal contact. Special eminence in Heaven did not belong to the family of Zebedee, any more than it belongs particularly to this church, or to some home here represented. There would be positions of honor — but the basis of this classification should be much more vital than the simple request of an ambitious mother — however sincere she may have thought herself to be.

What will the Master say to her — The Master, always so gentle and tender. Will he rebuke her? Strange as it is, the mother of Zebedee's children passes out of the story here. If her cherished sons had been mere boys, and she solely responsible for them, then he would undoubtedly have replied directly to her — but these two sons were John and James, foremost among the disciples.

He turns to them.

There they stand — smitten with chagrin over this unwarranted petition. They should have had the courage and the grace to disclaim, very courteously, any desire to force themselves into prominence above their brethren. And yet, the question had been asked, and still remained unanswered. They did not know — although they might have known — what reply would follow that selfish demand.

And so they are silent. Even their chagrin was not so strong as their hope that the Saviour might grant this unheard of prayer.

The Master waited for them to speak. He preferred that they should deny their interest in this question. But they are silent. Then this request is theirs also. The mother of Zebedee's children may step aside now. The Saviour will deal with them.

"Ye know not what ye ask."

How often God might say the same to us. You have prayed for something that would hurt you, or, the thing you wish that would make you happy would bring sorrow to another. I dare say many of our prayers are unanswered because we have asked unwisely.

And thus Christ spoke to John and James: "Ye know not what ye ask. Are ye able to drink of the cup that I shall drink of?"

And then they proved that they knew not what they asked by the effrontery of their bold reply: "We are able."

There was a note of finality and firmness in Christ's response.

"Ye shall indeed drink of my cup — but to sit on my right hand and on my left is not mine to give. It shall be given to them for whom it is prepared of my Father."

I would have you observe Christ's mysterious question: "Are ye able to drink of the cup that I shall drink of?"

"Ye would aspire to prominence — even to the highest gift at the disposal of God — are ye able to drink of the cup that I shall drink of?"

I find this question reaching out in all directions and proposing itself to ambitious men in every walk of life. We are all aspiring — or should be aspiring — toward some great aim. Count that man a failure who has no high ideal toward which his hopes and thoughts ascend.

Here is a man desiring to hold high place in a sphere of usefulness. He looks up to some hero and emulates him. For he, too, would be great. Aye, although ashamed to ask so great a boon, yet if the question were asked for him: "Grant that this ambitious one may stand next to thee in glory" — he would not deny his interest in the petition, but would await the reply with bated breath — and the reply is always the same: "Are ye able to drink of my cup?"

The shade of Louis Pasteur asks this question of the aspiring young scientist who looks up to him, wonderingly, if perchance he, too, might not hold a great position in the world's sight.

You remember well the achievements, if not the life-story, of Louis Pasteur. His father was a tanner of humble circumstance. The young man destined to become one of the earth's greatest scientists, in a sphere, too, that did more toward ameliorating suffering than any other in the history of men — acquired his education amid many hardships. His salaries, when at last he became a teacher, were mere pittances. His investigations were in a field too visionary for his contemporaries.

The use of the microscope was legitimate in its place — but

this theory of discovering, and classifying, and naming minute bacteria, which were presumed to be the sources of disease — this was theoretical. So thought his colleagues. And they scoffed at him. In poverty — with no aid, and practically no encouragement — this man persevered through the years till the medical fraternity, and the whole scientific world was forced to bow before his discoveries. At the age of forty-three, worn to a shadow with work and worry, just as earthly rewards began to be his, and the skies were bright, his sun set — and from then on till he had spent three years of borrowed time, after his allotted three-score and ten — he lived in the ever-deepening twilight of bodily infirmity, paralyzed.

And so the spirit of Pasteur says to the young scientist, who looks up to him, and envies him his fame: "You who would sit by me in the recognition of the scientific world — consider my hardships — count the cost — 'Are ye able to drink of my cup?' "

The ambitious musician — casting about for a hero — might select as his favorite star from that mighty constellation of famous musicians, the name of Beethoven. The man was peerless in his profession — but the cup from which he drank — "Are ye able?"

His father was a worthless vagabond, though a talented musician. His son, exhibiting marked precocity, was trained in mere babyhood that he might be a prodigy in instrumental music — which he was. But because he loved art for art's sake — and paid but little attention to his natural patrons — he lacked popular favor. A man of acute sensitiveness, he felt the stings and slights that the envious dealt him — and it ruined all the happiness of his life.

One biographer said of him: When he presented his matchless Grand Opera *Fidelio* it failed. In vain, he modeled and remodeled it. He went, himself, into the orchestra, and attempted to lead it, and the pitiless public of Vienna laughed.

To think of the Austrian groundlings ridiculing the sublimest genius who ever lifted his scepter in the sacred empire of sound — making him writhe under the torturing irony of so monstrous a reversal of their relative superiorities.

After this cruel outrage (Weber continues) he crept into his lair alone, like a wounded beast of the forest, to hide himself from humanity. Nothing could have been sadder than this mighty man's defeat. Think of it. At thirty-one, the greatest musician in the world. At thirty-one so completely deaf that not a note could pierce his deadened ears. And added to it all, the haunting dread that he had no friends — and the remembrance that the world had laughed.

Glory and eminence have their price. "Are ye able to drink of this cup?"

I see another hero — a Florentine priest — attempting to reform the debased institution of which he was a part. So high does he stand in the world's vision, I do not wonder that some would make him their hero, and, whatever be their reform — or their peculiar method for the earth's betterment — look to him as their inspiration: and though they do not beseech, they might stand silent were one to ask in their stead:

"Grant that these may sit on thy right hand and on they left in *thy* kingdom."

And then would come this awful, searching question: "Are ye able to drink of my cup?"

See him, Savanarola, the mighty — dragged from his pulpit to the cell — from cell to judgment — from judgment to the stake. He would uplift men, and men had slain him. 'Tis well to be reformers. All honor to the death he died. But you who would win his fame — and perpetuate his memory by deeds — must ponder deeply his query, "Are ye able to drink of my cup?"

I hear the spirit of Abraham Lincoln answering the young men today who would be statesmen: "Are ye able?"

There will be hardships in plenty — criticisms at every hand — "the carping of the lesser men who are feigning greater goals" — days of contention — nights of worry — and though some time the deeply-graven epitaph may tell, in glorious dignity, the story of sufferings endured — yet there are many steps between the ambition and the realization — between the striving and the glory attained.

"Are ye able to drink of this cup?"

And so the great ones of the earth continue charging their devotees and followers:

"Count the cost. Can you pay the price? Can you make the sacrifice — bear the sting — the hurt, the death? Are ye able?"

I do not bring these things before your minds, my friends, to urge your relinquishing ambition. Far from it. If you are made of the clay that has gone to form the heroes and martyrs whose fame you would possess — this will but be fuel to feed the flame of your high hopes.

Today, we ask for mighty gifts, and receive them as matters to be taken for granted. Do we know what they cost? Might not our benefactors say to us in sternest tones: "Ye know not what ye ask."

Review the comforts of life — the luxuries of our own modern day — and contemplate the mental toil, the worry, the self-denial — the lives that some men, somewhere, have invested that we might be possessors.

Our land of liberty and freedom, with its bloody purchase-price — our opportunity for education — our freedom of thought and speech — sum them all up into a mighty debt and then thank God for the brave men through whom they came.

And now — with our earthly comfort assured — we turn our

eyes toward the great future — and ask the Blessed Master if
we may sit with him in his kingdom. 'Tis the mightiest ambition
any human soul can know — to be with the Son of God in his
Celestial Home. And we sing of the Heavenly Mansions, and
the crowns we shall wear, yet ever and always does the solemn
question come to us — in the stress of care — in the quiet hour
of meditation — in the agony of trial, "Are ye able to drink
of my cup?"

Oh, this expectation we have is so marvelously beyond human
comprehension that many men deny its reality. You and I are
assured that eternal peace and happiness are possible. God has
promised, and God cannot fail — but we are now in the days
of testing and refining. At the church altar, we answered Christ's
question, and although we did not utter the self-righteous, and
wholly daring "We are able," yet we did say "We will try."

Our destinies are in our own hands now. God has spoken.
Christ has wrought. It is ours to complete the task. And the
Master continues the while with his earnest, pleading question
to the men and women who would share his kingdom. 'Tis a
mighty test — a wondrous sacrifice — a consecrated service —
Are ye able to drink of the Master's cup? Are ye able?

Sometimes, despite a natural inclination toward optimism, I
grow depressed over our modern religious life. Mind now —
I do not deduce these gloomy thoughts from your life any more
than from my own, but I am occasionally forced into drawing distinctions between Christianity and Churchianity — between the Master's requests and the modern interpretations of
the same. It seems that we are taking our religious life all too
comfortably. Too much performing it in companies, and squads
and platoons. Too much asking each other: "Are you a Lu-
theran, or Calvinist, or Wesleyan. Are you High Church or
Low Church?" And not enough answering the question: "Are
ye able to drink of the Master's cup?"

Is it possible that some of us have only been playing at Christianity? Can it be that this Master's cup holds a position in our religious thought as ill defined and shadowy as did the Holy Grail in our childish fairy-land of wars and pilgrimages?

Sometimes we are on the very point of losing our commission as disciples. Denominational rivalry — purposeful in its place — is carried to excesses that beggar the cause of Christ in the eyes of the world. Personal opinions clash and send the echo of their useless battle through the land. Church members stand ready to do battle with each other for the sake of personal tastes, and idle preferences. Whither are we drifting?

And through it all the Wonderful Saviour of men points to the first principles of discipleship. He would have us come back from our theorizing, from our useless controversies — from our petty jealousies and puerile strifes, and answer this great question:

"Are ye able to drink of my cup?" 'Tis the Master's test of discipleship: "Are ye able?"

Lancaster, Ohio

For whatever of valor we have, we thank Thee: for grace to endure pain; for strength to withstand adversity; for patience to wait, faith to hope, and vision to see the glory of our eternal home. We give thee praise for these great gifts.

to a storm

"Why are ye so fearful?" — Mark 4:40

IT HAD BEEN one of the most eventful days in the experience of the privileged fishermen of Galilee. And when, in the late evening, Jesus suggested a trip across the lake to Gadara, it was with a fine glow of spiritual fervor that they made ready the boat.

All day long fresh assurances were confirming their faith in their new Master — who was also their comrade — a relationship rare enough in this world where one's masters are not often one's comrades as well. It seemed that day as if the world's reticence about accepting the reign of love had spontaneously yielded: as if its resistance to the appeal of Jesus' idealism had suddenly broken down.

For they had no more than entered the little city of Capernaum, that morning, when the centurion in charge of the local garrison came saying that his servant was sick. Jesus cheerfully consented to go, at once. But the centurion had replied:

"You need not go. Give the word that my servant shall be healed. That will be sufficient. I understand the power that goes with authority. I myself have authority — of a sort. I command men to go, to come, to do — and they obey me."

In the opinion of the disciples, that meant something — coming from a centurion. Somehow it was as if the government had stamped its visé on Jesus' passport to public recognition. The story had quickly spread, and a crowd had collected — a crowd of needy people — and the mysterious rehabilitations of that afternoon's clinic were afterward remembered in that region as distinguishing the most significant day that the Province of Galilee had ever witnessed. Wonder had piled upon wonder, that afternoon, until even a scribe — of the caste that really dared not ally itself to this uncredentialed prophet, at the peril of losing its standing — came through the crowd, to Jesus' side shouting: "I will follow thee whithersoever thou goest!"

And then there had been spoken that great Parable of the Sower. And when the Parable of the Sower was finished, the day's work was done, and the boat was being made ready for the trip over to Gadara, the disciples asked some questions about this sowing of the seed. Not surprising, at all, that they should — for the Parable is by no means as simple as it seems on first reading. Not difficult to believe, of course, that there are souls hard as a macadam road, and souls resembling a thicket of briars — but hard to understand why some souls should be that way, while others are productive as a fertile field.

At all events, the Parable still lingered in the minds of these men — and Jesus retold it — with full explanations of the human types he had sketched previously, and added: "It is given unto you to understand the mysteries of the Kingdom — as it is *not* given to the multitude."

And that remark — if, indeed, they needed anything to make their self-confidence complete, that night — had the effect of distinguishing them, in their own eyes, more than ever before. It was in this mood that they entered the little fishing smack, hauled up a bit of canvas, and sloped off, gently, in the darkness, toward Gadara.

It turned out to be a bad night on their erratic little inland sea. Galilee was only a small body of water, but whimsical of temper, and, notwithstanding they had often dealt with its caprices, tonight they were at their wits' end.

Jesus, after a hard day — for the strain on him must have been incalculable — was asleep. He was not feigning sleep. He was — one likes to believe — morally above any pretences — even in the interest of illustrating some fact. He often resorted to fable and allegory, to make some truth luminous — but his own life was not a fable or an allegory. If he seemed to sleep, he slept.

Nor was this inconsistent with his reiterated statements that his life was lived above the level of fear.

Men live their lives on certain planes — geometrically speaking. In their attitude toward fears, men live on different levels.

The untutored savage understands so little about the phenomena of the natural world that his list of fears may be supposed to embrace almost every manifestation of physical energies.

On successive planes, above the savage, live people who have conquered certain elementary fears through knowledge and experience. They are not terrified by an eclipse of the sun. They expect it to pass in due time. They calmly set about it to deal effectively with a forest fire. On the mounting planes of understanding and the discipline of experience — dwell the types which have eliminated from their lives the major part of the torturing phobias which make such a pathetic figure of the savage.

One can easily conceive of a scientifically trained man — while guest in a village of mid-African bushmen — noting their abject terror in the face of a shower of meteors; one can easily conceive of the courage and confidence he might impart by a quiet word of assurance. Nor is it hard to imagine how puzzled this civilized European would be over the primitive fears of these untaught Africans. He would say to himself — if not to them — "How can anybody who thinks at all be so fearful?"

And yet it is possible that this emancipated scientist — who has outgrown the fear of meteors — and lives on an exalted plane of understanding where a considerable area of the old atavistic frights has been put under the cultivation of illuminating experiment — it is quite possible that even this scientist, in his lofty altitude of knowledge, gives hospitality to certain fears: fears of things which he, with all his erudition, does not understand.

Unquestionably, the distinguishing attribute of Jesus' moral supremacy was his utter freedom from fear. Not *fears* — but *fear:* fear — as a principle.

Humanity has been spending the best of its efforts trying to be rid of fears. As understanding increases, fears diminish in quantity.

Sometimes parents are impatient of their little children's fear of the dark. The big brother, who has found that he needn't drown in the water, finds it hard to understand why his little brother can't jump in and take his word for it that the water won't hurt him.

One of the main businesses of culture, and one of the chief activities of education, is to eliminate fears. Jesus was not especially interested in overcoming fears — but *fear*.

Of course a man could do much for himself by a progressive escape from one fear after another, until he had left behind him the silliest ones — like being afraid of the dark — and the costliest ones — like being afraid to fight a fire. And at the end of a long life of unloading his fears, he might have only a few left — like the fear of death, for example.

But, to the mind of Jesus, it was much more satisfactory for a man to make a clean sweep of all his fears by getting rid of *fear*. All that he had to do was to say to himself: "I am God's child. I am in His hands. As for my body — it was never meant to be permanent. As for my life — it is immortal. Why, then, should I be afraid of *anything?*"

Jesus slept.

One might have thought that this fact, in itself, should have been enough to restore calmness on board the little ship. But it seems to have had precisely the opposite effect on these stampeded people.

How he could sleep — through their dangerous predicament — was not only a marvel of personal assurance, but an equally baffling marvel of indifference. They woke him up. They did not do it in a very pleasant manner — for they were frightened almost to death, and could not be expected to be oversolicitous for the little amenities. They shook him roughly, and shouted: "Carest thou not that we perish?"

How often one sees it all enacted, again and again. How often it has been enacted in our own experience. A sudden storm breaks over us; and we go at it by the usual processes of taking in canvas, battening down the hatches; tying the cargo, and after a while pitching it overboard — and then, when everything's been swept away but our own self-pity, we suddenly recall that there is a presence on the ship. And when we remember, how apt we are to say: "Much he cares! Much he cares about me! Everything that I had is gone! That which I most dearly loved — *gone!*

"Hopes blasted! Sails tattered! Masts splintered! Rudder lost! Much he cares about me! Much he cares about anybody. Master, carest thou not that we perish?"

We have the record of three gospels for it that Jesus arose and spoke to the storm, and that there came a great calm. The minor incidents in the story differ slightly — but all are agreed that Jesus stilled the storm. Perhaps that is all we need know about it, for our own use. Jesus spoke; and there was a great calm.

The gospel writers say that Jesus spoke to the winds and the waves — and they obeyed him. But, had they stopped the narrative at that point, I presume the permanent value of the story might have been difficult to arrive at.

For — if that were all (Jesus' calming address to the storm) it would make our own predicament not much less difficult than it is. If that were *all* — the address to the storm — the net result to the world is of negligible value — however remarkable it may seem from the sheer standpoint of a challenge to one's credulity. Did the Sea of Galilee become any safer, after that night? It did not. Did the event add anything to the science of navigation? Not a bit. Did the disciples know any more about the handling of a boat in rough water than they had known before? Not at all!

No — if the story had ended on that note, it would have left us sadly bewildered. A Miracle Man has conferred a benefit for that date and place only. He has spoken to the winds and waves on the Sea of Galilee, but it has no effect on the Mediterranean Sea. He has spoken to the winds and waves on Galilee and they have obeyed him; but tomorrow night they will be as boisterous as ever — on Galilee.

A thousand ships will go down, in the succeeding ages, carrying terrified cargoes of men, women, and children to the slime of the ocean floor; but Jesus' great secret will be safe! In that case, his assistance is too local and transient to be counted on as a world-benefit.

But the narrative does not leave us in that perplexity. For, in the same sentence in which Jesus speaks to the storm on the sea, he speaks to the storm in the hearts of these frightened men! It was there — in their hearts — that the most menacing storm was raging; and it was there — in their hearts — that this great calmness must come!

Jesus rebuked *that storm!*

"Why are ye fearful — O ye of little faith!" Here they were, fresh from the most triumphant manifestations of faith in action, a day brimming with stupendous verifications. Pagan Rome had believed in it: and invoked its aid. Conservative Judaism had believed in it: and wanted to come along with it. A whole city had been swept with emotion.

How proudly had these disciples stood by their Master's side, witnessing the victories of faith in the all-goodness of God. But — how easily they had slipped back, within an hour, into the old grooves worn deep with years of timidity and self-protection!

Jesus rebukes them.

He might not have rebuked any other twelve men in the whole world — for being afraid, that night; but he rebukes this particular twelve on the ground of their failure to make his investment in them productive. Now, they could understand the Parable of Seed sown in unpromising soil. "How is it," he inquires, "that *ye* have no faith?"

One might easily understand how persons who have had no chance to learn the deeper meaning of Life, and for whom there have been but a few spiritual privileges — one can understand how they will succumb to panic, and lose their heads, and go into hysterics, and wind up with a savage shriek toward Heaven: "You don't care; do you? We can all go down, and out, and you wouldn't care; would you?"

One rather looks for neurotic explosions like that from people who have never benefited by any spiritual disciplines. But — why are *ye* fearful? You have surrendered everything humanly dear to follow the new Idealism! You, Peter, have left your home. You, James, have abandoned your occupation. You, Thomas, have dropped your skeptical philosophy. You, Matthew, have walked away from a good job in the revenue office. All of you have given up the normal pleasures of life. You sleep out-of-doors. You often go hungry. You have lost caste in your own synagogues. Your conservative neighbors think you a bit off. You haven't a penny in your pockets. And you are well aware you aren't going to have.

All this you have given up, because you were lured away from it by the gleam of a great hope! You wanted to live without fear!

Now look at you!

One presumes that the Spirit of Christ is still amazed at the curious lack of orderliness in the minds of the people who claim to be Christians. I think we can be confident that our Christ has the utmost patience with the spiritually underprivileged. And when one speaks of the spiritually underprivileged one may be speaking of those who — in most other considerations of life — are apparently quite fortunate. The rich farmer, in Jesus' parable, who had spent his best thought and all his time tearing down little barns to build bigger barns to hold more and better corn, was a fool only in the opinion of the angels. His neighbors doubtless looked up to him as one of our best people, who had done very well by himself.

I think that our Christ must be very patient in his thought of the spiritually underprivileged, whoever they are, in the same spirit with which he looked upon the multitudes — of his own country — with a brooding tenderness and compassion.

I cannot imagine him, in the role of an elder brother, swimming confidently in deep water, ridiculing his little brother for being afraid to take the first plunge. But — if that little brother had grown up to be a strong man, and had gone to the bother and expense of building a costly diving platform, where he invited his friends to come and hear him discourse on the joys of aquatics, and the benefits of possessing self-assurance and courage in the water, not only that one might be able to save oneself, but others; and if that little brother had grown up, with all this vast show of interest in trusting himself to the water, and encouraging others to trust themselves to it, but had never yet taken his first dive — that would be a different matter!

One presumes that the same Christ who wondered, in a storm on Galilee, how these spiritually privileged men *could* exhibit such an utter collapse of faith is still amazed at the whimpers of people who have talked so charmingly, in fair weather, about his saving grace — who give generously to build and maintain expensive churches where, they love to think, other men and women are encouraged to fling themselves, unreservedly, into the mysterious depths of the divine love, expecting its buoyancy to hold them up.

One presumes he is amazed to see how many well-meaning, wistful souls — who, to put themselves into harmony with a spiritual universe, have cut themselves off from many a pleasure and have denied themselves almost all of life's physical necessities, to promote what they lyrically refer to as Jesus' kingdom — are devastated by doubts and despairs and stampeded into hysteria when some unexpected storm disturbs the ordinary routine of their placid lives.

For the best that Christianity has to offer is the promise of a life without fear.

How is it that we — with all that we have seen and heard of God's Providence in our world — have so little faith, when there comes a sudden gale?

The Spirit of Christ still rebukes storms in the hearts of frightened men. He does not try to save men FROM storms; but IN storms. Good mariners never attempt to drive their ships on to dry land, to escape a tempest at sea. Their task is to keep the ship seaworthy *in* the sea.

The Spirit of Christ does not ask to navigate your boat. He keeps his hand off the tiller, and makes no suggestions. He is your passenger; and you can take him where you will, and do with him as you like.

It is quite customary for people to forget — in calm weather — that he is on board. To all practical intents, he is in his berth asleep. But — when all your own reliances have failed you, he is prepared to speak peace. He may have nothing to say to the storm without — but it will come to the same thing as if he had spoken to the storm — for, after he has spoken, there will be a great calm. It may not come to the winds and waves, in actual fact, but it will come to you.

And that's all that matters; for the tempest that endangers, is inside of *you!* And when the great calm arrives, it must come to *you!*

And when that confidence that gave serenity to the soul of Jesus shall have become our own, we may expect the blessings which accrue to the unshackled — and the mental majesty of that peace which surpasses all understanding.

Radio Address
Montreal
January 12, 1930
East Congregational Church
London
August 3, 1930

OUR FATHER GOD:
Whose ways we are not asked to understand, but whose wisdom we can safely trust, we come to Thee with all our hopes and fears, beseeching Thee to give us faith and courage to walk confidently even in the darkness that has spread over our troubled world.

part three

HOW A CHRISTIAN LIVES

can a man be born again?

Less than two hundred years ago the English Parliament decreed that barbers must discontinue their practice of surgery as a sideline.

Presently the Jacks-of-all-trades began to specialize. And today it is commonly taken for granted that if you want a reliable opinion on anything you should consult an expert.

Some witty fellow may propose that the conundrum at the top of this page might be referred to an obstetrician. Nobody would be silly enough to accept his suggestion seriously, but there are plenty of sensible people willing to have this question submitted to the geneticist who may reply that a man's aptitudes, aspirations, graces, and defects are inherited. This geneticist will add that a man is born (once only) with tendencies over which he has little if any lasting control, and that he is no more likely to alter the essential nature of his aims and behavior than the shape of his ears or the color of his eyes.

This problem, however, is not one that can be referred to experts in the study of heredity. It is just as foolish to ask this question of the geneticist as of the obstetrician. It is not in his field. The facts he has discovered in his experiments with fruit flies and guinea pigs are of no value here.

"Can a man be born again?" deserves to be thought about at Christmas time when attention is directed to the birth of an influence which — though the world was old, and had been reproducing and repeating its own blunders for ages — was to make startling changes in the whole structure of civilization.

So — whoever wants to think profitably about the problem of "rebirth" should make sure he knows his Christmas. You can't have Christmas at the same price as Thanksgiving Day or the Fourth of July. You have to come at it in a different mood.

Christmas did not originate one day at noon with clamorous publicity. It arrived by starlight and made itself at home in a stable. It was neither a scientific discovery nor an ingenious invention. The details of the story are better understood when sung rather than spoken. It was no mere happen-so that the epoch-making event was announced in the dusk by a choir of angels poised over a sheepfold. Indeed, Christmas is so distinctly an affair of the heart that any effort to make a critical examination of its lyrics and legends is as unrewarding as a chemical analysis to determine the value of your mother's photograph.

It is not important that you give your intellectual consent to the details of this strange occurrence. Persons who try to disprove these Christmas legends by the usual tests applied to an historical event get nothing for their pains, nor are the people any better off who try to prove them by such measures. When you approach this story with your slide rule and calipers, it makes no difference whether you are for it or against it. In either case, you won't know what it's about. Definitely establish it as a fact that a strange comet appeared in the Near East late in the Augustan Era, and you haven't done Christmas the slightest bit of good. Prove scientifically that there never was such an astral body, and you haven't done Christmas the slightest bit of damage. There is indeed a Christmas problem, but it has nothing to do with stars or angels.

The real problem is: Did the arrival of the Christ spirit give the world of men a "rebirth"? Can a man be born again when he is grown? Did anything happen to make it possible for a person to become a changed creature, so changed that old things are put away and all things are become new?

Of course, it is an easy and pleasant duty for organized Christianity to reassert its Christmas claims. It sings, "Joy to the world; the Lord is come!" And it stands up in the pulpit to say that anybody who thinks the Bethlehem story is a mere flimsy myth should remember that the day was important enough to require the beginning of a new calendar. The old record of blunders and savagery was closed and a new ledger was opened, and at the top of the first page civilization wrote, "Anno Domini, I." And if anyone thinks the Christmas story is merely funny, let him try to laugh *that* off! And so forth.

But that doesn't quite satisfy. For let it also be remembered, in spite of the new calendar that came in on the first Christmas, by the arrival of a new spirit of peace and good will, there is still a lot of work to be done in applying that message. Christmas didn't pick the world up by its muddy hair and lead it into a new path of righteousness by a single decisive act. Let us make no mistake at that point. A nation may quickly revert to the jungle, no matter how many spiritual privileges it may have enjoyed. It is quite possible for a nation to serve as home and host to a very powerful organization of Christians for nearly a score of centuries; and, in spite of that experience, become a menace to the world's peace. It is equally possible for a nation to devise and deliver another powerful organization of Christians to spread its cultus to the uppermost parts of the earth; and, in the face of that achievement, offer a world a very sorry exhibition of good will among men.

Christmas never promised that it would lift the human race, or any particular color, culture, creed or custom believing in it, from degradation into moral dignity with one spectacular tug, and insure its remaining at that exalted altitude. It simply pointed the way toward better things. And in all fairness it must be said that civilization at large, while still sorely in need of improvement, definitely shows the effect of having followed that Light, even though it has done so erratically, timidly, and afar off. The Hero of Christmas would never have composed the cherished hymn:

> *He rules the world with truth and grace*
> *And makes the nations prove*
> *The glories of His righteousness*
> *And wonders of His love.*

He would never have put an O.K. on that verse for the very good reason that it wasn't so, and has never been so. Perhaps it never will be so. The salvation of the world from its own mistakes wasn't quite that simple. He implored the nations of the world to go in for peace and good will, but they were never *ruled, and they were never made to prove anything whatsoever* — much less "the glories of His righteousness and wonders of His love." If we're going to talk about this business at all, we may as well be honest.

One fact, however, needs to be kept in mind when viewing the predicament of the "Christian" nations. It is a mistake to assume that a small minority of war-bent dictators, with iron hats and spiked collars, represent adequately the sentiments of their hapless subjects.

Peace and good will seem to be going through a depression, but it is safe to guess that the whole civilized world would be let in for a comforting surprise if every man of every nation, on the coming Christmas Day, were permitted to go privately and unthreatened into a voting booth to express his own ideas about a desirable way of life for himself and those who are dear to him.

Nor does this apply to the general public alone, that has been used to taking things as they come, with no expectation of being able to alter them. In every nation thousands of men in distinguished positions are unable to express their honest convictions. In one country, the Big Chief is candidly gruff, as he warns the legislator that he must obey orders or lose his head. In another country, the Big Chief is suavely polite as he warns the legislator he must obey orders or lose his seat. All down the line, men of every station hestitate to be themselves. At the top, the methods are different but the motives are about the same. Whether the so-called representatives of the people are kept in line by a purge or a picnic, it all comes to the same thing. In one land, men stand in line, wagging their tails for their dinner at the door of the relief officer. In another land they goose-step on the parade ground. One demagogue wears a steel shirt and a scowl, another wears a polo shirt and a smile. But the difference is a mere matter of taste and technique.

So — if anybody sneers at the way in which The Light is being followed today, let him reflect that if *the people* were permitted to say their say it might be shown that peace and good will among men — given a decent chance — would be manifested almost everywhere. Christmas didn't come in attired in asbestos. It never has made any demands; requests only. It never said that things would be put right in a day, a century, a millennium.

It is at this point that a great deal of muddy thinking has been done on the subject of an individual's "rebirth."

It is entirely possible for a man to become so impressed by his own failure to make a constructive use of his mind, his time, his hands, his capacity for friendship, his opportunities to give aid, that he rises one day to declare his determination to follow a new way of life. And it will be as if he had actually been *born again*. Life immediately takes on a new dignity and a new delight. He walks with a firmer step, speaks with a fresh confidence, wakes in the morning with a clearer head. His friends ask each other, "What's happened to Charlie?" His business feels it. Even his dog knows.

But that doesn't mean that this fellow is now sitting pretty, in a blissful state of imperishable moral grandeur. The upkeep of a second birth is increasingly expensive. Considerable talk has been going about, lately, concerning the high price of bearing children. Our pioneer great-grandparents used to call in Aunty McNab and the good old family doc. Babies didn't cost anything.

Now it is different. They still arrive F.O.B., but also C.O.D., with an alarming invoice of delivery charges: hospital, nurses, operating room, physician, surgeon, specialist, anesthetist, blood counts, metabolisms, X-rays.

But the modern cost of being born the first time, however exorbitant, isn't to be compared with the expense of a second birth, an expense which continues for life. True, the outlay may be reduced somewhat as the years pass. It's a little like the cost of life insurance. After a while you begin to draw dividends which may be applied to the premium. But you never stop paying. It's quite possible for an old man who, at forty, had been born again, to become very cantankerous at seventy, after he has gone to live with his daughter-in-law. Oh, he may still talk a lot about the second birth he had experienced, but his grandchildren will say that if this is what a second birth does to you they will try to get along with the one they had. As a general rule, the people who talk most about their second birth seem to be subconsciously aware that the phenomenon, in their case, needs to have attention called to it or their families and business associates might not realize the importance of this rejuvenation.

But it is still possible for a man to be born again.

The first practical step in this direction is the wish to live a more satisfying life. Clearly, this first step is not a very difficult one to take. Almost nobody is entirely satisfied with his life, either as to what he is putting into it or getting out of it. If *wishing* would give a man his second birth, the general state of society would be vastly improved in a day's time. However, the mere wishing isn't to be sniffed at, for this is the first necessary act in the achievement of a "rebirth."

The second step is an attempted return to the places where certain paths divided and the wrong way was chosen.

Much foolishness has been written and spoken on this subject. Sometimes this "parting of the ways" is explained as if there had been but one fateful option — a spot where he decided, deliberately, and in cold blood, whether he was henceforth going up or down. This is nonsense. Nobody makes such decisions. Nobody is asked to make such decisions. Most of the unfortunate choosings are made unwittingly, without one's knowing what will be involved.

There is no one place where a man faces the determining fork of the road, but rather a score, a hundred places where he may get off the right path. The map of his journey doesn't resemble an old-fashioned bootjack, shaped like a Y. It is more like a chart of the circulatory system on an anatomical chart, arteries branching off into small and smaller and smallest arteries.

Go back to the last place you came to where you feel that you lost the road to peace and well-being. It may not be very far away. Perhaps you will have to return only to the day you met good ole Bill Thompkins who persuaded you to join the Pigeons' Club. Ever since you joined the Pigeons' Club, you have been worrying your people at home. A little more of the Pigeons, and you won't *have* any home. Let us go back, then, to the Pigeons' Club and see how gracefully we can eliminate ourself, for it's a clear case that we can't possibly become a new creature in that atmosphere.

Now we can travel for quite some distance before we come

to another place where we made the wrong turn. That was the place where our nephew asked us to take him into our business and we wouldn't do it because his father made us mad, one time, in a political argument. We could easily have absorbed this young graduate, but we didn't, and he has never got on very well. And it has pretty thoroughly busted up the family harmony. A lot of them aren't speaking any more. Even our wife and her sister, who weren't in the row at all, haven't exchanged visits for six years. So — having backed up to the day we failed to do the expected thing by Tommy, we write inviting him to come and get into the game with us, which reconciles everybody, all the way round. And the "second birth" is beginning to make its reality apparent.

But this is no place to stop. It's beginning to be fun, now. Every time we arrive at one of the old junction points where we missed the road, we find ourself better able to deal with the problem. *One day we shall find the place where we first lost the way.*

To be born the second time may require even a longer period of development than being born the first time. It is not an act; it is a process.

And, finally, let it be remembered that a second birth necessitates proper attendance, same as the first birth. To be born the first time, we should be assisted into life by people who really want us to be born and are entirely sympathetic with our wish to be as they are.

If we want to be born again, we should avail ourselves of the kindly offices of persons who thoroughly approve of our wish to be born again. Some of them won't know anything else in the world but the importance of being born again. But, if they know *that much*, they can give valuable aid. Don't sniff at them because they don't know what you mean when you speak of the "Big board." Doctor Snatchem, the obstetrician, wishes he had never heard of the "Big board." Don't scorn them for a split infinitive. Doctor Stillem, the anesthetist, wouldn't recognize a grammatical rule if he met it at noon in the Sahara desert with a lantern in its hand.

Bel-Air
California

With becoming humility — remembering our own weakness — may we walk the paths of generosity, kindness, and magnanimity, with our minds becoming more and more swayed by the influence of the compassionate Christ.

AMEN.

exploring your soul

Your Soul: What It Is; How It Operates

ONE OF THE most interesting phenomena of history is the importance which every generation has attached to the affairs of the soul. Anyone in doubt as to the very considerable influence of religion upon the various cultures and urges which account for our civilization will comprehend the outstretch and tenacity of religion's grip upon the imagination of all mankind by surveying the fields of thought and action wherein it has been at once a motive and a machine; an ideal and an aim; a first cause and a final goal.

Leave religion out of the story of the great migrations, which, by their very tax upon men's courage and ingenuity, explain the most notable of their achievements, and these epoch-making movements of whole races would stand on the books practically motiveless.

Omit religion from the story of the most strategic of the map-changing wars responsible for social and economic emancipations, the founding of new political states, the creation of new *esprits*, and the reappraisals of systems of thought, and these vast struggles would be, almost without exception, utterly inexplicable.

Delete religion from art and letters — song and drama, legend and folklore, architecture and reliquary — and all these time-binding pursuits of men's creative imagination would be impoverished of both mission and meaning to their successive legatees.

Religion is, and has ever been, the central theme; the motivation; the driving *élan* of life — and religion is the concern of the soul.

Yet; if you were asked for a brief, cogent, adequate definition of the soul, you might be troubled for a suitable phraseology to express your conviction on that subject. To define as "soul" that which is of "spiritual" quality in our composition, and (further pressed for explanation) to define as "spiritual" everything within us that is not material, is only to muddle the problem, hopelessly — seeing how large a territory of human thinking has to do with the ways and means for the satisfaction of desires and demands belonging to our physical bodies.

Investigate your own thought-processes, and it may amaze you to discover what a considerable amount of your thinking deals with mere socialized and civilized elaborations of such thoughts as the animals entertain, in order to safeguard their physical welfare. How much of our intellectual effort goes into the business of providing ourselves and our dependents with daily food — the difference between such thinking, and the thinking of the tiger and the dog and the seagull, on that subject, being rather a difference of technique than of essential quality.

How much of our intellectual effort goes into solutions of the problem of physical shelter — the difference between such thinking, and the thinking of the beaver, on that subject, being only a difference of process (with the odds, quite frequently, in favor of the beaver's methods).

How much of our intellectual effort goes into the zealous desire for the perpetuation of our species; a desire no less strongly manifest among all creatures, no matter how relatively insignificant, or apparently useless.

So, if the soul of man should be defined as that which is spiritual within us, and that which is spiritual should be defined as everything in our life not strictly material, tangible, measurable — one has automatically thrown the whole question away by ascribing spirituality to every living thing.

Perhaps we may arrive at the discrimination we need to observe, here, by predicating of the soul only such attributes as are not to be explained by any apparent demand or desire of our physical bodies.

It is of no possible advantage to my body, for example, to speculate upon where I came from, or where I am bound for. My interest in the origin and rise of the human race; the history of its strivings for liberation from its various slaveries; my zeal to discover what other men have thought about life, and recorded for the benefit of their unborn successors — these longings of mine have nothing to do with the welfare of my physical body.

Indeed, the pursuit of such knowledge may be a serious distraction from my efforts to promote the welfare of my physical body, as is evidenced by the fact that most of the world's remembered philosophers have been poor men, lean of jaw, simple of garb, and short of bank credit.

My interest in the future drift of our civilization, and my efforts to have some share in the plotting of the next curve of social progress, cannot be explained as an animal instinct, backed by a desire to improve my own physical comfort or security; for it concerns a period when the problems of my physical existence shall be no longer at issue. All such questions arise at the instance of some institution within ourselves which transcends the needs and desires of physical life.

We may properly assign such longings to the soul. And perhaps there could be no better place to begin, in an exploration of our souls, than to ascribe to them this insatiable zeal to relate themselves to the past and the future, as far as their vision can reach in both directions. Doubtless it was this longing that first gave man the idea that his soul was immortal.

Of course, eternity is a very long time, and we do not seem equipped to comprehend it in its fullness. We may have moments when we think we can conceive of existence as endless. But not many people can draw a sharp focus upon a fact which had no beginning. Eternity, with us, is a more or less relative term, meaning as far as we can reach, imaginatively, both forward and backward in point of time.

Deep within us, we have a strange, persistent, albeit unsubstantiated desire for the everlastingness of ourselves — our souls; and not only do we nourish that hope of the future of ourselves — our souls; but we are haunted by a belief that we have come forth from that which is without beginning (as we understand beginnings): that we are emanations of and tributary to a conscious Creator of our souls.

Now, a man may arise in the morning and wash his face, for the same reason that a cat washes hers; and eat his breakfast, for the same reason that the dog eats his; and work all day to earn his victuals, for the same reason that the horse works all day to earn his victuals; and store up necessities, like the bee; and organize into social groups to promote the mutual welfare of the tribe, like the ant; and share his ideas of all these pursuits with his fellows, like the monkeys. But, when he sits down, quietly, to contemplate the everlastingness of himself, and comfort his mind with his firm belief that he is of eternal stuff; that he proposes to outlive all the material things he sees about him because his essential self was existent long before any of these material things came to be, he immediately puts himself in quite another category than that of the animals. It is his soul that he is dealing with, now.

On superficial examination, this unique attribute of the human creature — this consciousness of his essential oneness with The Eternal — would seem to be primarily a great compliment and a high privilege.

Examined more critically, it is seen rather to be an almost terrifying responsibility. A man's soul, being immortal, must be held in a far different manner than he regards his body, which (let him do his utmost to preserve it) gradually goes more and more out of repair until he is finally obliged to put it down as of no further use to him. A little at a time, under the best possible circumstances (for disease or accident may precipitate a crisis at any moment, regardless of his years), he wears out, physically. His eyes lose their capacity to analyze objects close at hand. Once upon a time it did not matter so much that his lenses had flattened. He could still shape earthen pots, tend his sheep, and whack ripe sheaves with a flail. Perhaps nature had arranged that as he grew older, it were better for him to have a clearer gaze on the far distance — even if it was had at the cost of a blurred vision of things directly under his nose.

But, recently, mankind has been squinting at fine print; and goading the flattening eyes to their difficult task under lights unprecedentedly glaring, so that men take to artificial optical aids in their mere youth. Nothing daunted, then, by the warning that his eyes are playing out, the modern provides himself with lenses to correct the difficulty; and carries on.

At length his eardrums thicken, and he finds accessories to overcome that. His teeth fall out, and he puts in others which serve his purpose with even less bother and expense than the outfit supplied by Nature. He loses an arm, and buys himself another. His appendix hurts, and he has it taken out; after which he gets along as well, or better. His heart cuts capers, and he teaches it to behave with digitalis.

But, no matter how prudent and careful he is about making all these repairs, as necessity arises, he knows that it is only a matter of time until the whole machine will have to be abandoned.

It's somewhat like an old car. It can be tinkered with just about so long. Every little while it has to have new tires, a new battery, a new set of friction disks; perhaps a new generator. And he's certainly willing to give it new fan belts and spark plugs, valves and piston rings; but the day comes when, despite all the driver's zeal to keep the machine running, everything goes to pieces at once. The carburetor has quit; the differential has lost its cogs; the transmission will not transmit; the water pump is out of business; the oiling system is stopped — and what is left of the machine has to be towed to the junk pile. But, fortunately, *the driver does not have to go along to be junked with his car.*

The same thing occurs with his body. About so much mileage, and it is ready to go out of commission; *but the owner of that body does not propose to go down to defeat with it;* and be junked when it is no longer useful. He proposes to abandon it; exactly as he abandoned the successive, outworn garments with which he has sheltered his body from the weather.

Spiritually, he is not only not disintegrating, but the chances are that he is becoming really more effective, spiritually, as his years increase and his body weakens.

Frequently, the frustration, or utter failure of some physical sense organ, will only intensify and stimulate the remaining vehicles of perception. An old adage has it that if one would fully appreciate the world, one should possess the eye of the deaf and the ear of the blind.

So, the breakdown of the physical does not involve the soul, at all, unless to strengthen it, as is evidenced by the fact that some of the most radiant and masterful souls we have known are obliged to objectify their beauty and strength through physical bodies racked with pain, or hampered by organic and functional imperfections.

Now, to be aware of this — that the soul, far from following the natural course of disintegration inevitable to the body, goes forward without diminution of power (adding to its own importance, indeed, as the physical disintegration occurs) — may be either a very comforting, or a very alarming thought, accordingly as one has estimated the value of his own soul.

To become aware that, daily, the part of one's life that came out from eternity and is presently to return to stand in the visible presence of its source, is growing, and destined increasingly to grow more and more aware of its own importance, as the physical demands and distractions fail, either through satiety or disrepair, and that eventually one is to go onward with none of the normal reliances of physical life left, must give any man pause who has been so occupied with the affairs of the body that he is unacquainted with the needs of his soul.

So, while a man may accept with a warm glow of satisfaction, the ancient, racial assurance of an immortal life for himself, and think it all very fine indeed that, instead of being hauled slowly to the cemetery by sorrowing relatives, he, in actual truth, shall have abandoned his body, and is en route to some winged estate to live forever beyond the reach of pain and care, the fact is that, unless he shall have discovered what his soul is; how it operates; what it can do; what it must not try to do; what sustains it; what makes it stick; what it likes; what it hates — he may, in his utter bewilderment, bereft of every device and tool and weapon on which he had accustomed himself to rely, have moments when he heartily wishes he had gone to that cemetery — all of him — slowly to mingle with the primal clay.

If he lived the same kind of a life that a dog lives, construing it in terms of so much scouting for food; so much playing about in the sunshine; so much sleep; so much fight; so much barking at his enemies; and so much tail-wagging for his friends — then he may be pardoned for wishing to die as a dog dies; and have done with it; for to be caught out with nothing but a soul, and not to know what it is; what it is good for; how it works; or what one might reasonably expect of it — would be a most embarrassing predicament.

Personally, I am not disposed to have any traffic with spiritualism or spiritualists, but that tenet of spiritualism which holds that the souls of the average departed go into their new life utterly confused; and wander about, for a long time, dazed, lost and panicky, unable to speak the language of souls, unable to read the names of the streets on the lampposts and unable even to tell who they were, back yonder in the bright, blinking lights of the good old U.S.A., sounds to me very plausible; and seeing nobody knows anything about it, I presume the spiritualists have a right to think that, if they want to.

And when we complain to the spiritualists that the messages they receive from the departed are inane, stupid, incoherent, and muddled, they retort: "Well; what would you? They have yet to learn to find their way about; and as for their proficiency in estimating their new environment, how do you think you would feel and talk and think, if you were suddenly turned loose without any of the attributes of physical life upon which you had staked your all?"

Now, assuming that there may be some commonsense in this very practical manner of viewing the problems of the future, what better thing might we do for ourselves than make the acquaintance of our souls, and discover, insofar as we can, what may be confidently expected of them.

I have been heartened to take up this subject by the new popular psychology edited by Dr. Albert Edward Wiggam, entitled *Exploring Your Mind*.

One doesn't have to agree fully with Wiggam to be stimulated by him. Let it be conceded that his theories on eugenics as

propounded in such books as *The New Decalogue of Science*
and *The Fruit of the Family Tree* arrive at conclusions which
leave everything like idealism and character development out
of debate — the data he has painstakingly collected and analyzed are quite beyond the reach of any man's sneers.

In his latest volume, Dr. Wiggam merely writes the captions
for the chapters, and serves as a clearing house for the opinions
of a dozen noted psychologists discoursing, in laymen's language, of the affairs of the mind.

And Wiggam is sportsmanly enough to let them have their
say, and help them to an audience, even when they puncture
some of his own gayest balloons. He himself is a confirmed
behaviorist, believing that character is in the blood stream and
that a man is what he is (like a spotted leopard). But, one of
his collaborators, in this book, hops off by declaring that an old
dog can be taught new tricks.

One of the most informative papers in this compendium is
presented by Professor Edward Lee Thorndike, of Columbia. I
shall attempt no review of it further than is necessary to making
an adaptation of one phase of it to our own study of the soul.

Professor Thorndike begins his paper on "The Mind" by stating that we are now in great need of knowing exactly what the
words "intellect" and "intelligence" mean. I presume the same
query would be entirely pertinent if applied to the words "spiritual" and "spirituality."

We have had a lot of vapid and meaningless talk about spirituality meaning "the state of religious emotion in which I find
myself." If your experience differs in any way from mine,
you haven't any spirituality! Not much wonder if many persons
of refinement shy off at the word. It has been used too often by
the wrong people.

Up to 40 years ago [*writes Professor Thorndike*] *people
thought of the animals as having minds that were merely rather*

poor human minds. They believed that animals do reason, once in awhile; not as often as we do, nor as well; but they would tell you many an interesting story about dogs and horses that seemed to prove their case.

More recently we have carried on some experiments with animals leading us to a different point of view. It appeared, at first, from our experiments, that animals learned by what we call trial and success.

By that, we mean that they just fumbled around and learned to do a thing, much as we do in getting exactly the right amount of force into a golf or tennis stroke. Our experiment indicated that when the cat, in fumbling around, chanced to lift a latch, or turn a button, and the door opened to some food, he remembered it; and next time did not need to fumble so long to achieve the same reward.

Later, in experimenting with apes, we discovered that instead of merely happening, accidentally and at random, upon successful ways of doing simple things, they did have a capacity for putting two and two together.

The chimpanzee will learn to do all sorts of things with a stick. If you hang a banana up beyond his reach or place it outside his cage, he will pick up a stick and knock it down, or poke it until he gets it within reach. In certain highly developed specimens, he may take a hollow stick and push it inside another hollow stick to make it longer.

However, when it comes to piling boxes on top of one another to be able to climb up on them to reach something, this is quite too much for the chimpanzee. Give him one box and he will mount it; but he has no notion what to do with two boxes.

From all of which, and a score more of illustrations, Professor Thorndike concludes that animals possess a specialized intelligence. It takes even more ingenuity for a chimpanzee to insert one end of a hollow stick into the end of another hollow stick to make a longer stick, and thus increase his reach, than to pile one box on top of another to increase his height, but, the animal's intelligence being specialized, he can manage the sticks but not the boxes.

A dog is clever enough at dodging obstacles; remembers exactly where is the hole in the hedge large enough to go through and will dash for it when the rabbit enters the field, even though it retards him temporarily from the pursuit of his quarry, but finds it very hard to learn to open a gate, even if the action involves but the lifting of one bar. Dog logic isn't equal to that kind of problem.

From this point, Professor Thorndike moves along to a discussion of people. One type of mind is adequate to handle a given group of situations, problems, obstacles; but falls down when faced by another net of perplexities.

He loosely catalogues some common types under such code phrases as Mechanical Intelligence, Social Intelligence, and Abstract Intelligence.

The social intelligence knows how to manage, organize, and get willing effort out of other people, but, if shown all the pieces of a complicated machine, and asked to put it together, could not do it at all; while the mechanical intelligence would delight in assembling the machine; but would have trouble assembling the people.

I wonder if it is not the same way with souls. May it not be that souls can be codified, after a measure, under such heads as, say: Socialized Souls; Cloistered Souls; Inquisitive Souls; Aesthetic Souls; Mystical Souls: each having its definite genius for the accomplishment of certain tasks, to which, if it is wise, it will commit its special talent, without reserve.

If there be any truth in this, then it becomes quite important that we should discover what spiritual talent we possess, in order that we may put it to its best use. Unquestionably, most human failures in business, and in life at large, can be traced back to a maladjustment between a man and his job.

Environment, home persuasion, and the counsel of friends may have pushed him through a law school and out into an unhappy practice of law when all his slumbering gifts wanted a chance to write poetry, direct an orchestra, or paint portraits.

I know a man who married a wholesale grocery business, who ought to be writing detective stories. I know a man who owns a haberdashery and wants to be an ornithologist. I know a young purser on a ship that runs to China who majored in political science at Harvard, but hasn't found out yet what he is good for. I presume that the position of purser on a ship is as good as any for a man who doesn't know what, if anything, Nature had meant him to be.

And, by the same token, I know men who might have taken a prideful interest in the development of their souls had they been differently environed and directed. One man had the soul of a mystic. As a mere child, the consciousness of God's living presence in his life was at times quite overpowering. He could sit, quietly, in rapt contemplation, and sense a kind of inner illumination, a warmth that was other than thermal, an awareness of the Divine affection. It was a very fine, high-grade, potential soul — and needed expert handling. His parents were zealous about his physical welfare; and saw to it that he knew his hygiene; were careful that he should have balanced rations, and his full quota of sleep, and the right amount of exercise and reaction. Equally mindful for the training of his intellect, which was quick and precocious, they were inquisitive about his school, his teachers, his outside reading. But, it never occurred to them that his soul demanded direction. He learned about souls at the Sunday School.

There was no discipline in that Sunday School, for the reason that not only was the instruction voluntarily offered, but as voluntarily accepted, and a good deal of the teacher's efforts and ingenuity were spent in the sheer task of keeping her wriggling charges quiet enough to avoid disturbing the class adjacent.

To capture their attention, and command interest, it was necessary to tell stories of Hebrew magic resident in the folk tales of a primitive people, dating some thirty-five centuries ago. Religion was something that used to be. It used to perform queer tricks. And certain men used to hear celestial voices; but, apparently, it had gone out of such business, long since, for the teacher made no effort to connect this antique lore with present possibilities.

Obviously, what this lad needed, to develop the type of soul he owned, was the direction and influence of some mature person who, like himself, was of sensitive, mystical quality. As he grew up, and went to the services of the church, he learned that the main business of the institution was to raise its annual budget (which is not often accomplished, probably for that reason) and around the family table he heard discussions of the main issues which commanded the attention of his parents' church, and no one of them even remotely impinged upon the problem of his own soul hunger.

In later adolescence, he became absorbed in the affairs of his physical world — his vocational problems, college, love, the new home, his business — and forgot he had a soul. Now and again, it throbbed, and stretched and sighed, but he ignored it and it went to sleep again. He had the makings of an important spiritual leader; but lost his chance to be that through mishandling — mishandling largely charged to the church, and the church's misguidance.

Another man had a definitely aesthetic soul, but was so unfortunate as to be taught what passed for spiritual culture at the hands of people to whom the love of natural and moral beauty, for its own sake, had never been evoked. Religion was a sheer matter of conduct — their conduct. They had their own little table of mores, and the business of religion was to make everybody behave just like that. As for the loveliness of life, the livableness of life, the profoundly stirring majesty and wonder of the divinely co-ordinated beauty of life, they couldn't teach it, because they had never suspected it.

Religion was the gospel of *don't.* It began and ended with Thou Shalt Not. It had no sunrises or sunsets; it knew nothing of great music; great literature; great drama. In short, it had nothing to offer to an aesthetic soul, and this particular aesthetic soul hungered awhile and dropped off, through sheer under-nourishment and anemia, into a rather fitful slumber — occasionally haunted by longings and dreams, but colorless.

Then, there are the inquisitive souls — eager to learn as much as they may of God's will as apparently deducible from Nature, scientific discovery, and the ripest thinking of other inquisitive souls — people who, falling into the hands of confirmed Traditionalists, have been warned that inquiry is infidelity.

Highly socialized souls, who believe only in a gospel of work, should get themselves into some connection where there will be lots of committees to attend, and speeches to make, and hats to pass and cards to sign and resolutions to enact — a perpetual procession of things accomplished. For them to find themselves in a mystical atmosphere of quiet contemplation might not benefit their souls at all.

But, before a man can pick his company and his technique of developing his soul, he must find out, by careful investigation, what kind of soul he is. He must discover what his soul wants; what it lives on; what appeals stir it to satisfactory reactions; what kind of human contacts fills him with desire to be better than he is; and what kind of inspiration results, with him, in aspiration.

One might suppose, from a survey of the churches of the day, that there is abundant room for them to do some constructive work on this subject, in assisting men and women to a discovery of the paths to their own souls.

Too many of our churches are so busy regulating or — to speak more accurately — too busy attempting and failing to regulate the public conduct, that they have about left off dealing with spiritual matters. All that Religion is about is souls, and their culture. Most of our modern religion concerns itself with practically everything else but souls and soul culture.

Spiritually hungry people come, on Sundays, to our churches, wishing they might learn something that would improve their celestial contacts, and help them find out their peculiar soul-powers; and they go away pretty sure that they'll have to muddle along without help. For every normal man would really like to know exactly what is on the inside of him — what his soul is; how it works; how he might make it strong. Let organized religion begin talking about these things, and see what will happen to the churches. And to the people who compose the churches.

Have you ever explored your soul? It is not too late to do so. The pursuit is quite rewarding. To do it properly may mean the temporary ignoring of many concerns of latter-day religion which the churches think vastly important. But it is worth the trial. I heartily commend it to you, as a noble enterprise.

It would be a great thing to feel that one had contrived to find out exactly what one's soul is good for; what strains and stresses it can endure; how well equipped it is for the strange adventure upon which it is ultimately to set forth; how fit it is to stand in the white light that beats against the throne of God.

Los Angeles
January 6, 1928

EXPLORING YOUR SOUL

II

Your Soul: What It Lives On

IN MANY RESPECTS, there is clearly epitomized, in the life of an individual, the history of a whole social order.

In that constricted orbit described by the normal career of a man, from cradle to grave, we find, as if in miniature, the immeasurably larger cycle of a race, from its dazed uprising out of the elemental grapple with the ground, on through its conscious successes in refashioning its environment to suit its increasingly exacting ambitions, to the hour when, jaded, sated, and enervated by the very rewards and possessions so dearly bought, it sinks into lethargy and dissolution.

Shakespeare, in his Seven Ages of Man, has traced progress of the individual from helpless infancy in its nurse's arms, to the final *sans* everything stage of infirm senescence. And Froude and Hegel long ago postulated the same progression of nations and races.

More recently, we have added to our knowledge of such matters. Spengler, in his *Decline of the West;* Keyserling, in his *The World in the Making;* and John Dewey in his philosophical survey of ethnic history, specifically in his study of China, have mapped the rise and flowering and fruiting and decaying of civilizations, in a manner that makes us half skeptical of the hardearned riches of progress — seeing how inevitably the ripening of a race into sophistication and self-adequacy lacks only a day of the period when dissolution is assured.

All these studies in the cyclical movements of civilization, however, are essentially materialistic. They concern largely what may be seen by a thoughtful tourist, and recorded in what he may be self-confident enough to call The Travel Diary of A Philosopher — superficial symptoms, diagnosed hastily and in short cross sections of narrow vistas.

The case they make is convincing enough, viewed on the surface. In the frontispiece, there is perhaps a picture of a multitude of heel-dragging coolies wheeling reluctant barrows of sand and rubble from a pit beneath whose floor lies the forum, the stage, the throne room of Babylon: a mute but indisputable testimony to the inexorable fact that what goes up must come down — whether it be a pebble idly flung into the air, or a nation raised by Herculean effort into pomp, power and prosperity.

Nor have we been less forehanded in our investigation of the progress of the individual, in the plotting of his curve. Biology, not content with starting man where Shakespeare found him, helpless, in his mother's arms, traces him from the first, faint stirrings of his prenatal life; discovering a startling analogy between the successive physical changes in the form and structure of the unborn child, and the early mutations of the evolving human race, from lower forms — reptilian, feathered, amphibian, arboreal — until mankind walked erect and shaped a stone into a dish, an axe, an awl.

Nor does biology stop with its research in the beginnings, endeavoring to show that the life of an individual is but a tiny, complete, replica of the life of a race — exactly as the microcosmic universe comprehended by a single drop of water, is but the infinitesimal portrait of the spatially superior sidereal universe to which our world belongs. It points to the striking similarity of a man's waning strength, his hardening arteries, his progressive sluggishness of response and reflex to the stimuli of sensations, and the progressive apathy and slow reaction of old nations, obviously death-bound.

But, in all these strictly scientific approaches to this most absorbing subject of man's relation to the race, and the individual's span as related to the cycle of a civilization, spiritual forces are not reckoned as factors in the equation of human destiny.

However portentous may be the photograph, taken on the spot, of modern Archeology, spade in hand, at the grave of Classic Greece, and the sarcophagi of Imperial Egypt, Proud Persia, and Rich Phoenicia, the fact remains that the aspiring spirits of these buried civilizations, far from being entombed, fled — unimpaired, unimprisoned — upon the decay of their physical tools, weapons and vehicles, to seek further triumphant expression in adolescent social orders, elsewhere.

Nothing of essential truth is really demonstrated by the history of Rome's utter destruction of Greece as a world Power — on the battlefield and on the sea and in the market place, and at the council table of kings — unless it be remembered, also, that after all that work of ruin and rape, sack and pillage was accomplished, and Greece had been reduced to dust and ashes, no Roman could call himself a gentleman unless he spoke Greek, and conversed in the terms of Hellenic culture. The body of Greece was crushed, broken, dead, if you please; but her soul went marching on.

And when Goth and Vandal had similarly disposed of Rome, and jackals and hyenas prowled by night among the sprawling columns of the Forum, the soul of the Imperial City had already flung out its tenacious tendrils over the northern marshes of the Adriatic, promising the rise of that new civilization which was soon to flower in the most brilliant outpouring of men's creative imagination — in art and architecture, drama and song, which the world had ever known.

And if there be, as there unquestionably is, an inevitable parallel between the life cycle of a civilization and the life story of an individual, surely the same spirit which, having activated a nation to the achievement of its full fruitage, spreads its wings and escapes to find lodgement and expression elsewhere, is of the same essential stuff — divine and immortal — as that which drives the individual over his course, and, having made full use of his physical resources, speeds away to seek a larger fullness and freedom in some other form.

And when, with the history of such spiritual mutations outspread before our eyes, we view the migrant soul of a tribe or nation abandoning one set of physical tools and devices, to quest a better expression of its aims in other realms and by means of other vehicles, we are entirely warranted in echoing Browning's triumphant credo:

> *If I stoop*
> *Into a dark tremendous sea of cloud,*
> *It is but for a time; I press God's lamp*
> *Close to my breast — its splendour, soon or late,*
> *Will pierce the gloom: I shall emerge one day!*

Now, all this inspirational logic may be sound enough, at base; and yet, in its practical eventualities, mean little unless it be able to survive the case method of criticism.

It is simple enough to point theatrically to brilliant examples of a migrant spiritual urge abandoning the broken massiveness of stone. Meneptahs and Amen-Hoteps in the Valley of the Nile to find jubilant rebirth in the more beautiful classicism of the Athenian groves, and, when Destiny had tolled another hour on the dial of progress, again setting forth, from pillaged Athens, to seek hospitality in Rome; and again fleeing ruined Rome to breathe into the nostrils of Venice the breath of life that it might become a living soul; easy enough to trace that migrant spiritual urge, embarking at Palos, and sailing westward to reconnoiter for fresh liberties on an unmapped continent, and later taking passage on the *Mayflower* with a few dozens of the desperate. These dramatic occasions speak for themselves; chiseled an inch deep in proud monuments, and as enduringly fixed in heroic verse and epic frieze and eternal song. They speak as cogently and convincingly as the great biographies point to the influence of the famed discoverers of facts and molders of opinions over the aims and achievements of their spiritual lineage.

Some think it not without significance that Isaac Newton was born on the night that Galileo died. Or that the lives of successive brilliancies in the veiled realm of discovery should have been laid end to end, with almost mathematical precision — as if there were an actual transmigration of one highly dynamic soul through a royal line of descent commandeering the talents of a spiritual family composed of a Galvani, a Volte, an Ampère, a Franklin and a Faraday — as if they were born to it not by flesh and blood — or by the will of man — but of the Spirit of God.

But, after the roll has been called, from the bronze and marble tablets in the halls of fame, of these meteoric displays of supergenius and master-mindedness, both on the part of races and their seers, one gazes out over a rather bleak terrain of apparent inconsequences, both in the story of whole peoples and their natural leaders.

There are huge social orders in Asia and Africa, which, in the course of a history so hoary with age that they were bowed with the weight of antiquity when Eden's flowers bloomed, have contributed nothing to the progress or enrichment of their world. No aspiring spirit ever fledged wings and soared, expectant, from the body of their indulged and indolent flesh. No jealous barbarian horde had ever done them to death to possess their treasure; for they had amassed no fortune worth a covetous glance. They never died, because, in very truth, they never lived.

Not meaning that their successive generations were utterly

unpossessed of that which, nourished and encouraged, might have made for the greatness of a social order; for the occasional traveler, grateful for a night's hospitality at their hands, discovers that they have a code of morals and a tribal pride; that their men are as careless of life, in defense of their honor; that their women are as spendthrift with their sacrifices on behalf of their children; that youth is encouraged and age venerated; as well as — and sometimes better than — in civilizations which regard them only with a mocking smile.

But, however they may have possessed a slumbering national soul, they have not discovered the rations that makes a national soul fledge wings and outgrow its nest; and seek new fortunes in new forms.

They have never fed that national soul the stimulating meat and heady wine of discontent with things as they are, until it found its cramped quarters too stifling to be endured, and demanded fresh housing; even at the price of abandoning the humble place of its nativity. In sluggish ease and smug complacency they beat their tribal tom-tom; built high walls about their worthless stuff; inbred their rulers until all their kings had rickets and epilepsy, and were satisfied with their world. They never learned that *that which thou sowest is not quickened except it die!*

In similar mood, one surveys the generality of individuals, including oneself, who happen to be swarming the stage of life for a little while in the theater of Destiny. Poe, drunk, sick and in despair, preferred to think we were only the audience in that theater, watching a puppet show whose grisly actors stalk in the shadow of a drab tragedy; doomed to finish at the tomb.

> *Out — out are the lights — out all!*
> *And, over each quivering form,*
> *The curtain, a funeral pall,*

Comes down with the rush of a storm;
And the angels, all pallid and wan,
Uprising, unveiling, affirm
That the play is the tragedy "Man,"
And its hero the Conqueror Worm.

And Omar Khayyám, Poe's spiritual patriarch, rebelling at the scheme entire, fatuously wishes we might conspire to shatter it to bits, and then remold it nearer to the heart's desire.

But, without too broad a glance over the human scene, when one takes reckoning of the lives most of us live, it is small wonder if we speak with deep humility, if not chagrin, about our souls.

Here, again, the life of the individual epitomizes the history of mankind. Listen to the earnest queries of your four-year-old child about God — queries that startle you for their bland irreverence; and their savage sacrilege. He talks about God, the Absolute, with a blunt candor that brings you up with a gasp, and you hush-hush him with a caution that one doesn't speak that way about God.

Who doesn't? The sophisticate! He doesn't! The maimed, and stained, and brow-beaten soul: it doesn't! But, to the little child, one's relation to God is something that one takes terribly in earnest. It is only after we have put ourselves at a remote distance from our Source that we begin speaking of Him softly, and in whispers — or, preferably, not at all.

As with the Babel-builders, who, out of their naïve, elemental passion to see God's face, essayed to climb to Him with brick and mortar, but, having perfected their technique of masonry, decided on second thought to build a monument to themselves, our childish curiosity about God swiftly gives place to a haunting anxiety lest we might find Him, and relate ourselves to Him in some manner demanding more of us than we care to pay. Perhaps the Babel-builders, realizing day by day that they were achieving the heights, feared that once they had arrived in the presence of God, they might not be able to climb down again to carouse with the neighbors.

Perhaps we hesitate to feed our souls on a stimulating diet for fear they may become bold in demand and audacious of mastery, threatening at any time to hurl us into hazard of those things which temporarily guarantee the welfare of our bodies.

What *does* the soul live on? What manner of nourishment makes it conscious of its strength, and eager to quest adventure with its powers?

First of all, it must be definitely assured of its own importance!

Out! on all these pale and sickly ballads that timidly chirp of "You in Your Little Corner and I in Mine" and "Oh to Be Nothing" and "For Such a Worm as I."

Quite off pitch is the timbre of a feeble voice like that, when it tries to attune itself to the Galilean: "Ask What Ye Will, and It Shall be Done! Seek, and Ye Shall Find! Knock, and It Shall be Opened!"

Let a man concede, if he wants to, that his body is whatever he cares to call it in the general category of things that do not much matter. To me, it has always been an amazing inconsistency in the more passionately fanatical among our latter-day religionists that they should so vigorously rebel against the idea that our bodies are the slow product of an evolution from things not quite so complicated as they are now!

Let the body come from where it will, by whatsoever road it finds most convenient — when we are done with it, it goes to its original elements: a little lime, a little carbon, a little phosphorus; a little iron, a little salt; a bit of this and a bit of that — so be it! With a body headed for such an inglorious wind-up as that, how matters it where or what it came from?

I heartily acclaim the noisy troubador of Tarsus when he declares (in a rather free translation), "We owe no debt to the flesh; nor are we under any obligation to live according to the desires of the flesh. For, if we live under a sense of obligation to the flesh, we shall die. But if, by attendance upon the Spirit, we do sublimate the demands of the body, we shall live. We are heirs of God; joint-heirs with Christ; in all things more than conquerors; and I am persuaded that neither that which men call death, nor that which men cherish as life; nor angels; nor governments, nor the past nor the future; nor height of ecstasy nor depth of despair can exclude us from our Father's love."

Let your habitually recumbent soul stand up, and rejoice in its importance. Let it flex its biceps, square its shoulders, and expand its chest. A Child of God!

But, just on the point of feeling that I have bitten of the fruit of the tree that makes men great as God, let there be quiet pause to consider that this hypothesis that I am a child of God is erected on the assumption that all men everywhere are the children of God. For, if all other men are not the spiritual children of God, there is no sense or significance to my claim that *I* am.

If the only way I can account for my personality is to trace it back to a Divine Source, then the only way I can account for any other man's personality is to trace it back to a Divine Source.

Now, that is not only good food for my soul; but good discipline, as well; for the business of calling every other man in the world "brother" is no trifling contract. Not much wonder that Jesus had so much to say about the importance of brotherhood. No brother; no Father. Take the doctrine or leave it, on these terms. Everybody a Child of God, or nobody a Child of God.

That is — potentially!

We all have times when we certainly don't act much like it. But the thing is to assume that every other man is a child of God, and if he seems something other than that it is because he has repudiated his heritage. Or, perhaps he is unaware of his heritage. One of the blunders of our frequent phraseology relating to Christ's mission to the world declares that he came to make men the Children of God. What we mean is that he came to make men aware that they already were the Children of God.

Jesus was so fully aware of his own Divine paternity that Peter when he first met him, growled: "You'd best not have anything to do with me. I am a sinful man."

Jesus' Divine Sonship showed through. His errand was to help other men to such an awareness of their Divine Sonship that it would also, in their case, shine through; until the glow of their souls would not be as a candle hidden under a bushel measure, but as a light to all who came into their house; increasing in power until they would be as a city on a hill whose light could not be hidden.

Jesus was fairly aflame with desire to see this news spread. His latest injunction to his friends begged them to go to all the world and teach this gospel — this good news — that we are all of us, spiritually, the Children of God.

And whenever and wherever a Christian messenger has failed to make the gospel convincing and beautiful, it has been because he approached a prospect, saying: I am a child of God, whereas what he was really sent out to say, was: You are a child of God.

And the more people you can persuade of the reality of their own divine lineage, the more assured you become of your own.

Of course, there are ways and ways and ways of doing this. Unquestionably the most tiresome and fruitless way to do it is the way I am doing it now — making a doctrine of it and inviting you to believe it. People do not like to be invited to believe things. They prefer to see things in operation; and if they like them, they will believe in them.

Perhaps the easiest and most natural and beautiful way for me to assure you that you are a child of God is for me to recognize and identify, in your life, some noble quality; and, not in the tone of raw flattery, or with fresh impertinence, but by direction, call your own attention to it, and help you see how valuable it is.

Sometimes one man can point out to another man how wealthy he is, spiritually, by making mention of it to a third party. Occasionally, the news gets back to him. And he stammers that, after all, it was a mere nothing that he had done — not worth talking about, surely; but, all the same, it puts a little more force and direction into his next experiment with whatever kind of altruism it was, and his soul grew an inch or two in the process.

And, curiously enough, the soul of the man who imputed this added power to him, grows also, by as much.

It's really a lot of fun, after a little practice, this business of giving other people hints about how fine they are on the inside, and what they might make of their souls, if they took the time and trouble.

Presently they find some reason to come back to you, to see if you can notice anything else in them that is worth cultivation. I know I always do. If a man deftly hints that he sees something of value in me, I keep wanting to have another sitting with him. I am at my best in his presence; high-minded, sympathetic, idealistic; confident. And naturally I like him because he makes me like myself. I recognize him as a child of God because he helps me understand that I am.

Most of the people in this world who live poorly, wretchedly, meanly — proceed, unaware of their heritage, because they are not looking for the essential values in other people's souls — or trying to make them conscious of their divine sonship; but seem, rather, on a crusade to discover what ails the other people.

They, too, are apostles; but not of good news. They, too, frequently become skilled technicians in the imputation of motives, but, unfortunately, the motives they impute are not desirable.

They do not often face up to a victim and say, bluntly, "I don't like you because of this, and because of that, and because of something other," but confide it to a third person, and take a chance on its getting back.

The most powerful stimulant my soul can receive is an assurance, produced somehow, that it is at one with the Divine Life, and the best way for it to retain that assurance is by making other souls aware of their oneness with the Divine Life; of their inherent longing to be as God obviously meant them to be.

It was an ennobling thought that appears in that sublime prose poem we call the Fourth Gospel, where the mystic is saying, after long contemplation upon the nature and destiny of the soul:

"Beloved, we are now the children of God. It doth not yet appear what we may become, but we may be assured that when God shall have been made clearly manifest to us, and we see Him as He is, we shall be found to be like Him."

Like Him! How many of us? Like Him? In what particulars?

Not much wonder the prodigal postponed his going home, until every resource of his life has been exhausted. Afraid? To face his father? No; not afraid; but ashamed. Once he had been the heir to a fortune. He had been his proud father's son. Latterly, with his legacy squandered, he had become so poor, so lost to all self-respect, that he would have shared husks with the swine. There was nothing for it, now, but to go home, but he would not have the effrontery to go back as a son. He would ask only to be a hired servant.

But, when his father, on the lookout for him, saw him coming, afar off, he ran to meet him; and, embracing him, cried, "My son." And made him a feast, and said, "Let us rejoice, for this, my son, who was thought dead, is alive again. Was lost, but is found."

Not much wonder if the prodigal was ashamed to go home and face such a father.

But, on second thought, if he was aware that in his veins

coursed such noble blood, and in his heart dwelt, potentially, such capacities for a lofty idealism, he can be sure that no matter how poor or ragged he is, or how lowly has been his occupation, or how disgraceful his mendicancy, or how far toward hell he's blundered, he will be recognized as his father's son; at least by his father.

And that's all that matters. Other people may not notice the resemblance; but his father will. He may start toward home, a dirty swineherd; but, by the time he arrives there, he will be his father's son — who, though thought dead, is alive again; who was lost, but is found.

It is our heritage to be the spiritual children of that kind of a Father.

Sometimes we find it hard to believe of one another, and, in our more introspective moments, we find it even more difficult to believe of ourselves; but that is what we are; and while it doth not yet appear what we may do with our heritage, whether our awareness of it shall make us beloved and immortal in at least two worlds; or whether our indifference to it shall keep us on this earth-plane in rags and wretchedness, we can be sure that when God has been made clearly manifest to us and we see Him as He is — we shall find ourselves like Him.

Los Angeles
January 13, 1928

Teach us Thy will for our lives, and point out to us new avenues of self-expression, that we may invest ourselves — with all the powers Thou hast given us — in labor and love for the sake of the vineyard.

pERSONAL pOWER

Ask, and it shall be given you; seek, and ye shall find; knock, and it shall be opened unto you. — Matthew 7:7

WITH AN ALMOST painful twinge of nostalgia, many of us will recall the lines of a tender hymn, crooned by our mothers in the dreamy days of our early childhood, when their devotion was so feebly requited.

It was a song sentimentally reminiscent of gracious deeds in Galilee where little children were trustful in the arms of the world's Best Friend; and in every stanza this wistful thought recurs: "I should like to have been with them then."

Only a cold and surly pedantry would parse a mother's cradle song, or cavil at its logic. It is significant to note, however, that the obvious implications of this refrain have been everywhere present in our conventional estimate of Christ.

In a certain remote epoch, in a certain eastern land, astounding benefits were conferred by a Person possessed of supernormal power. By his command the lame were made to walk, the blind to see, the deaf to hear. Lepers were cleansed, the dead were raised; and — what was almost as unprecedented — the poor had good tidings preached to them.

Persons to whom full credence in the highly improbable is achieved — if at all — only by hard mental struggle, have occasionally experienced rather rough treatment at the hands of zealous Christians, bent upon commandeering belief in Jesus as a wonder-worker.

To the best of my information, no skeptic has ever been excoriated for expressing the doubt that Christ performs miracles today — but church history is red with the records of tragedies due to doubts expressed that Jesus worked wonders in Galilee.

By no means would I attempt to convey the impression that the Christian Church has dated and located the entire service of Jesus to first-century Palestine.

It has been confidently taught that the Master's life was so inextricably related to the Spirit of God that he was and is forever in a position to speak for his Father and plead for us *to* his Father; that so necessary is his intervention between humanity and God that no man cometh unto the Father, *except* by him.

As for the practical outcome of our belief in Jesus as the Christ, the bulk of traditional Christian teaching on this subject has restricted its interest to the rescue of the soul for a burden of hereditary guilt; and a guarantee of heavenly bliss to all who accept the rescue thus arranged for.

But when any inquisitive believer rises to inquire by what process the aid of Christ may be invoked in the solution of present problems, relating to daily experience, the voice of the church is hesitant.

So long as it is discoursing of what Jesus did in Galilee, nearly twenty centuries ago — or of what Christ has provided for all faithful souls in the Beyond — the church speaks in the firm tones of assurance. It is fully convinced of wonderful blessings conferred in the Past — and to be conferred in the Future. But if you query it about the actual, factual, amply proved and properly vouched for *benefits* which believers are receiving as a result of their *supplications* — *here and now* — the reply is vague and unconvincing.

If one is disposed to investigate such stories as are afloat, in every generation and every community, relative to miraculous

Restorations to Health — Inexplicable Conferments of Favors —
and Extraordinary Outcroppings of Divine Power in the Experience of one's contemporaries — one is dismayed to learn that
these events are too often predicated by or of neurotic persons
of unstable judgment, whose emotional interests appear to have
had such priority over their intellectual pursuits that their testimony — however well meant — would receive but scant respect
on the witness stand.

As for the attitude of the church toward such reported benefits — miraculously bestowed — it is customarily a policy of
dignified silence.

The practical light offered by the church concerning the technique of availing prayer is projected through a thick fog. Prayer
has been a sort of hit-or-miss adventure — not subject to any
regulations, or amenable to fixed conditions.

The chemist knows that if he pours sulphuric acid into water,
he will get a far different reaction than if he had poured water
into sulphuric acid. The physicist knows that if he projects an
electric current into a vacuum tube he will get quite another
result than if he had projected it into a spark plug. The navi-
gator knows that if his chronometer is three seconds off, he will
miss his transatlantic port by six miles.

The modern world is operated by instruments of precision —
and physical laws of stern inflexibility. To such an extent, indeed, that this age has less respect for — and less interest in —
any loose, indefinite, unauthorized counsel than any previous
generation. It is not much to be wondered at, therefore, if
there should be a waning regard for a pursuit so nebulous and
tentative as prayer.

If your own experiments are typical — you asked God, in
the name of Christ, to confer a specified favor upon you. The
chances are that you were rather hard pressed for assistance; and
that your zeal was made active by your need. . . . So far as your

earnestness of desire was concerned, it lacked nothing. . . . Your faith, also, was probably as strong as your capacity for faith could muster.

If you got what you asked for, you were pleased. Perhaps your prayer had had something to do with it; perhaps not. You never knew. There was no precise method of checking up. You had put your requisition through — but it was not what the telegraph companies call a "repeated message." You got what you had asked for; but, despite your most gallant efforts to be devoutly grateful, the question arose whether you might not have got it, anyway, in the natural course of events.

If you didn't get it — well, perhaps it was not God's will that you should have it; though that was, of course, mere guess-work on your part — seeing you had had no evidential reply to that effect.

But, if you were eager to retain your faith in prayer as a prin-ciple, you settled upon that explanation as the least unsatisfac-tory of the probable answers to your dilemma. If your faith was a frail affair, exercised seldom, and then only in moments of desperation, when you weren't really capable of thinking straight about *anything* — you probably decided that there was nothing in prayer — for *you* — whatever it might accomplish for others.

You continued to pray, regularly, in conformity to a custom which you had observed until it was easier to comply with than to abandon — but your prayer was rather a loyal declaration of patriotic allegiance to the Kingdom of God than a supplication for definite favors.

The possibility that Jesus — having disavowed all other avenues of approach to God with a finality that said, "No man cometh unto the Father but by me" — had issued some cogent rules and regulations governing the act of prayer has rarely been recognized in our Christian teaching. Oh — we have spoken with much determination about the obstacles which make prayer *impotent*. When it comes to informing people how and why they *cannot get anything that way*, we have done very well. Nothing is surer — we say — than that the heart filled with prejudice, hatred, greed, envy, and uncharitableness is merely committing an impertinence when it asks a gift of God.

But — we have been more efficient in invoicing the negations — than the affirmations.

Assuming the relatively good life — good conduct, good attitude, good motives — assuming an outpouring of as great faith as the candidate is capable of, and a reasonable request, what have we definitely to offer as a reward for the very best prayer a faithful heart can project?

If you will turn to the sixth chapter of Matthew — about midway of the sermon on the Mount — you will discover a fixed formula for effective prayer. There is nothing haphazard about the recommendations — and nothing vague about the promise of results.

It is as exact as a problem in chemistry. You can have what you want, and be what you would like to be, and realize full value on whatever latent powers are resident in your life.

Just what do you make of the sentence: "When thou doest thine alms, do not sound a trumpet"?

It has frequently occurred to me that the pictures which embellished the Bible story books of our childhood have done us a very doubtful service. Adjacent to the passage, "When thou doest thine alms," there was a drawing of a rotund, smug, insufferable Pharisee ostentatiously dropping a coin (probably one of those large, bright, promising nickels like ours) into the basin of a flea-pestered mendicant. A crowd stood about, open-eyed, and interested. A self-righteous man had done a trifling act of charity in a very vulgar manner. We were presumably invited to take heed that this was the wrong way to make a gift.

But — after all — this didn't stir us, deeply. . . . Surely it didn't require the ineffable wisdom of a Son of God to inform the world that this sort of generosity was abominable. It is to be regretted that we miss much of the uncanny wisdom of Jesus just for lack of understanding the Oriental mood — and habits of speech.

"Alms" — on the lips of Jesus — is a code word for the investment of one life in another. "When thou doest thine alms" is a phrase not to be comprehended by the picture of well-fed egotism bestowing a penny on starved inferiority.

"Alms" is my projection of myself into the community to which I belong. "Alms" is my practical declaration of belief in human brotherhood.

There are two processes by which I can declare this belief in the essential Brotherhood of Man. I can — in the first place (and this is the customary process) — declare that belief publicly. Indeed — a great deal of my investment in human society, in an attempt to promote the general welfare, cannot be *other* than a public declaration.

The financial federation which serves as a clearing agency between those who have and those who have not, solicits my subscription toward its charitable institutions. It is very foolish for me to reply that I am doing my alms secretly; and therefore have conscientious scruples against the technique of organized charity. . . . If the world had had to depend — for its practical relief — upon persons endowed with consciences like that, every great city would be a plague-spot and an eyesore. Deliver us from people whose conscientious scruples always get in the way of their capacity for co-operating with movements based on the best judgment and experience of skilled social workers.

But — whatever is to be said in behalf of organized charity, and the opportunity it affords the benevolent to declare his belief in the brotherhood of man — this public confession of faith

in that theory doesn't really get you the *personal* results necessary to the establishment of that contact which you must seek,
if you wish to approach God in His capacity of Father — to
you!

Draw a check for twenty pounds to the associated charities;
and you have tacitly confessed an obligation to society, and declared your belief in the brotherhood of man — as a theory —
as a good, working hypothesis; but it has not enabled you to
project your own personality into the life of another individual.

This type of public charity is a good deal like public worship.
There's a lot to be said for *corporate worship*. It is very hearten-
ing, to a Christian believer, to go into a church, of a Sunday
morning, and observe how many other people — besides himself
— recognize their filial obligations and privileges as the spiritual
Children of God. In corporate worship, however, we make our
devotional approach as a community.

Jesus insists that when we are bent upon asking for Personal
Power, we must establish *a more intimate bond than this* with
our Father. We must not be content with a declaration — however sincere — that God is the Father of all mankind, ourselves
naturally included as small units of this countless host; but I must
seek a direct, private, insulated line to the spiritual source of *my*
life as an individual — as if I were his only child, and He exclusively concerned about *me*.

In other words — if I am seeking favors, through prayer, "I
must enter the closet, shut the door, and pray in secret."

This marks a long step, in spiritual attainment, in advance of
the prayer that merely postulates the theory that God is the
Father of all mankind.

Now — the problem of putting oneself into a mood of actual,
personal, heart-to-heart intimacy with the Divine is the important question which Jesus faces, in his counsel on the investment
of one human life in another.

Public charity — performed in the open — done in the bulk — was a tacit confession of the donor to the general theory in the brotherhood of man. Exactly as public prayer, in the course of public worship — done in the mass — was a tacit confession to the general theory of the Fatherhood of God.

When you do Public charity, you are concerned about the improvement of people, considered in bulk. When you do Public Prayer, you are concerned about God's favor to be exercised upon His Children, considered in the mass.

If — therefore — you want personal power, as an individual, for the achievement of some specific favor, you will have to make the approach of an *individual*.

The problem is, therefore: How are you to establish that intimate contact with your Father? You are not now going to be content with reading from a prayer book the very commendable wish that God will bless all sorts and conditions of men. You are, instead, going to ask for specific light on a given problem that relates to you, personally; not as all sorts and conditions of men — but one unique individual.

How better could you prove your belief that God does sustain that personal relation to you — than by establishing that *same* type of relation to an individual brother-man?

Pursuant to this advice of Christ, you look about you for an opportunity to invest yourself in some other life that needs rehabilitation. You will probably perform this task with *money*. Not because all human problems are to be solved with money — by any means — but because your money is your own static-power, earned by your work or genius.

If you have no money, that does not mean that you have no power to rehabilitate another's personality. Sometimes an optimistic word of hope and good-humor and joyful adjustment to things as they are, will send another man on his way with a fresh grip on his own weapons; *and the less money you have in your pockets* when you advise another man to be of good cheer, the more your counsel amounts to, naturally: for when the rich advise the poor to be of good cheer, it only makes them laugh.

It is to be carefully understood, however, that if you propose to make a private approach to God — on the basis of His Fatherhood in relation to you as a person — whatever preparation you do for it, in the way of an establishment of human brotherhood, must be *private, too*.

Let whatever you do for your beneficiary be performed so secretly that your own left hand will be unaware of the benevolence offered by your *right hand*.

Of course — this whole subject is vastly more extensive than can possibly be touched upon in the course of a brief Sunday morning sermon.

To appreciate its full meaning, one would have to make an excursion into the field of human personality. Our personality — after all's said about it that psychology has to say — is just another designation for soul.

Souls grow, and souls shrivel. Systematic exercise and proper nourishment will do the same thing for a soul — a personality — that exercise and nourishment will do for the body.

Souls — or personalities — grow strong through projection. Every time I make contact with another personality to its hurt, mine is *damaged*. Every time I make contact with another personality to its improvement — its expansion — its increase of power — my own personality is enriched by that much.

If I propose to intrude my personal affairs upon my Father God — it behooves me to go to Him with the strongest spiritual equipment I can devise. If I expose a shriveled, scarred, defeated little soul to the rays of Divine light and energy — it goes without saying that I can't hope for much. My *reception* will be faulty.

It will not be the fault of the projection energy. The trouble all will be at my end of the line, where I am asking for power, and have no instrument capable of receiving it.

How do I make my soul — my personality — effective? By exercising it, in the lives of other people, to their own increase of power. Every time they exercise more power — if they were inspired to it by me — it is actually *my* power that they are using. An alert, constructive soul can — if it wants to — be operating through a score of other personalities.

There are many benevolent people who are accomplishing more — in actual world-effort — in the amount of foot-pounds of burdens lifted, and lives rebuilt, after they are to all seeming *dead and gone* — than while they were alive.

They had set in motion certain forces which outlived them. They are more alive than they were when walking about in the flesh.

But if you want to go to God in the hope of establishing a secret relationship — you would better have some secret to confide. . . . You may have many secrets, that are not confidable to Him.

Prepare yourself with some secrets relating to private investments of your soul in the souls of other people. Very few persons deliberately contrive such secrets. They do plenty of good things — but not in secret. They may not consciously brag about it — but it gets out. And then it is no secret.

They do some really fine, constructive act, which reinvigorates another soul — and it makes them so happy, and pleased with themselves that they can't help talking about it — perhaps to a best friend — or a member of their family: and then all the joy of it is gone.

Make your investments so secretly that nobody knows. . . . Your Father will know. You will have a secret between you.

It will give you the kind of intimacy you desire with your Father.

Then — go to Him, in secret, and ask for what you want — and see what happens.

Had it ever struck you as a singular thing that certain persons of your acquaintance seem to live lives curiously immune against petty worry, lives so poised that ordinary irritations do not matter — and sudden crises do not alarm. Personalities so powerful that they seem supernaturally endowed with a gift for smoothing ruffled situations — and inspiring hope — and setting crumpled people up on their feet?

No — they will not tell you how they came by it — exactly. It is a long story — and they are under contract not to tell it. But *they* know how they came by it — and are persuaded that He is able to keep that which they have committed unto Him — against the day when there shall be no need for secrets — and all God's purposes shall be made plain.

Radio Address
Montreal
July 20, 1930

OUR FATHER:

We thank Thee for all the agencies of good that spring from the gospel of Thy Christ.

That we may accept these blessings — and translate them into peace, power, and plenty, for ourselves and our world — is our prayer, this night, for Jesus' sake.

AMEN.

◦ia◦ems an◦ ƒagots

It is with a sense of almost distressful inadequacy that I take
my stand upon this holy ground where, on occasions similar,
prophetic words have recently been spoken by one whose voice
is stilled.* And while it would only be a shallow affectation in me
to pretend insensibility to the honor implied by my commission,
it would be a mere impertinence to adventure upon it otherwise
than with humility, and the honest wish that so grave a trust had
been more worthily bestowed. But if the things I shall be saying
serve only as a feeble echo of his voice who so often pleaded,
in this place, for a deeper consecration to the truth; for duties
transmuted into deeds of valor; and for an idealism that transfig-
ures daily a recognition of the claims of a fearless selfhood, I
shall have fulfilled my promise to him, even if my words are not
so felicitously phrased as his, or spoken with such high authority.

In the little poem which probably represents the Sage of Con-
cord at his utmost, our days are pictured as "barefoot dervishes,
marching singly in an endless file, bearing diadems and fagots in
their hands." The casual reader hastily concludes that diadems
are symbolic of honor and success, while fagots, obviously, stand
for failure. A closer inspection of this metaphor, in the light of
experience, discloses quite another meaning. For diadems have
so often been the symbols of an empty pomp. Never have they

* Dr. Douglas is undoubtedly referring to Dr. Marion LeRoy Burton, Presi-
dent of the University of Michigan, who died on February 18, 1925.

been worn so lavishly or ostentatiously as upon tottering thrones; while the most valorous names in the story of man's ascent from dust to dignity have been associated with fagots. The diadem emits a feeble glow for an hour. The fagot gleams with an inextinguishable flame visible for thousands of miles across the centuries. The diadem merely reflects a light that cannot survive the shadow of a passing cloud; but no chemical has ever been discovered that would put out a fagot fire.

Now I think I know what is in your mind at this moment, who have yet to make adventure into the activities of business and professional life. You fear I am tilting at windmills — wasting precious time talking of matters obsolescent. You question the value of any serious comment on diadems in a world where, of late, regal symbols have meant so little; or of fagots in an age that exacts no martyrdoms. But you will be learning, before long — and the more rapidly you arrive in positions of usefulness, the more quickly you will learn it — that every age gathers fagots for its intellectual leadership; that our age is no exception; that perhaps no single group of years, in the past two centuries, are comparable with the last decade, in this fagot-industry.

You go out, now, to face a public that has been living, for some time, almost exclusively upon sentiment. Such a public is always erratic, neurotic, impulsive, and volatile. It is your right and your duty to know something about your public, if you would serve its needs acceptably. That this public means well, is beyond all question. That it is fired with zeal to do the right thing, and arrive at high blessings by the shortest possible routes, demands no proof. Indeed, its very zeal constitutes the most serious factor of its problem. Were it afflicted with a touch of Laodicean listlessness, you might sit down in the shade with it and talk things over, dispassionately; and, peradventure, arrive at some mutually agreeable logic in the calmness of approximate sanity.

But this public is almost frantically conscious of its crying needs. And the while it piously holds aloft the symbols of an idealistic Golden Rule, and shouts loudly of its aspirations to know the Truth, it is to be doubted if ever a more disturbing intolerance or a more dangerous iconoclasm has been at work, in our republic, than at the present hour.

Perhaps — to know that public in its current mood — it is well for you to realize, first, exactly what it thinks of You, as the finished produce of Higher Education. This public knows, by its own experience of elementary education, that, at the tender age of six, you were caught in the gears of a huge machine bent upon grinding into you a certain volume of information concerning the world in which you live, the stellar universe to which that world belongs, and various conjectures about the world to come. At the earliest moment consistent with the claims of the law the bulk of this general public wriggled out of the machine and went its way into the active affairs of life, leaving you fast in the clutches of the mill where, it thinks, you have remained under the same sort of discipline that had made its youth time hard to bear.

It has visions of you toeing the pedagogical chalk line through at least a half dozen years while it has been out driving hot rivets, piling brick upon brick, and pouring molten metals. It believes that not unlike the Strasbourg goose, which sits supinely in its narrow pen, receiving hourly lozenges of rich food, to the end that it may develop a liver of startling dimensions, it has been your lot to accept, resignedly, whatsoever pabulum has been thrust down your throat; and that your reputation as a student has been determined by the degree of docility wherewith you have swallowed your intellectual manna. The public believes that like a chunk of malleable steel, in the grip of an automatic machine, you were slowly fed through — the evident aim being to drop you out of the exit-end of the device, at length, diploma in hand, resembling one another as nearly as possible in temper, mind, and mood.

It thinks that at the last minute, just before your release from the inexorable clutches of that machine which had been devised to mill you all into standard parts, some fear was expressed lest there be left on you, somewhere, a shred of metal, not properly sheared off, emery-wheeled, and chamoised; and that, for this reason, and to insure against the possibility of such accident, caps and gowns were put upon you to make the loss of your personal identity complete. And there is just enough of truth in this, unfortunately, to make the whole sophistry difficult to deny. It is a truth that too little time has been put at your disposal for independent thinking and the natural development of your personality.

You have taken your milling, as it came, day after day; and because the modern educational program leaves very small blocks of time uncharted, you were in poor case to resist the process.

We have it on the testimony of no less eminent a naturalist than Mr. Bernard Shaw, that "if you once wash a cat, it will never again wash itself." I do not know whether this be true or not. My own experience of such pursuits goes no farther than my conviction that if you once wash a cat, you will never try to wash another. Mr. Shaw was attempting to say that our faculties for assisting ourselves into wisdom are dulled and incapacitated in direct proportion to the amount of aid we have received from other people bent upon guiding us into knowledge.

The public stands in awe of the prodigious quantity of theoretical wisdom you possess, but its appraisal of your practical value to society does not flatter you. And if you and the public are to become acquainted, sufficiently to put you in its confidence, the initiative to that friendship had better be undertaken by yourself. The common canons of hospitality imply that the public should be waiting, outside the stadium, tomorrow, with outstretched hand, to welcome you into the rough-and-tumble. It will not be there. You are not to wait, either, for it to make the first call upon you — seeing you have moved into its neighborhood. You will be expected to make the overtures; and it is well if you inform yourself as to its mood before making that adventure.

You will find the majority subsisting upon their emotions. Of course, the general public, at all times and in all places, arrives at its decisions more frequently through its reactions to sentiment than reason. But certain circumstances have arisen, in these latter years, tending to overestimate the emotions, to the enfeeblement of the intellect. About eleven years ago, there began the most devastating and spectacular tragedy ever enacted in the world. Through the days of our attempted neutrality, our people were kept in a fever of anxiety and alarm. Then, to speed our official action in the matter, it became imperative that we should be sold our stock in the war — a negotiation which required the utmost of perfervid propaganda, achieved by a frank appeal to sentiment.

I do not wish to be misunderstood here as denouncing what we did at that time, or the manner in which it was done. If proof were necessary, I could easily secure from many persons in this presence a certificate stating that among those who indulged in the appeal to sentiment, through the tumultuous days in question, few were noisier than the speaker himself. It seemed necessary that we should do it that way; and, had we to do it again, I doubt if we could hit upon a better.

So, presently, we were into the war, and right valiantly too, albeit the processes whereby we were required to build an army overnight, and win the public's wholehearted support of it, would not exalt the function of the human intellect, or stimulate the pursuit of pure reason. Every device that propaganda, salesmanship, and professional mob-hypnosis could remember or invent was practiced on a scale so stupendous that nobody tried any longer to think calmly or clearly. Indeed, we candidly declared that men who could think dispassionately while the world was on fire only indicated their own patriotism; and maybe that was so, but it registered a definite setback to the operation of the public's capacity for any mental exercise — a capacity all feeble enough, even in normal times. Then came the peace — only slightly less disturbing than the war; with governments tottering to a fall, and insolvent states hoarsely and impotently shouting maledictions at one another, while the whole economic structure of civilization seemed ready to clatter down like Yokahama.

Remembering, then, how effectively the skilled devices of propaganda had been invoked, in the hour of our great emergency, to the necessary welding of our people into a common cause, every organization extant — plus a legion more born for that exclusive purpose — launched upon noisy campaigns for the promotion of this-that-and-the-other alleged prophylactic or remedial program, devised either to rescue us from our predicament or insure against our experiencing another. Never was there such a volume of discordant clamor, clatter, and chatter heard in the world before. Never were there so many societies, committees, commissions, drives, campaigns, Tag Days, slogans, pledge cards, petitions, mass meetings, resolutions, and processions in the long history of the so-called human race.

But you can't keep people on a strain like that — in a perpetual state of stampede and alarm — shouted at from every corner either by self-anointed prophets of doom, who see a ghost behind every tree, or the excited high priests of four-score different brands of social salvation, each howling that he was the official Messianic hope of the world; you can't keep that up for eleven consecutive years without seriously affecting the general public's mental habits and shattering its nerves. The inevitable result has been that the people are half hysterical. No longer disposed to sit down, pipe in hand, to think things through, the public expresses itself now mostly through its primary instincts.

Practically every appeal made to it these days is atavistic — directed to the most elemental of the human passions and motivations.

Recognizing the conditions but hoping to lay the blame at the door of something sufficiently solvent to warrant our getting a judgment of society against it, and collecting an indemnity, we have charged various tendencies with the alleged moral breakdown, which, when a study is made of them, prove not to be causes of anything, but effects themselves.

The recreations, amusements, and entertainments affected by the public's liberal wing (composed of such as are not piously congregated in huge wooden tabernacles to seek light under the guidance of shirt-sleeved prophets, endeavoring to build an ark for the rescue of their particular cultus when the predicted deluge of divine wrath shall have inundated this befuddled world) — the recreations of the liberal wing are distinctly pathological and should be of interest to you only as students of abnormal psychology. Certain professional moralists would have us believe that the blatant eroticism of the movies may be held responsible for much of our moral turpitude — which is, of course, arrant nonsense. The movies are not a cause of anything, but a natural effect; for the public has been nourished on the sentimentality of sentiment until only the rudimentary urges of undisciplined physical life remains sufficiently active to be stirred. The superheated fiction of the day and the raucous squawk of the ubiquitous saxophone are not causes of anything; they are the inevitable achievement of an age that has fed its emotions on red pepper until its jaded palate refuses to react to any dish unless served with nitroglycerin sauce and garnished with firecrackers.

Impatient of the tardiness and apparent reluctance of its obvious leaders to speak words of certitude as to our best course (for they, too, have been perplexed by this unprecedented plight of the social order), the public has listened to voices of quacks and exploiters who would heal, with magic and miracle, that which only time and patience and simple faith can mend. Bewildered by the complicated problems of the future, the conservative wing has set up a mighty shout, at the behest of its hastily ordained seers, that it means to go back — back — to the mind and mood of our tranquil fathers. That, of course, is impossible. Even if it were the right way, which we doubt, it is no longer ours to take. Statistics may demonstrate that oxcarts were safer than motorcars are; but we are through with oxcarts; and are not going back to them, though the casualities on our streets were multiplied by ten — which Heaven forbid!

One hears loud lamentations in many quarters to the effect that we are sadly lacking in leadership. Maybe so; but the main trouble is that the people are so utterly put to rout with fears, and so completely exhausted as to their neural resources, that they are not disposed to follow wise leadership. They have no patience with men who wish to think calmly. They have no time to put themselves through a clinic, or wait the report of an honest diagnostician. They prefer a well-advertised patent medicine, three bottles of which will put the patient either on the first line of the pepful smilers, or definitely under the sod — but in any case, there will be a tang of finality to the stuff. It will at least guarantee certainty, and that's what the public wants. It has been undecided and bewildered long enough.

So it is a trying day for wise leadership. Moses can come down from his period of exultation on Sinai, bearing a new code which he expects will set things right again, but he will find the people dancing and chanting around a golden calf or its equivalent. For the public is always easily distracted from the main issue, to pursue mere minor matters of passing concern. One day it dances about the Egyptian calf, proclaiming that this is, after all, the god who had led it up out of bondage. And on another day it dances about an alleged Darwinian monkey, asserting that "this, after all, is the devil that has been subversive of light and truth." These are days, consequently, when any mountebank can gain a respectful hearing, any fakir make a living, any charlatan recruit a clientele, any quack enlist a waiting line of patients. And that is because the public wants surety; and these people are sure. The public has had enough of anxiety. It wants now to know the truth from voices who speak with a "thus saith the Lord" impressiveness, and the only man who can do that, in these troublous days, is a quack.

When the honest scientist is haled into the witness box by the irascible majority and is obliged to answer to certain queries which it has conceived in stupidity and brought forth in impertinence, and candidly replies, "We do not know," the public shouts: "Aha! just as we thought! You do not know. Very well. We will go to somebody who does know," and scurries away to the chiropractor (until very recently the driver of a jitney bus); and the man with the Abrams machine (who has just retired from the tonsorial profession); and the owner of a neuro-calomotor, who, by an examination of a lock of hair, a drop of blood, and a certified check, can diagnose any ill to which mortal flesh is prone; and draw from a slot in the device a prescription that will guarantee a lasting cure by Thursday at the latest.

In every department of life, small men willing to make capital of the public's psychoses; and unsuccessful men, who have tired of being honest at the prevailing price of that commodity, are arrogating to themselves large leadership. They speak with conviction. They never doubt, or wait, or hesitate, or ask the patient to come back next day for a decision. They put their dogmas down on the table with a bang and a growl. The public has been beaddled, mentally, just long enough to like that school of thought. It goes to a novelist for its information on history; to a journalist for its education in social science; and to a real estate auctioneer for light and learning in the field of anthropology. And the flattering attention which the public accords such quacks only inflames the fevered egos of these busy mountebanks until they themselves become sincerely convinced that Jehovah is communicating to the world through them — a very dangerous state of mind, indeed, for no fool is quite so great a menace as a zealous fool who has fallen victim to what the psychiatrist calls "grandiose paranoia" which is, I understand, the next to the last stop on the road to "hallucinatory omnipotence."

Given, then, a so-called intellectual leadership offered by people suffering from a fatty degeneration of the first personal pronoun; and accepted by a public that is nursing a bad case of "floating anxiety," and the young graduate who wishes to be honest either as a producer or retailer of truth must not be too much startled if he confronts a dull market. For the public, unwilling and afraid to go forward, has turned back. It has reverted to the old days of mob-stampede and the torchlight procession. It apostrophizes the little red schoolhouse which was one of the sentimental properties of our grandfathers' ballads; and shouts for the same literal acceptance of the Scriptures in the schools as that with which the Hopis grovel before their totem poles.

Its untutored prophets even have the audacity to howl their anathemas at science, by night, over the radio, which shows them to be lacking also in humor and reminding one of Huxley's remark that certain objectors to science made him think of the Abyssinian who was said to carve steaks from the ox that carried him. It invokes the effete dogmatism of two centuries ago, and stakes its last crust on minor creedal profundities, concerning which one man's guess is as good as another's; and no practical outcome in faith or character promised, no matter whose guess is right.

Massed assemblies meet to pledge their common hatred of all persons not so fortunate as themselves in the selection of parents, birthplace, racial background, and ancestral religious beliefs. Laboriously, sympathetically, tactfully, we had built up a process of Americanization through the schools, whereby we might impress our foreign imports with their duties to one another and the state. We were beginning to make some headway. But the panic-driven mass, unaware of this, breaks down in the course of three years of organized ill-temper all the nascent tendrils of faith and trust that this patient work had achieved in a half century. One would think that any man, realizing that he was unequipped either by natural gifts or mental training to pull his share of the load, and who knows that he will be always obliged to sit in the vehicle wherein the big bulk of humanity is ever to be hauled by its betters into a larger liberty — sitting there, doing nothing but adding to the weight of the burden — one would think he would have at least sense enough to sit still. One would think he ought to have at least sense enough not to drag his feet.

This, then, is the general public to which you are to minister. You can make more money being a quack, a pettifogger, a spiritualistic medium, a phrenologist, a palmist, an itinerant tent evangelist, a patent medicine peddler, or a plain second-story man than in any honest, self-respecting vocation.

It will not always be so. Presently the public will regain its reason. For the time, however, it is sick — desperately ill — and you must approach it as you would any other invalid — patiently and sympathetically. For it means well. It sees our morality and disarray, our laws unkept, our patriotism wandering; and would cure anarchy by urging upon its harried representatives in the legislature and Congress the enactment of still more laws — a process as illogical as the further issue of more billions of paper money to correct the precarious monetary system of a government which had already printed too much paper money; and would stimulate its sluggish patriotism by class and clan insularities which tighten up a parochial consciousness to the defeat of the national unity.

This is the befuddled public with which you are now to make adventure; and I charge you, by all that is good and right, by all that is decent and sportsmanly, by all that is holy; I charge you, in the name of your high privileges, in the honor of your alma mater, whoever is going to be a quack, it dares not be you. Whoever is going to make money by imposing upon a heart-sick and unbalanced public, it must not be you. Whoever is going to make capital of the fact that this generation would rather be lifted up to the magic and miracle of soothsayers than through the honest ministry of scientized altruism; whoever is going to teach the mob to howl sentimental slogans, and incite stupidity to hate — *it must not be you!*

Solomon remarked that on certain occasions it came to pass that servants went on horseback and princes afoot. Had he lived another ninety days, he could have seen it happen again, seeing he left his laurels so badly withered that his own heirs and assigns had to revert to the oldest known method of transportation.

We have seen this, latterly, at its utmost! This is the drift of a democracy in which too much pains have been taken to explain to the multitude the richness of their privileges, and not enough care has been exercised to teach them the nature of their responsibilities. We live in such a time as that, with Demos in the saddle; ignorant insolence imperiously making large gestures with hands still blistered from rough contacts with the useful, but lowly crowbar; and its helpmeet displaying costly jewels on hands still red with honest, albeit humble dishwater. Every morning, Demos and his spouse load the cart with their intellectual betters and rattle them over the cobblestones to the place of execution, hoarsely shouting for a liberty jeopardized by every fresh outburst of their passionate ignorance; for an equal-

ity which, to their mind, is arrived at through the elevation of
a dull stupidity; and a fraternity founded on unreasoning hate.

Here come your days — like barefoot dervishes, muffled and
dumb, marching singly in an endless file, bearing diadems and
fagots. Take up your fagots and let Demos have the diadems.
It may come to pass that you go out, at length, unjeweled, un-
crowned; but it will have been something to go out unashamed!
And I would have you take up your fagots, emblematic of the
inevitable martyrdom of an honest and fearless mind, in an age
that would rather trust to its emotions than its intellect — I
would have you take up your fagots without a whimper.

In one of the most subtle of *his* parables — he who spoke as
did no other man — the story is told of a wealthy landlord who
owned a vineyard. It was the season of harvest — a period of
heavy industrial stress. The grapes must be gathered. He went
into the market place, at early morning, and found men waiting
to be employed. He asked them to go to work in his vineyard,
and they said they would do so for "one denarius." It was a
high wage, and they knew it. And he knew it. But without
parley, he accepted them. The old Greek text says: "He har-
monized himself with them for one denarius." So they went
into the vineyard and to work, with the honest industry of
men who thought highly enough of themselves to ask for a dignified reward. At nine o'clock the landlord went again into
the market place; for it was obvious that his crew — no matter
how fast they toiled — could not gather the grapes before they
were ruined. There he saw men standing idly about — not looking for employment — merely lounging; and asked them if they
would go to work in his vineyard. They said they would; and
he told them to go. Whatever was right he would pay them.
And they were content. They knew their service was not worth
much and had rather leave the matter to his generosity. At
noon, noting, with increasing anxiety, the magnitude of his problem, the landlord again sought the market place; again hired

casual laborers; again promised to pay what was right. And at three, and at five he took on additional help, of doubtful character, with the same promise of a just wage. All day long, it may be conjectured, the early morning laborers, who had dickered for one denarius, witnessed the advent of these various groups of unprofessionals, learned that these casuals had not thought enough of their service even to inquire about the reward; frowned upon them as a lot of unclassified loafers and, by tacit understanding, resolved themselves into a little organization promptly known as the Loyal Order of Hardworkers.

At length six o'clock came, and the blast of the horn. It was time to quit. According to an eternal custom, the last to arrive were the first ready to leave; and, as they passed the gate, each of them was handed one denarius. By this time the Loyal Order of Hardworkers had neared the wicket and stood waiting while the casuals filed out. The five o'clock delegation had gone away, rejoicing over the receipt of one denarius, and now the three o'clockers were departing, each with one denarius. They who had arrived at noon were paid each one denarius and the nine o'clock crew had been accorded the same. So, when these, who had borne the burden and the heat of the day, approached, heaving long sighs of fatigue and very ostentatiously mopping their faces with their sleeves, they thought they should have more. And each of them received, according to compact, one denarius. Whereupon quite a large scene was staged. They staged speeches. They were professionals. They had borne the burden and the heat of the day. The landlord was summoned to hear the tumult; and he asked, "Did you not bargain with me for one denarius? Was this not your own price?" They confessed that it was true. "Then," said he, in a tone of finality, "Take what is thine, and go!"

Judged by sound economics, this parable does not, of course, have a leg to stand on. And whoever proposes to measure his value to the world in terms of wages will not like it. To him there will be no justice or reason in it. Nor is there justice or reason in it. The man of far vision does not expect to be dealt with justly or reasonably. People who insist upon being dealt with justly and reasonably always bear names which can be written with lighter tools than chisels. But I fancy that it is a parable you will often be reverting to if you are honest; and the more honest you are, the larger truth you will find in it. By the acceptance of your privileges you have automatically committed yourselves to a certain bargain with Destiny.

I should not be so unconscionable as to state — even in the interest of being polite — that one hundred per cent of you will achieve high place. Such things do not happen in this world. For some of you, tomorrow will be in the nature of a commencement; for others of you, perhaps, it will be regarded later more nearly as a finish. But, today, you are to have the benefits of all the doubts; even of your own! You are the professionals of your generation. Your training has made you so. You are not the mere casuals, sitting idly in the market place whittling sticks and swapping yarns at 3 p.m., willing to work for a couple of hours at almost anything, provided the job is brought to you and urged upon you. No, you are the professionals, out early in the morning to dicker for a whole day's work picking grapes in a vineyard. You are willing to give them the best you have; but they will have to pay you well for it — not a farthing less than one denarius.

Now, if it happens that — in a time of grave emergency, when the vineyard of our social order is fairly bursting with seasonal problems, certain casuals, untrained — casuals who in normal times would never be thought of by anyone looking for employees — if some of these should come drifting into the vineyard at noon, or at three, or at sunset, and go out presently with as much to show for it in the coin of the realm as you will have who dignifiedly negotiated for a wage, play the game according to the rules. No whining! No envying! No whimpering! Take what is thine and go! Now do not, in a sudden flare of anticipatory martyr's valor, tell me you will find it easy to be a good sportsman in the face of these conditions. For there will be drab days when a quiet honesty — in the face of sneering competition with flashy quackery — will seem hardly worth the plaint of him who, in Emerson's poem, met the days — and made his choice — and never lived long enough to cease regretting what he selected.

For — says he:

> *I, in my pleached garden, watched the pomp,*
> *Forgot my morning wishes, hastily*
> *Took a few herbs and apples, and the Day*
> *Turned and departed silent. I, too late,*
> *Under her solemn fillet saw the scorn.*

There will be temptations in plenty waiting for you — even in the face of your good resolutions at this hour. There will be tests of valor, addressed to you, comparable to the martyrdoms of old. And even if a manifest injustice should rob you of the material recompense you know you should have had, in consideration of your industry and courage, you are to face your situation with heads high and firm voices, as you shout to a haughty Demos, "We who are about to die, salute you!"

> *For so the ark is borne to Zion, who heeds how they perished or were paid that bore it;*
> *For so the shrine abide — what shame, what pride, if we, the priests, were bound or crowned before it.*

Baccalaureate Address
University of Michigan
June, 1925

the correct time

If a bit of boasting does not annoy you too much let me tell you about my watch. It is, as you have already surmised, an unusually accurate timekeeper. I feel that one should be right about something in this confused world; and, having neither a talent for prophecy nor a very good memory, it comforts me to know where we are at present. So, I carry the correct time. It is known as Pacific Standard Time.

I am aware that there is such a thing as Greenwich Time and Eastern Time and Tokio Time, but the right time is Pacific Time. Perhaps, if you live in the Midwest, you may feel much the same way about Central Time. Let us be broad-minded about this. If you will concede that Pacific Time is the right time for me, I'll concede that Central Time is the right time for you. Our watches will still differ by two hours, but each of us carries the correct time.

Now that we have settled this matter, some cantankerous old heckler inquires, "How do you mean — correct time? Correct time for what?" He seems to think that it is silly of us to be so particular about keeping the correct time unless we have some definite plans for what is the correct thing to do at that time. So, we proceed to inform him, though it really isn't any of his business. "It is now," we reply, consulting our fine watches, "time to get up, or go to bed, or give Aunt Annie her medicine, or leave for the eight forty-two."

"Yeah — I know all about that," drawls the old pest, " — and it's time to pay the gas bill, and time to turn on the news commentator. I agree that you're well equipped to decide when it's time to feed the cat, and when it's time to take a bath if you hope to find any hot water. What I'm asking is this: Do you know when it's the correct time to believe certain things, and expect certain things?"

"Well, Uncle, you'd better be a little more specific," we suggest. "What's on your mind?"

"I'll be glad to tell you," obliges the heckler. "What did you believe, in 1917, about our participation in the war? You thought it was the right thing to do, didn't you? If you didn't, I'll bet you kept your trap shut."

"Of course we believed it," we hasten to assure him, "and we said so. We thought we were helping to save civilization."

"Quite proper!" he comments. "That was the correct time to believe in enforcing the claims of a civilized society. Now, how did you feel — in 1921 — about the big war to save civilization?"

"We were disillusioned!" we reply, with a growl. "We had lost thousands of men, billions of dollars — and hadn't accomplished anything. Apparently, civilization wasn't to be saved that way. So, we decided to liquidate our military machine and go out of the war business. We urged the government to cut down our expensive navy, demobilize the army, and attend to our own affairs."

"That's right," remembers the heckler, "and almost everybody thought so. It was the correct time to believe that. It wasn't what we had believed in 1917, but couldn't we have been right both times? You have agreed that a man in Pawtucket shouldn't think a man in Walla Walla is a lazy loafer because he doesn't go to work until half past eleven, according to the clocks in Rhode Island. By the same sensible reasoning, two entirely different beliefs — dated four years apart — might both be correct. But we felt that the only way we could prove we were right in 1921 was by flogging ourselves for what we had believed in 1917. We came to despise war so bitterly that we even hooted at the high idealism everyone had felt when we sent our young men abroad 'to save the world.' They had believed it, too. At least, they believed that we believed it; and we did. But they weren't much more than out of their uniforms until we told them we had all been mistaken. Well — it was a pretty serious thing to make a mistake about; wasn't it? What must the young soldier have thought of us when he came home with an empty sleeve to find us saying, 'Excuse it, please. We made a mistake when we sent you. All that "saving civilization" stuff was the bunk! We don't believe in war any more. It's murder. And you'd better forget what you did, as soon as you can, for we intend to forget it, as soon as we can.' No — we would have been much wiser if we had said, 'It is apparent now that in the future we should stay at home and mind our own business; but we still insist that we believed we were right at the time we entered the war. That was the correct time to believe what we believed. Now we believe something else — and it's the correct time for that, too.' "

"It's a wonder our boys didn't lose faith in everything," we reflect.

"Maybe some of them did — if they had time to think about it," comments the old man. "It just occurs to me," he continues, "that it might be a fair question to ask if you think it is now the correct time to believe what you believed in 1921, or 1931, or 1936? For instance: didn't you think that Mr. Chamberlain was justified in the efforts he made to preserve peace? Almost everybody did, you know. We said, 'Good for old Chamberlain! Maybe he can appease those fellows — and stop the war.' You thought the word appeasement was respectable. It means 'to pacify, to soothe, to calm.' I know, I know, the word stinks now; but it doesn't stink in the latest dictionary. Our trouble is that when we are forced to a changed belief, we begin to revile what we believed before. We haven't sense enough to understand that 'new occasions teach new duties.' When obliged to take on a new belief, we jeer at the people who administered our former belief; gallop about, shouting, 'How come we haven't a bigger navy? Why haven't we ten thousand bombing planes? Who let us get into such a defenseless position?' The correct time? Keep this fact in sight: when you are obliged to travel far, you must reset your watch; but that won't mean that you were wrong before. Any man whose motto is 'Cheers for the Present; Fears for the Future; and Sneers for the Past' isn't carrying the correct time — no matter how reliable is his watch."

Bel-Air, California

Give us sympathy for all mankind — whatever may be their degree of progress, their blunders, their fears.

If we find within ourselves higher capabilities, better ambitions, and swifter advancement — than in others less privileged — may we humbly and devoutly give thanks for our blessings, and disclose the sincerity of that gratitude in the promptness with which we extend the helping hand to the backward and unprivileged.

Forbid that we should grow stern and frowning in our attitude toward others not of our faith or code.

the penalties and rewards
of wishing

Then Jesus turned, and saw them following, and saith unto them: "What seek ye?" . . . They said unto him: "Rabbi — where dwellest thou?" . . . He saith unto them: "Come and see."
— John I: 38;39

ONE OF THE MOST charming allures about the Spirit of the Great Galilean — as interpreted by the gospel story — is his willingness to meet the questions of inquisitive people.

It was a distinct departure from the attitude of humanity's leadership either in the fields of statecraft, education, or religion. The people were not asked: What do you want? What are you looking for? What is your idea of a goal worth the journey? The people were always told what was best for them. The people did not always think so, but it was more discreet to accept and say nothing.

The State never inquired whether the people wanted something other and better than the laws provided. The schools never asked what the students wanted most to know. Religion not only discouraged questions, but considered them impudent, sacrilegious.

There was sound precedent for all this. According to the Jewish account of the world's beginning, Jehovah had not inquired about the first man's wants. He had not solicited questions. He was flatly *down on inquisitiveness*. But He had made a very inquisitive pair of people, and for this questing trait of mind, they were expelled from Eden.

Jesus of Nazareth, as a messenger of God, reveals his Father as an entirely different type of personality. The God of Jesus does not frown when questions are asked. It was the old gods of the primitive days who disliked to have queries raised. Jehovah puts Adam out of Eden for fear the man's curiosity will lead him to invade some divine secret. Exactly as Zeus, god of the ancient Greeks, had chained Prometheus to a rock for daring to bring fire from the sun to warm men's damp and dismal caves.

The God of Jesus encouraged human curiosity: "Ask and it shall be given you. . . . Seek and ye shall find. . . . Knock and it shall be opened." The old gods would have kept man forever in a state of mental and spiritual infancy. The God of Jesus wanted them to grow up to the stature of the fullness of His Christ. No eminent exponent of any religion had ever turned around, on his path of leadership, to inquire of his followers: "What do you want?"

Jesus is the explorer's best friend. He listens to questions. He makes an *open bid* for questions! He turns, and waits, and asks: "What seek ye?"

So — viewed from a strictly Christian standpoint — there is nothing essentially wrong with wishing and wanting and asking and seeking and knocking. We are at our best when wishing most earnestly, and seeking most diligently. All discovery — all invention — all human progress — is in debt to these inquisitives. And it is not too much to say that Jesus Christ set the mind of man free of the old taboos against curiosity . . . and sanctioned wishing and wanting and seeking.

No further inquiries need be made as to why Christian civilization has given birth to human progress; nor is it difficult to see why all the other religions lie quite off the path of enlightenment. Granted: a beckoning God who invites you to inquire — and you have progress and liberty. Given: a frowning God who threatens punishment if you explore — and you have apathy and pestilence.

All growth of the mind and the spirit is the outcome of wishes. And that being true — it becomes us to discover what kind of wishing is profitable. Perhaps a good way to come at it is by a process of eliminating the wishes which are not likely to take us any place, except into disappointment, disillusion, and despair.

Shortly after the carefree and more or less consciously irresponsible days of adolescence are past, many people begin to organize a program of defeat for themselves by wishing for things they know they are not going to have.

In their more sensible moments, they reflect that it is time ill spent . . . but they keep on wishing, just the same. Sometimes the wishing is quite candidly hopeless; but even *that* does not deter them from wishing.

"I wish," says one, "that I was born with plenty of money; lots and lots of money. . . . For I love beautiful things, and could appreciate them if I had them; and I like to make other people happy, and could do it if I had the means. . . .I should have been born rich. . . . Why *wasn't* I born rich?"

"I wish," says another, "that I was possessed of some distinctive talent. . . . If I had some gift like that, I would give it the best of my energy. I would work day and night. There is no sacrifice I would withhold to develop that talent."

"I wish," says another, "that I had been able to provide myself with a better education. If I had only myself to provide for, I would do so yet. . . . If only I had the technical knowledge, I could succeed."

There is a great deal of this kind of wishing — tragic, hopeless, futile wishing — that makes life a bitter and corroded thing.

The editor of a magazine wrote me, last week, enclosing the copy of a letter he had just received, and asked me to send him an article that would try to answer the question in the letter. This is what the letter contained:

"After one is thirty, and especially if one has dependents, life becomes a struggle. One can do nothing about it. Everyone I know has to endure, rather than enjoy. . . . We all seem prisoners; you in your city, with all your advantages, and I in my little village. But why do so many people have to endure life without enjoyment?"

Now . . . if *you* were asked to write two thousand words about that, what would you say? I haven't written any of it yet, but if I do, I think I shall begin by disputing the letter's primary thesis: namely, that life has to be endured rather than enjoyed.

This man, who writes the letter — if it is a man (which I'm not any too sure of) — says, "Everyone I know has to endure, rather than enjoy." Now, how did he come by this singular invoice of repining friends — all of whom unanimously testify that life is an endurance, and not an enjoyment?

I have a feeling that in the conversations which developed that idea, my unknown friend helped shape the mood, and the other people fell in with it. I can conceive of his wishing that he had plenty of money, and some distinctive creative talent, and an adequate education, so that he might be in a position to bring more happiness into the world. But life has been difficult for him; so difficult that he does not attempt to enjoy it . . . but only to endure it; and he starts out on a definite campaign to discover how many of his acquaintances are as soured on the whole business as *he* is.

How did he find out that everybody else he knows is just enduring? Perhaps he proposed his questions in the wrong place. Perhaps he phrased his questions to bring that sort of answer. Maybe he has been wishing for impossible things — to the extent of failing to appreciate what he has: what he is: what he might become.

Of course, if there were all the time in the world — instead of a mere half hour — one might easily prick the opalescent bubble of these vain wishes . . . and show that the fulfillment of any one of them carries very irksome responsibilities.

Not always are the people happy who have been born to wealth. Many of them are quite oppressed by their problems. They have great difficulties assaying friendship, and they wonder and wonder whether they are really loved for what they are . . . or what they have. The poor man may not be sure of much; but he can be confident of his friends . . . If they seek him, they seek *him;* not *his!* Any time, the rich may lose all, and there is nothing so pitiable as a poor rich man.

And, more often than otherwise, people who have been entrusted with some singular talent are so bestraddled and ridden and harried by the gift that it comes to be a mild psychosis — and presently they are considered peculiar, and a bit uncanny; if not, indeed, half crazy. Adulation and attention make them self-conscious. They begin to be afraid of the arrival of a day of staleness in their work — or the indifference of a public that has been fed up with them, and has turned to other objects of devotion. They tell me it is very exacting and wearing to be conspicuous, and many people who are would welcome obscurity.

And education is no guarantee of great usefulness . . . as any college alumni secretary could tell you if he cared to — after looking over the records of graduates for twenty years or so.

But there is another kind of wishing that serves any man or woman well. . . .

First: The wish that I may be able to identify my strengths . . . and give them a chance to expand.

Again: The wish that I may add . . . by my attitude and conversation . . . something of happiness and hope and courage to the time in which I live.

And: The wish that I may follow my best ideals into a

beautification of my mind and the exultation of my soul.

Here — for instance — is a portrait in John's gospel of two men following Jesus. What does that mean: following Jesus? The phrase is common enough among us. One says: "Following Jesus means obeying his commandments; submitting to the influence of his personality." I fear that definition is a bit too vague and nebulous.

Getting down to practical facts: just what is it that we *want*, when we follow? What do we expect to *get*, by following Jesus, that we did not have, and will not have, unless we follow him?

That was exactly what Jesus wanted to know of the men who trailed him on that country road in Galilee. He did not turn to inquire: "What philosophy of life are you most interested in?" or, "What ideals do you entertain?" He simply asked the fundamental question: "What do you want?"

Naturally — they were somewhat embarrassed, as we would be, if we had been following him and he had stopped to inquire why. They were as much embarrassed as we might be, if the question were asked of us at this moment. They fumbled for a reply that might sound plausible — and finally one of them said: "We just wanted to see where you live."

I think it was an admirable answer. It was unquestionably an honest answer. They had recognized him as a great man, who knew the secrets of triumphant living. They saw that he was fearless; that he was in complete harmony with the universe; that he was somehow in league with God.

Of course, he was calm and brave; of course, he was personally charming; of course, he spoke with authority; of course, little children loved him — and the Roman consul said, seriously, "Art thou a King?"

Naturally — they wanted to see exactly how these strange gifts of his had reacted on his immediate environment — and whether his environment had somehow helped to make him what he was. They wanted to see the bed he slept in, and the books he read, and the desk where he did his writing. They wanted to see what kinds of flowers he grew in his window boxes — if any — and whether they grew any taller or gayer for him than they might have grown for them.

It did not occur to them to question him about his views on theology, or any of the profound speculations that have so seriously attracted his more recent followers. They just wanted to see how he was geared up to his daily life. Without doubt, the formula by which he lived would affect everything he touched. He knew how to live! He had found life good.

They wanted to run an inquiring thumb along the blade of his adze, to see if it was more effective than the dull tools they used. They wanted to inspect his spring, to see if it was less likely than theirs to go dry in midsummer. They wondered if he had a dog; and, if so, was it a surly dog that barked at strangers — or would even a *dog* react to Jesus' kindly code? They felt that if they could see him in his normal environment, it would be a great satisfaction.

He had said that men, at their best, lived without fear. That was quite a revolutionary idea. Their own lives were full of fears, riddled with fears. They wanted to see the home of a man who lived beyond fear. Would there be a bolt on the inside of his door? They had heard him say that if a man possessed two coats, he should give one away. It would be interesting to take a peep in Jesus' wardrobe.

They had heard him talk about the importance of doing unto others as you would be done by. They wondered if he kept a servant; and, if so, it would be interesting to see what was the relationship between them. They wanted to hear him give orders to his servant; and see if *his* technique of getting service performed was any different from theirs. They wondered how much he paid his servant; and whether there was a lock on the cupboard. They wondered if Jesus' neighbors ever let their chickens loose to scratch in his flower beds; and, if so, what he did about it, if anything.

It was one thing for a man to declare himself independent of worries and anxieties and fears; it would be quite another thing for him to demonstrate his theory in the rough-and-tumble of daily life.

Said Jesus: "Why are you following me? What do you want?" Said they: "We would like to see where you live. We want to see you at home. We want to come into your house — and see."

And Jesus replied: "Come — *and see!*"

I would like to think that it is in some such mood that we all are wishing we could follow Jesus — trying to find out how this ideal is related to the homely problems of our everyday life.

The trouble with most of us is that in our well-intended efforts to glorify Jesus — we have glorified him completely out of our reach. The pictures we have drawn of him are mostly unsatisfactory. We try to make him look serious, and succeed only in making him look sad. We try to make him tender, and succeed only in making him fragile. Occasionally, some radical young artist breaks with all the conventions, and draws him with an athlete's biceps, and the flush of youthful vigor and joy on his face — and yet that leaves so very, very many important things out of account.

Perhaps the best we can do is to draw a mental portrait of his principles at work in some environment with which we are personally acquainted. Perhaps "following Jesus" is the pursuit of a consistent program of dealing with our problems as we might expect him to deal with them, were he in our place.

It is difficult for us to do this for the reason I have cited. We have glorified him until he is out of reach. . . . It seems a sacrilege to wonder how he would handle some of the little difficulties that keep us irritated and jeopardize our peace. It seems so flippant and vulgar to wonder what Jesus would do if his neighbors ran their radio at full blast, late in the night, when he wanted to sleep. It seems like demoting him to try to imagine what he would do with a servant who habitually stole from him, and slighted his work.

And what would Jesus do, if he owned a house, and the tenants not only wouldn't pay the rent, but had gouged the plastering full of holes, and left the windows open so that the rain came in and damaged the ceilings, and chopped kindling wood on the kitchen floor, and let their goat chew the bark off the young maple trees. Would he put them out?

And what would Jesus do if he was working as a carpenter, and was told that he must use *pine* where the specifications had called for *oak* — or lose his job? Yes — I know — that would be easy enough, if Jesus were looking after himself alone; but suppose he was the only support of his mother, and a half dozen young brothers and sisters, and jobs were scarce: — what then? *Oak or pine?*

I presume one of the most effective ways for the Christian, today, to define his own convictions, is to make himself acquainted, in so far as he can, with the Man of Galilee, in the most practical and homely and workaday relationships of life.

We have allowed our estimate of Jesus to be too much cluttered with utterly impractical considerations. When we want to know how he was spiritually in league with God, we have been disposed to spend most of our time in speculations about his birth — and philosophical explanations of his divinity. Why not assume that he was divine — and pass on to the nature of his practical alliance with God. We have allowed ourselves to be diverted from the main issue.

When we have discussed the process by which people become

Christians, it has been so easy to date the hour of discipleship from one's *baptism*. And to be still further detoured from our course by debating how and when and by whom and in what phrases that baptism must be performed. When we have talked about the *salvation* that Jesus offers, we have been too often intrigued by the complicated theories relating to the atonement.

When we have discussed how we might appropriate unto ourselves and assimilate into ourselves the living spirit of Christ, through participation in the ancient rite of the Holy Communion — we have too often been distracted from the real purpose by theories named Transubstantiation and Consubstantiation, to say nothing of the arguments we have had about the mere technique of the ceremony.

Happily — the church is outgrowing this mood; and is questing the spirit of Jesus with something of the practical interest expressed by those who followed him in Galilean days.

We are eager to learn how he feels about the little difficulties of life at home, on the street, in business, and in social contacts. We would like to be of good conscience. We would like to feel that we are following him. We would like to sense the joy of his approval. If he lived, today, what attitude would he take toward social life? Would he hold himself aloof from it? Would he content himself without friends — except those on whom he meant to confer some favor?

As I look over the conventional pictures of him, and poems and songs about him, it is difficult to imagine him doing anything that goes to make up the sum total of our life.

He has been made too remote for practical association with our affairs — either at work or play. Jesus at a hockey game! — why the very idea! Jesus, out in front of his house, hilariously returning a snowball hurled by a passing neighbor! — how sacrilegious! Jesus on a tram, going to work in the morning, hanging on a strap: how dreadfully offensive! Jesus at a little dinner party: — what in the world would he talk about — and what would the other guests dare to say to him — and what would his hostess do to amuse him?

Two interested men in Galilee are following him. He turns and inquires, "What do you want of me? Why are you following?" And they reply, "We want to see where you live, and how you live, in your own house." It is a natural query. Jesus did not — and presumably does not resent it. "Come and see."

Are you living a "wishing" life? *What* do you wish. Do you think it might smooth the road for you if you took to wishing, very earnestly, that you could live like *him?*

St. James United Church
Montreal
November 20, 1932

We beseech Thee to make known to us more and more clearly each day the duties we are expected to perform if we are to fulfill our destiny. We plead for that serenity of spirit which trusts confidently that Thy will may and must and can be done on earth as it is done in heaven.

Beyond command

We are unprofitable servants: we have done our duty.
— Luke 17:10

IF THE GALILEAN GOSPEL ever sounds trite and commonplace, the fault rests not with its author, but its interpreters.

One of the popular fallacies about this gospel holds that it is so simple any little child can understand it.

This is an illusion that has done us no good; for, in the regard of thoughtful and aspiring people, no merit attaches to a subject by virtue of its simplicity.

In secular education, the chief lure to the serious interest of an inquiring mind is the promise that continued research will find the subject more rewarding in direct proportion to the difficulties encountered.

The period of counting with wooden blocks is quickly followed by the technique of counting with figures . . . figures move along from simple combinations to bewilderingly complicated problems: — and presently, mere signs are introduced to represent groups of figures — and facilitate their handling.

The *ABC's* promptly resolve themselves into names of common objects — usually taught by sequence: ice — sled — boots — mittens — ear — nose — toes — home — fire — bed. Within a week we are moving on to the *doing* words: awake — dress — eat — play — run — slide — shout — sing.

Then we proceed to something not quite so easy — because you cannot point to it — and say: "There it is!" We have arrived now at abstractions: sportsmanship — sympathy — discomfort — contentment — justice — mercy — anticipation — repentance — remorse — satisfaction.

And, after a while, if we happen to have fallen in love with our mother tongue, we go back to the languages whence it was derived, and, learning where our words came from, we understand them more fully and use them more discriminatingly.

We begin Geography at four by learning that the earth is approximately round, and approximately three-fourths covered with water. We are handed a little globe, which we endeavor to lick the paint off of — until we discover (like Adam) that this fruit is neither pleasant to the taste nor guaranteed to make one wise. We are informed that the *green is for water* — albeit such water as we noticed was not green — and the *white is for land* — though we had not seen any white land.

Surely we have a lot to learn in this topsy-turvy world — where blackberries are green when they are red — and white is the colors put together — and black is no color at all.

But they assure us, at four, that is all very simple. Nobody goes to the bother of explaining that this little globe in our small sticky hand is co-ordinated with a quite tremendous scheme of planets in space; that the whole galaxy is whirling in five different movements, so fast that our earth has not only been hurled forward in space at dizzying rush, on its solar revolution — and on its axis — but skidding sideways into realms it never visited before. . . . They do not hand us any of the planets. The planets are only "Twinkle, twinkle, little stars."

It will be a long time before anybody talks to us about latitude and longitude and logarithms; and the moon's mutations — and the periodicity of the tides — and light-years — and relativity.

But — eventually — they *do* tell us that story — unless our I.Q. turns out to be so small that no one cares to waste any valuable time on us.

As for the gospel — it usually gets a hearing only in its primer stage. Jesus is born in a stable. The idea intrigues our childish fancy. We promptly catalogue it alongside the Ugly Duckling that grew up to be a Swan — and poor little Cinderella, who left her pots and pans to be a princess. . . .

We early get it into our heads that Goodness is somehow the product of poverty, despite the fact that Napoleon was born on a doorstep in Corsica — and Rasputin was born in the front wing of a pigpen in Siberia.

We easily fall afoul of the delusion that valor and integrity are derivatives of bleak poverty, resignation; limp, listless, apathetic, underfed penury.

Presently we discover, from our contacts with society, that everything is correct about this conclusion except the *major premise* — and it's always very hard on a conclusion to have its major premise abandon it.

After a while, we decide, not by any definite mental resolution, but by a gradual process of erosion, that while the gospel makes a nice, safe anesthetic to numb the hurts and humiliations of underprivileged people, who aren't getting anywhere — and are on the books to live small, pinched, timid, insular lives — *it holds out no inducement*, no difficulties, no risks, and no rewards — for the abundantly fit.

Of course, this is a vast mistake, but the people who entertain this delusion came by it honestly. By custom, the church keeps on steadily appealing to the early adolescent mind. We hear over and over again (stated with brittle redundancy) that the gospel is very simple — as if that were any credit to it.

Did the teacher of Arithmetic brag that the science of numbers is very simple and, therefore, ought to appeal to a mind like yours?

Surely not much of a compliment for the teacher to say of Geography, "Now here is something that is about your speed:

any little child can master it, the first day. Looking over this class, it occurs to me that you would all enjoy it mightily."

Or — didn't it rather thrill you, and make you square your shoulders when the professor said, on that memorable afternoon in September, when you returned as a sophomore:

"Now, beloved, we are going to engage with Differential Calculus — and if you will believe me, it is no picnic. Whoever has elected this as a snap course, to pad out his program on Tuesdays and Thursdays at ten, has let himself in for something he would gladly exchange for leprosy inside of a week. Strong men have spent nights in agony over this affair, and a few have gone quite permanently mad. This is heroic diet — for which the soft-spined and the loafers and the dunces should never apply."

Too often the preacher says: "Friends, the glory of this gospel is that any little child can grasp it." Nothing is clearer about Jesus' gospel than that it moves quickly along from the elementary rudiments of Purposeful Living — to the treatment of combinations of circumstances, where motives are all jumbled, and you can't tell whether to serve Church or State or either of them; and where obligations tug in a dozen different directions — and you can't decide whether to stay at home and look after the old folks until they die, or cut loose and live your life; and where you think you ought to dicker for a living wage — and then find out that the people who had come to work at 5 P.M. were paid as much as *you,* who had arrived at 9 A.M.; and it is wrong to go to war, but, if you go to war, you would better arbitrate than pit your 10,000 soldiers against 20,000; and it is better to give up your coat, plus your cloak, than have a lawsuit; and better to have your eyes plucked out than look at things that demolish your ideals.

Anything simple about a gospel like that? . . . I like to hear the gospel referred to — about once a year, on Christmas, as the "sweetest story ever told." But it has been called that too often. That phrase somehow keeps it in the nursery — along side the hobbyhorse and the dolls. . . .

In its initial phases, it is, indeed, the sweetest story ever told — and deserves to be told as such. But and if you get a chance to see it when it has arrived at the parable of the unjust steward — or the unjust judge — or the episode of the rich young nobleman — or the fable about the sower — or this private talk with the disciples recorded in the seventeenth chapter of Luke — you change your mind about the gospel as the sweetest story ever told — and decide that it is the *severest* challenge ever hurled at mankind.

Of course, I shall be misunderstood by some. . . . But the number who misunderstand what *I* am saying about the *severity* — as against the *simplicity* — of the gospel, will be very small, compared with the number who misunderstood the *author* of the gospel when he said substantially the same thing — only more clearly — and more strongly.

Let us forget, now — for a moment, at least — all this fatuous talk about *a simple gospel*. True, Jesus said: "Take my yoke upon you, for it is *easy*." But he did not say: "Accept my theory of life, for it is simple."

Jesus said: "Except ye become as little children" — but that was when rebuking the Pharisees for the fine-spun sophistications of their theology.

That there were degrees in a spiritual progress — according to Jesus' own belief — is almost constantly in evidence. "Unto you," said he to his disciples, "it is given to understand the hidden mysteries — as it is not given unto them" — meaning the general public.

The trouble — let me repeat, the trouble with our interpretation of the gospel — has been our indolent willingness to rehearse, again and again, the *ABC's* of it. The doctrine of Nonresistance has been viewed more as a supine acceptance of the world's bites and kicks and stings than as a positive, dynamic program demanding more energy than the energy of the fighter.

Conquering the world by faith has been taught as an easy and simple thing to do. . . . But it has been neither easy nor simple for people *who have done it!*

In the episode before us today, Jesus has taken his disciples into a private conference.

It is obvious from the nature of their talk that some one of them has said — with a sigh — "Oh, well, speaking of social injustices — when weren't the poor in hard luck? When weren't the people with property inclined to lean on it — and hoard it — and boast of it? When weren't rulers dragging their people into wars? It's the same old story: as Solomon said, 'There's nothing new under the sun — and all is vanity.' "

But Jesus was not in a mood to accept the world's defects exactly as they stood, and take them for granted. He replied — to whatever variant of that sentiment had just been expressed: "It is necessary that offences come; but woe unto him, through whom they come!"

And so they got to talking about offenses against society.

Let us keep it in mind that these men were of very limited social experience. . . . They couldn't talk much about what Rome was doing in the destruction of culture, by smashing the art treasures of Greece — for all that was outside their mental horizon.

They did not talk about the political smash-up down in Egypt where Augustus was making himself conspicuous. There was a great deal going on in their world that they knew nothing about — at all.

Such offenses as they were best familiar with had been the injuries done to themselves and their neighbors. They recited some of them.

"What would you do?" they inquired — "in such a case as this, to-wit . . . "

At that point Jesus gives them a formula for dealing with the offender. If a man injures you, rebuke him. If he repents, forgive him. If he repeats the offense, rebuke him. If he repents again, forgive him. An offence is always entitled to a rebuke; and repentance is always entitled to forgiveness.

"And how long are you to keep this up?" somebody inquired.

"*Indefinitely.*"

"Seven times?"

"Yes — seven times *a day!*"

And they said: "Lord — increase our faith."

I think they all smiled — at that juncture — including the Master, himself. It was, as we might say, a pretty tall order.

So — they got to talking about faith.

Note, please, this was no stiff and stagy conference around a directors' table. This was an informal chat, under the trees. One topic leads on to another.

They begin by talking of social injustices, and are diverted by somebody's report of a bad thing that had been done to *him*, as an individual. . . . And that leads to the question of how often shall I pardon people who wrong me? . . . And someone says, "Lord — increase our faith" — and now they are talking about *faith*.

Jesus said: "If ye had faith as a grain of mustard seed, ye might say unto this sycamine tree, 'Be plucked up —root and all — and cast into the sea,' and it would obey."

The simple and most common interpretation of this cryptic language is: If ye had faith the size of a little mustard seed. In the same mood with which we might say, "If you had faith the size of a pinpoint — the size of a needle's eye — the size of a gnat — you could do wonders with it."

Looking a bit farther into this, we find that Jesus did not mean *that,* at all. He was not referring to the diminutive size of the mustard seed, but to the nature of it in its possibilities for expansion.

"If ye had the faith of the mustard seed — which (as he had explained on another occasion) albeit is the smallest of all the seeds, grows to a tree so large that the birds of the air nest in its branches — ye might say to this sycamine tree — "

We will never know why he happened to single out that particular sycamine tree, but there must have been a good reason. Someone in the party had been irritated at this sycamine tree. Perhaps Peter had bit into one of its fruits and found it green and astringent. . . . The sycamine bore a figlike fruit, of doubtful edibility, except when carefully tended. . . . *Indeed — unless* the fruit was pierced on the tip, early in its development, it rarely came to anything at all.

Somebody had tasted one of these fruits and found it bad — nasty — and had spat it out; and the others had been amused; and Jesus had remembered. . . .

If ye had the mustard seed's faith, ye could expand it until it would enable you to conquer all your difficulties. Even if this *sycamine* tree had offended you, you could wipe it out of your consciousness; *obliterate it* as a disturbing factor; you could order it into the sea.

And it would obey you!

So — they got to talking about obedience.

Of course, it is beyond all reasonable expectation of ours that the entire conversation should have been recorded. . . . One suspects that the perennial question came up about one's obedience to the government.

It makes quite a difference — in one's attitude toward government — whether one has a *chance* to say something about it — at the polls. It makes quite a difference whether one is governed by laws *made for and by one's own people* — or a haughty class of aliens a thousand miles away.

The Romans made the laws for the Jews — and enforced them

under Roman banners. Should one obey such laws?

Precisely. That was a good way to keep out of trouble. Obey the laws! Render unto Caesar the things that are Caesar's.

And then there were the ancient Mosaic statutes — the *deca- logue*. But they were sound and satisfactory. Nobody ever got into any difficulty obeying *them*.

I think this discussion was carried on mostly among the disciples — and that Jesus was silent.

But when they were through talking about the various kinds of law to which they were obligated, he said:

"If you had a servant, would you consider yourself in his debt for cooking your dinner? Not at all. He had done what was required of him.

"So, likewise ye — when ye shall have done the things demanded of you — say, 'We are unprofitable servants. . . . We have but done our duty.'"

Now this is the real spirit of the gospel message in its dealing with the issues which make for life's success and satisfaction. To do less than one's duty means to live wretchedly and in constant difficulty with the laws, the customs, and the general sentiments of society.

To *have done* one's duty means to live without actually *colliding* with the regulations which keep society within bounds, for its own safety. To have done one's duty, means to have had all the hard work and no profit and no pleasure.

But to live *beyond* the laws — beyond duty — beyond command — is to live supremely. . . .

You begin to live an abundant life at the exact moment when you pass from the duty stage to this freer atmosphere of voluntary investment. The difference between living in shackles or at liberty is mostly a matter of mental attitude toward one's responsibilities.

It is the margin of effort that brings success and satisfaction.

That is good gospel. If you are commanded to walk a mile —
walk two miles, and you are proceeding beyond command.

Don't meet life grudgingly, but give it good measure — and
see what it does for you. If you wish to advance into the insured
joy of Christian living, escape from the commandments. Live
beyond them!

Unfortunately, there has been a great deal of duty done by
professing Christians. They have had much to say about their
duty, and what they have said about it has made it sound irksome
and unprofitable.

There was, first, the duty they felt to believe certain doctrines.
Sometimes the doctrines seemed flat against nature and sense —
but they believed them because it was *their duty*. Sometimes the
doctrines were inconsequential — and meant nothing — one way
or the other, so far as their own personal lives were concerned
— but they believed them — or said they did — because it was
their duty.

Then there was the whole range of philanthropy — *support-
ing missions* in faraway lands, not because one cared a farthing,
personally, for the people who seemed to be benefited, but because it was one's *duty*.

There were the charities to be supported at home — shiftless
folk who never had made a go of life and never would; but had
to eat, nevertheless, and mustn't be left to starve — *so one might
as well toss something* in the basket for them, because it was
one's *duty*.

There were all the various things to be supported about the
church, not that one had any particular pleasure in such business, but it was commanded — or at least entreated — and —
well — one must do one's *duty*.

I do not think that Jesus liked that word "duty." It was a
sour word; it was a smug word; it was apt to be a nastily *self-
righteous* word. People who had frequent recourse to it — to

define their motives and their actions — were not congenial to him.

So — he said — when you have done everything that the state and the church and society at large *command* you to do — say: "We are unsuccessful. *We have done our duty!*"

Wouldn't that be an eye-opener to a lot of gloomy Christians, if they ever happened to run on to it here in this seventeenth chapter of Luke, and stopped thinking about their sacrifices and their toil long enough to read it with some real consideration for its meaning?

Yes, they say, we have obeyed all the law from our youth up; never did this, that, or the other which many people do, in defiance of law. We have kept all the commandments enjoined by religion; have avoided the appearance of evil, and kept away from it as much as possible.

We have believed everything that our religious cultus told us it was our duty to believe, in order to qualify as Christians of a certain name and order. We have heeded the calls of the church, and they have been many and costly. We believe in doing our duty — and we have done it.

And Jesus replies: "Now you should add to that statement, 'We have been unsuccessful!'"

For the joy of Christian living begins at the exact point where duty has been overtaken and *passed.*

Out there where service has become a delight, and investment a source of exaltation.

Our church where there are no Ten Commandments, any more — no civil statutes — no demands.

Out there beyond the law — where the margin of Christian faith and effort work their wonders in the soul.

Now — there is nothing *simple* or childish or elementary about that feature of the gospel; and only a comparative few ever arrive at it.

Most Christians go trudging along — more or less consistently doing their duty.

You can generally spot the minority who have escaped from the mere realm of duty — and are living *beyond command*. It is in their voices, and on their faces.

In seasons of stress, they furnish the ballast and the steam to see society through the storm.

They live the *abundant life!*

They are not driven into it by law — but lured into it by Love.

Queen's College
Kingston, Ontario
November 16, 1930

We do not ask to see, or to know, but only for the grace to follow in faith believing.

what the LORD thought
of the PRUDENT

Is ANYTHING new to be said about Jesus of Nazareth? The world has had the written record of his life for nearly twenty centuries. Nothing authentic has been learned of the details of his career since the four gospels were compiled. Yet the literature concerning him grows more rich and voluminous.

It is so with all significant energies. The use of electrical power is comparatively recent; yet our word "electricity" is twenty-three hundred years old. It is derived directly from a Greek word meaning amber.

All the Greeks knew about electricity was the queer phenomenon they observed when a chunk of amber was magnetized by friction. Ergo: electricity was a property of amber. You couldn't have electricity without amber. Electricity was amber.

That was the extent of their wisdom on this subject, and it was not enough to do them any practical service.

What a vast amount of reappraising of the nature of this strange power was necessary before electricity became of active service in daily life. For literally ages of time, there was no progress whatsoever in this field. And then, when it finally achieved a feeble momentum, it seemed that each new generation had this power to evaluate, again, the same electricity all the time, but put to new employment, as the demands increased.

Something of this same progression of knowledge and practical development is to be observed in the world's understanding of Jesus. Every generation reappraises him, and finds new uses for the spiritual energy he possesses.

Nor have we by any means reached the end of discovery in the nature of Jesus. For ages he was understood by Christians as the Lamb of God. He was called the Lamb of God in conformity to the belief that his sole errand in the world was to serve as a sacrificial offering on the altar, to satisfy his Father God.

His whole mission was comprehended by that act of dying, sacrificially, like the lamb in the temple shambles.

Jesus, the Lamb, was, to that ancient Jewish Christian thought, somewhat like the electricity in the amber that was understood by the Greeks. Jesus' power was in the lamb, as electricity's power was in the amber.

You could be awed by it; and wonder about it; and compose poetry extolling it; but there was a latent power there, unrealized.

The Lamb and the Amber were possessed of two important secrets. It was sufficient to let them remain so. Mysteries? So be it.

But mankind is increasingly inquisitive about its latent forces. More and more it inclines toward the practical utilization and adaptation of all the forces it can lay hold upon. Today, we proceed to the practical employment of electricity in a spirit of businesslike investigation.

As to the underlying essence of it, we know but little more than the Greeks who said it was a property of amber. It has not even occurred to us as important to our use of electricity that we should give it a new name. It still stands, on the books, as electricity, and electricity means amber.

But we have entirely left off treating it as a vague mystery, defiant of our investigations, and too deep for our intellectual plumb lines.

Something tells me that we are nearing a day of remarkable

and radical reinterpretation of the power resident in Jesus of
Nazareth.

As to the essential nature of his being, we may be content to
let that matter remain as great a mystery as the essential nature
of electricity. We can properly count that question out of our
calculations; and do no more speculating about it.

As to the theological terms in which he may be discussed, let
him still be referred to as the Lamb of God, in the same manner
in which electricity is still amber, in the dictionary.

But, more and more, we are going to be evaluating the actual
ability of the Christ Power to solve the common problems of
daily life.

I say, we are now coming into a period when such experi-
mentation is likely to go forward, with fresh impetus. The modern world has become accustomed to reliance upon forces which
it does not pretend to understand. It does not ask to see these
energies but is content to witness their effects. It will be more
and more painstakingly analytical in its estimate of the spiritual
power of God as interpreted and perfectly understood by the
Man of Galilee.

I point you, today, very briefly, to just one feature of Jesus'
life which, I presume, will be the first point of contact we make
with him when we endeavor, practically, to use his power in
our own pursuits.

*It is his splendid audacity in assuming that he has a right to
live beyond the reach of fear.*

That is the high spot of human achievement. To be *free of
fear*.

I do not now refer to *specific* fears, but *essential* fear.

Some people are afraid of deep water, who are not afraid of
thunderstorms. Some people are afraid of the photographer who
are not afraid of the dentist. Some people are afraid of getting
old, who are not afraid of dying. Some people are afraid of

being poor who are not afraid of being dishonest.

One man is afraid of this, and another is afraid of that; and A cannot understand why B should be afraid of *this*, while B cannot understand why A should be afraid of *that*.

But nobody is ever going to do much in dealing with his fears until he has handled the general problem of fear.

Jesus lived at complete liberty. The poise of his life, his absolute command of himself, his capacity to confront every exigency of his career with calm, wise, unworried, unhasting discrimination, was due to his entire independence of fear.

Not meaning, either, that he had arrived at some static position where he was forever unassailable by the various threats which life holds over every man. The general upkeep of his mood of fearlessness made certain demands. He was required to keep himself constantly in the confidence of his own source of spiritual supply. Once he was asked by a Samaritan woman where, in his opinion, was the best place to seek God. Some said, she remarked, that God was to be sought in the holy mountain; others, the Jews, said that God was to be found in the temple at Jerusalem. Jesus told her that the time would come when men would not attempt to give God a localized address.

Jesus was not distrustful of the temple, as a fine memorial to man's reverence. He saw the point of that and commended it. He, himself, visited the temple frequently, and found it worth while. But he had to have a closer contact with God than that, to keep himself empowered with spiritual forces. He couldn't be in the temple all the time; and yet he knew he had to be conscious of God all the time. So, he conceived the practice of *living in the presence of God.*

While aware of that contact, he was beyond the reach of fear — not fears considered item by item; but *fear*. And to the maintenance of that mood, it was imperative that he keep himself free of fear-concepts. If you will go through the recorded gospels with a blue pencil and underscore all the admonitions he offered on the subject of eliminating fear from human thought, you may be amazed to discover how considerable an area of his teaching was comprehended by this counsel.

And not only was he constantly urging other people to be fearless, but he was careful to avoid the contamination of their fears. He was indignant when they came howling in a panic to hurl their cowardice at him. In the storm on the Sea of Galilee, he sleeps. So confident of his own independence of physical forces was he that it was no longer necessary for him to brace himself against fear. He slept through the storm. His disciples shake him awake. What was the matter with him, anyway? Here they were, frightened to death, and he was able to sleep. Apparently they want him to be frightened, too. It is not enough that they be scared. He must wake up and see how serious is this menace that has stampeded them.

"Oh ye of little faith!" How often that phrase was on his lips. "Why are ye fearful . . . oh ye of little faith?"

A few days before he met his tragedy, Jesus, with his disciples, spent some time on the seacoast, near Tyre. It was a brief vacation from the wearing drain of dealing, daily, with great crowds of needy people. One day, without warning, Jesus announced that he was about to start back, now, for Jerusalem. He would attend the Passover Feast. Aware of the enmities which, in Jerusalem, were being brought to a sharp focus, and would unquestionably strike at his Master on the occasion of a day of enthusiasm for the old orthodoxy, Simon Peter begged Jesus not to go. It was by no means safe. He didn't really have to go. Let him stay where he was out of the reach of his enemies. "This must not be," said Peter. Jesus pushed him aside — and not very gently, either. Peter was getting in his way — Peter with his cowardice; with his program of safety first. Jesus did not consider that an act of friendship at all. His idea of a helpful friend was someone who stimulated you to free yourself of your fears; not someone who called your attention to them.

Constantly, he was endeavoring to encourage other people in their faith and fearlessness. Really, the only thing he seemed to be impatient of was caution; timidity; prudence. One man said to him in Galilee, "I would like to come along with you. You have something I want; and I think I could get it for myself if I associated with you. But, you see, I am rather unfortunately situated just now. My father is an old man. He has lived his whole life under the old orthodoxy. Its conventional routine is sufficient for him, and he wants it to be sufficient for me. He will die, one of these days, and then I will come and follow you. Let me bury him first." Jesus said: "Let the *dead* bury the dead."

Jesus was for burning the bridges after him to insure against retreat. "Whosoever putteth his hand to the plough and turneth back, is not worthy of me." His really delightful experiences were had when people made brave adventures with their faith. He liked their reckless disregard of old traditions and conventions on that occasion when the friends of a sick man, unable to get into the house where Jesus stood, crowded about with the multitude, tore off the roof, and let the bed down into the room by ropes. That was a great day for Jesus. He must have felt that his new gospel was really doing business, that afternoon. He liked to see people taking risks for their principles.

One day he sat in the temple hard by the big golden urn where the people dropped their contributions for the support of the institution. Most people made quite an elaborate ceremony of offering their money and were anxious to have the public take note. And that all this might be attended to conveniently, there was a sort of low mezzanine box over against the treasury, where people could sit and watch the donors. It was a good place to study character; and Jesus was there, that day, watching.

All sorts filed by — the rich pouring in gold, and the not-so-rich pouring in silver, and the poor dropping in their coppers. I suppose the rich sometimes dropped in coppers, too: humanity being pretty much the same, the world over.

Along came, presently, a poor widow. She put in two mites. Two mites made one farthing. It was approximately nothing. Beside a Jewish farthing, a French *centime*, which is the tenth part of a franc, which is worth four cents, is a lot of money. But it was all the widow had; and when one gives up all, it doesn't have to be much to be everything.

Jesus noticed the gift, and turning to a companion, said: "The widow has given much more than any of the rich. They gave some of their abundance: out of her poverty, she gave all."

If somebody had been writing the story who did not know Jesus very well, doubtless we would have had a nice little sequel to this episode. Jesus would have called her back. He would have recovered from the box her poor little coins, and handed them back to her, magically transformed into gold, and commanded her to go, and live happily on them, for the rest of her days. But Jesus did not call her back. He did nothing to relieve her poverty. He knew she had her full reward.

Never did he try to get between people and their sacrifices. Never did he caution them against doing too much or against working too hard, or investing in life too deeply. He liked to see them taking up their crosses. He liked to see them making adventures; and battering down their fears. And if we would be like him, and become to others, in friendship and assistance what he was to his acquaintances, it is important that we do not try to talk other people out of their adventures.

For many of us, we have a notion that it is a mark of friendship and loyalty to be forever cautioning one another against risk. We think we are doing them a favor by attempting to step in between them and sacrificial deeds.

Somebody is devoting himself, tirelessly, to a mission that

keeps his nose to the grindstone, and prohibits his enjoyment of what we think is pleasure — and we consider it a friendly act to counsel him to give it up and live his own life and have a good time.

How large a part of our attempted friendliness is taken up with efforts to keep people from doing really brave and adventurous deeds. We counsel them to prudence. We urge their taking it easy. We are afraid they may work too hard. We riddle their morale by contaminating them with our own fears, our doubts, our timidities.

Ah, but the time will come when we shall have more adequately understood Jesus, as a great spiritual dynamic, that the supreme act of Christian friendship will be expressed by the ardent zeal with which we commend other people's sacrificial labor, and the enthusiasm with which we counsel them to hurl themselves into bold and brave adventures.

What a poor and drab thing life is, for many people, pursuing petty rounds of safe routine — a little work, a little play; a little wishing and day-dreaming; dodging the calls to important service; fearing to step aside from the well-worn sheep trail to investigate some burning brush; ambling along through their days, clutching at one another's sleeves and shouting: "Look out! Be careful!"

Tear loose from your fears. Keep yourself clear of people who counsel you to seek ease; who pity you; who see no reason why you should make investments of yourself in pursuit of duty.

Stern Daughter of the Voice of God!
O Duty! if that name thou love,
Who art a light to guide, a rod
To check the erring and reprove;
Thou, who art victory and law
When empty terrors overawe;

To humbler functions, awful Power!
I call thee: I myself commend
Unto thy guidance, from this hour;
O, let my weakness have an end!
Give unto me, made lowly wise,
The spirit of self-sacrifice;
The confidence of reason give;
And in the light of truth thy bondman let me live!

First Congregational Church
Los Angeles
July 8, 1928

If we have lived poorly, if we have lived grudg-ingly — lift us up into the larger liberty of Jesus Christ our Lord, in whose name we pray for this emancipating grace.

living in expectancy

WHEN MYLES COVERDALE made his English translation of the Bible in 1535, he said in the preface, "I am convinced that there cometh more knowledge and understanding of the Scriptures through their various translations than by all the doctrines of our sophistical theologians."

In recent times, our estimate of the Scriptures has been improved, and our interest stimulated, by the large number of new versions which clarify many passages otherwise destined to become obscure — if not indeed quite meaningless — as times and customs change, and words shift their values.

To such men as Doctors Weymouth, Goodspeed, and Moffatt, who have lately made fresh translations, we are in debt for many a new conception of the ancient lore of our Bible.

Sometimes a single radiant phrase will serve to light up a whole paragraph that had seemed either too cryptic to be practical, or too cloudy to be viewed with interest.

I call your attention, this morning, to a specimen. Professor Goodspeed, translating the second chapter of Luke, which, you will remember, deals with the tender and beautiful legend of the Nativity, gives something new to think about in his reference to the mental attitude of the people at the time of Jesus' coming. He says, translating the thirty-eighth verse of the second chapter of Luke: "They were living in expectancy of liberation."

I invite you to concentrate on that phrase for a little while — *living in expectancy.*

I do not ask you to keep the phrase locked in its New Testament significance, where it refers to an enslaved race, which, for hundreds of years, had chanted of a departed glory, and yearned for a great liberation. It is more to the purpose that we should discover how much our own lives might be enriched by a practice of expectancy.

For many, many people, the significance of life, instead of growing brighter and richer, as their years go by, seems rather to narrow into dull routines and a dumb acceptance of things as they are. For them, the zest of life is gone. There was a time, in their adolescence, when they did some valiant daydreaming. Here they were, in a big, wonderful world, having just one try at it — one life to live, one course to pursue. For a while, the world was something to be explored — adventured with, savored, enjoyed. And then, little by little, disillusion came. The dreams faded. The vocation settled to an economic necessity; so much work, for so much pay, to square for the cost of existing. So many hours, at so much wages per hour. That was their stake in the work of the world, and the manner of their actual contribution to the world. Gradually the huge orbits of their dreams tightened into restricted little circles, around which they padded along, with heels scraping, like animals in a treadmill; like caged squirrels on a wheel, making excellent mileage but going nowhere.

Now, religion, if it be good for anything in the life of the individual, ought to lift a man out of these deep grooves, and teach him to live *expectantly*. For the man who entertains the hope of a larger life in some future home of the soul, religion should minister with the expectant mood that is on the alert to find more rewarding experiences here.

Religion, especially if it should be so beautiful an idealism as our Christian religion, founded by one who had the mind of a pioneer and adventurer — calm and fearless — should aid a man in conserving the radiant hope and zest of his dreaming youth.

If ever a man is to be immortal, that immortality can only be established on the fact that he is immortal *now*.

Surely there would be no logic in a belief that this present life we live here gradually wears itself out and fades until there is nothing to it of any interest whatsoever, and then Death, and, later, somewhere, somehow, another life, of another kind, with other hopes, dreams, and aspirations. To believe in a future life, on that basis, is a mere speculation with no experience or information to warrant it.

But, to believe that our own life here continues to grow richer and fuller, every day bringing its fresh interests, its new discoveries, its new appreciations, its new evaluations — at length briefly punctuated by one's passing through an eventful turnstile known as Death, into even fairer landscapes and greater possessions, and keener enjoyments — to believe that is to illumine life for ourselves, and all who in any way derive their thoughts about life from us.

I promise it could be shown that the hindrances to our living in such expectation are really quite simple when analyzed.

Some people do not live in expectancy because they are asleep. Long ago, they decided — maybe not by a definite mental act of decision, but by gradually accustoming themselves to the idea — that they had got out of life about all there was in it of any interest. They had learned all there was to know about their job, and decided to continue doing it, for the rest of their working years, according to knowledge and experience already in hand. As for getting about — they had seen everything they cared to see. As for new ideas, of other people, one felt more at home with the ideas one had already collected.

Asleep and satisfied! To eat three meals per day, and spend eight hours in bed, and read the papers in the evening, and start to work in the morning — a little round of humdrum duties. No longer alert; no longer on tiptoe; no longer expectant! But, like jaded old Solomon, saying: "There is nothing new under the sun. The thing that hath been is the thing that shall be."

Some people do not live expectantly because they have prac‑
ticed caution and conservatism and timidity until the thought
of anything new happening to them is disconcerting. There
might be a chance of something happening that would be hazar‑
dous; or make them temporarily uncomfortable; or break into a
rigid network of habits. And, because they do not care to take
that risk, they do not lift their eyes to scan the horizon for new
experiences or new phenomena.

In *Alice in Wonderland*, the White Knight, who was the last
word in prudence and caution, is said to have loaded himself so
heavily with insurance against dangers and discomforts that he
could proceed only at a snail's pace. He even took along a
mousetrap, in case he should be troubled somewhere with mice;
and a beehive, in case he should come across a swarm of bees.

They cannot live expectantly, these people, because of their
dread of encountering something different — something new.
Their old *thoughts* — oh, but how they do hang on to them, and
fight for them, and raise loud outcries should anyone suggest
another idea.

I think it could be proved, by psychological experiment, that
a considerable volume of conservative opinion on antique social
justice, political necessity, economic ways and means, and re‑
ligious creedalism is ardently maintained, declaimed for, and not
infrequently defended with a zeal worthy of a sprightlier cause,
by persons who conscientiously feel that they ought to *think
something;* and *stand for* something; but have lost the capacity
for absorption or adaptation! They have used their mental brakes
so constantly that they have worn them out; and dare not now
risk any intellectual bursts of speed but must travel at a snail's
gallop.

The way they have always done things: that is the way to do
things. The things they have always thought: those are the
things to think. People cannot live expectantly who snuggle

down into that manner of smug prudence.

Jesus described our spiritual estate as a *kingdom*. No matter how a man might think of his aspirations, what he was really striving for was a kingdom of his own. Jesus said there was a kingdom of the spirit, into which, if a man entered, he would be at peace; not *apathy*, but a power-filled *peace*.

Not every man discovered or appropriated this kingdom in the same way. One man stumbled upon it accidentally, like a traveler suddenly coming upon a chest of treasure hidden in a field. Another man saw how this kingdom served the life of a resourceful friend, and deliberately negotiated for it, as a man might sell all his jewels to buy one extraordinary pearl.

Some people kept themselves out of their kingdom because, like the foolish virgins debarred from the wedding feast, they had failed to carry along with them a margin of patience and poise to cope with life's emergencies.

Some people kept themselves out of their kingdom, and out of the joy of their Lord's bequest, because, like the one-talent man, they were too cautious to risk anything they owned, and buried their capital where it had no use.

Some people kept themselves out of their kingdom because they had allowed the greedy little merchandisings of life to absorb all their attention. Invited to the great feast of adventure in the larger endeavors of existence, they were obliged to send regrets. Too busy to come: had bought a yoke of oxen, and must spend that day seeing if they could pull; had bought a farm, and must go see if it was a good bargain.

Some people kept themselves out of the kingdom because they were too shy to ask for what they wanted. Instead of bombarding life, like the importunate widow who demanded a favorable decision of the indifferent judge, they gave it up, without half trying.

Some people kept themselves out of the kingdom for sheer cantankerousness. Invited to the great feast of opportunity, they balked, in the lobby of the banquet hall, against putting on dinner clothes. No, sir; if they weren't good enough to come in, ragged and uncombed and muddy of shoe, they wouldn't come in at all: so they stayed out, or, if they crashed in, were thrown out.

But, after calling the roll, interminably, of the things that keep men and women from getting into and enjoying the kingdom, Jesus settles down to a larger reason than any of the others for failure to realize the kingdom. This was the *tense* of the kingdom.

Some people, he said, had the kingdom located somewhere else than here — somewhere else than now. Either it was away out yonder, nebulously appearing, now and again, like a mirage, enough to make people shout, "Lo: here comes the kingdom." Or it was something that had once been active, like David's glorious administration, and was now gone, so that the people said: "Lo: there goes the kingdom."

Some people have always been dating their happiness and satisfaction as something that would come to pass at some future date.

Today, thousands of persons talk of almost nothing else, in religious connection, but the second coming of Christ. "He is to appear, one of these days, and vindicate my ideas," they think. "Anybody who doesn't agree with me, is going to be dealt with. I have my little set of habits and my little code of morals and my little handful of ideas. Christ is coming! And whoever doesn't have my habits, and my morals, and my ideas, is going to be pushed off the deep end into a steaming lake of brimstone." A very nice comment on the character of Christ — the Son of God — to believe that he would become a party to so inexcusable a transaction.

And today, even more thousands of people talk of almost nothing else, in religious connection, than the excellency of the good old days, when the churches were really pious, and family wor-

of life, the minor annoyances and losses and disappoint-
ts cannot have their way with us.

here isn't so very much difference, after all, between the
ht of stumbling blocks and steppingstones. Whether they
to serve as something to climb up over or fall down over,
nds upon our own mood as we approach them.

we've done it all; seen it all; thought all the thoughts we
propose to have; garnered all the experience we need, then,
ping is pretty serious business. And losses, when one has got
the point of developing any more capital, are very costly
ed.

ut, if the evidence is not yet all in; if the work is not yet all
e; if life is still full of eagerness, and the lure of adventure
the hope of discovery, the little hindrances and vexations do
matter much.

> *My life is crowned by three consummate things;*
> *Love that may worship, blind though unafraid,*
> *Some votive Being that the mind hath made;*
> *The spread and beat of bold Creation's wings*
> *When, poised above the blast, the Spirit sings;*
> *The moment when the storms of matter fade,*
> *And, clear as cloud-washed heavens, are displayed*
> *Replies to our bewildered questionings.*
> *No Magi brought these treasures from afar;*
> *They were engendered by that Inner Lord,*
> *The Expectant Soul, the veritable Me,*
> *Who, when the prison gateway swung ajar,*
> *Pressed, like the pallid woman in the horde,*
> *To touch the hem of White Reality.*

st Congregational Church
Angeles
tember 9, 1928

ship was the vogue in respectable homes, and children were in
the family pew on Sundays; and look at us now, will you. Lo:
there goes the kingdom!

Jesus said: "The Kingdom of God is within you." Now!
Here! Within you!

But once we have accepted this kingdom as our legacy, and
are living in it, we may confidently expect more and more happiness to be derived from our citizenship. It is a great thing to
be conscious of the essential bond that links our life with the
life of the eternal. To desire to do His will for us, not in any
egotistical little hope that our praise of Him will make Him
happy through flattery; but to do His will because it is the best
thing for ourselves.

Not to worship Him because we have a notion it does Him
some good, but because it opens our own lives to increasingly
closer contacts with the source of our power. Once we have
made such connections, we may live expectantly. Every day
brings its fresh exultations, its new tidings of joy.

Sometimes it seems to me that our own American brand of
religion, instead of being presented as a strength, guide, and
comfort, is mostly a source of intellectual anxiety and angry
argument.

General Feng, for many years known and extolled by missionary forces as one of Christianity's most outstanding and out-
spoken advocates, now publicly announces that in his opinion
all religions are equally authorized and equally adequate if sincerely believed and practiced.

This is, of course, in defiance of the fact that only Christianity
is identifiable with intellectual progress and philanthropy.

And what led General Feng to his conclusion? He accounts
for it on the ground that Christians are overmuch concerned
with the subtleties of metaphysics — to the extent of being disturbed over matters which not only cannot be settled, but have
no practical outcome in faith and conduct if they were settled.

To have done our best to arrive at truth, and then to torment oneself and others about the result, is to bring down the Holy Ghost, not in the form of a dove, but a vulture!

Ninety-nine times out of a hundred, the religious disputes which keep the church in a ferment of discord and uneasiness relate not to what one should do, but to what one should think. How much misery might have been spared Western civilization if Christians had been contented with the Sermon on the Mount.

We shall want to be giving our attention, soon, to an attempted recovery of the waning radiance of that spiritual culture which found its brightest and clearest effulgence in the tranquil certitude of Christ.

To live expectantly!

How full life has become, recently, with the things that minister to the spirit, if we really care to single them out and possess them. How rapidly the old hardships and discomforts, which sapped our fathers' and mothers' strength, making them old and bowed with their drudgeries, how rapidly these carking cares have been disappearing.

And now, at one's elbow, interesting tidings of the big, outer world — how other people live; what their national and racial ambitions are. It is only a little while since we knew almost nothing about any manner of life but our own neighborhood. An immigrant was just a man from the Old Country. As a lad, I recall that that was about as far as local information went concerning the hemisphere where our own ancestral background was located. It was the Old Country!

Now the world has suddenly become aware of itself, and the mutual interests of its component nations. New bonds are being created daily that unify and synchronize the aims and moods of all men.

How interesting if we, in these strategic times, can live expectantly, mentally on tiptoe, aware of the high importance of being present in the world, and an integral part of the world, at

a moment when it is discovering itself, and, a discovery will be staking off new claims to th of life! In that mood of expectancy, most of t pass into complete eclipse.

Thomas Hearne, in his journey to the mout mine River, wrote that a few days after they ha expedition, a party of Indians stole most of th comment on the apparent misfortune was: "T baggage being so much lightened, our next d more swift and pleasant."

Hearne was en route to something very int portant; and the loss of a few sides of bacon and of flour meant nothing more than an easing o Hearne been holed in somewhere, in a cabin, r his last days eking out an existence, and living viously collected, the loss of some of his stores b probably have worried him almost to death.

Most of the troubles of life loom up large b motive that propels us isn't big enough or strong its momentum when it encounters a bit of cros people are enisled with what they have gathere and things, and when any inroad is made on t of thoughts and things, they are instantly impc have scrapped all their machinery for creating n things; and are aware that any loss occurring thoughts and things is irreparable. Their old h mildew and ferment and, owing to seasonal cha tional and intellectual climate of their world, t of ideas becomes unusable; but they can't c ideas, for they have ceased to live expectantly. A are subject to moth, rust, and theft, and if los placed.

But, living expectantly, eager for new con alert to new tidings of life, awake to new hopes,

the challenge of immortality

THE HALLOWED FESTIVAL we are celebrating today defines the farthest outpost of adventure and audacity ever achieved by the human spirit. Whoever finds his pulses stirred by the glamour of the Easter hope, and his courage fired by the promise of Easter faith, is testifying to the potential greatness and goodness and gallantry of The Soul of Man.

In the fact of an inexorable dissolution at war with every flower and bird and beast and tree; and in the face of that stark inevitability which has swept each successive generation of men into the mystery of the great silence — this radiant idealism that is Easter has the breath-taking impudence to shout: "Nevertheless — I live! O Death — where is thy sting? Where, O Grave, thy victory! — For though I stoop into a dark, stupendous sea of cloud, it is but for a time . . . I press God's lamp close to my breast. . . . Its splendors, soon or late, will pierce the gloom. I shall emerge one day!"

Let whosoever will speak dismally of his own disabilities, his misdeeds, and his doubts — or, if of a smaller caliber, let him speak dolefully of the imperfections and unfaiths of his neighbors — Easter clamors for one's optimism.

Sometimes I may have brief periods of being ashamed of the human race as an institution, and depressed over the fact that as an individual I have done little to improve its standing in my own esteem. But — today — I celebrate with pride my human heritage and my present membership in a social order that can rise, on certain high occasions, to a forgetfulness of its own infirmities.

It is a great thing to be of a race that can (even if very briefly) ignore its pains and worries, its frustrations, its disillusionments, and remember only that it is indestructible.

I have had — and I am almost certain I shall have — plenty of occasions for remorse, repining, and repentance. I shall be examining my frail flesh to discover how insecure and helpless it is. . . . I shall often examine my mind — as I have to examine it — and sorrowfully reaffirm my discontent over its sluggish reactions to unwanted facts, its cowardly refusals to acknowledge the reality of inconvenient and disconcerting truths, its indecisiveness when faced with expensive obligations — but today I am proud of My Soul, and I am glad for you if you are proud of Your Soul. . . . If we can say — on this Easter Morning — that, all natural appearances to the contrary, we know ourselves to be of immortal stuff — nothing else really matters much.

For the implications of this faith in immortality bind us integrally to the life of God in a unity so dear that neither temporal government nor physical powers, nor past misfortunes, nor future threats, nor ecstasies nor depressions can separate us from that Source of Love. Perhaps we should pause to ask ourselves how we came by this audacious thought.

In the eleventh verse of the third chapter of Ecclesiastes, a reflective old cynic — traditionally held to have been King Solomon, though this is doubtful, for the author of Ecclesiastes was a very shrewd and thrifty old diplomat, while Solomon left his country bankrupt and ripe for civil war — ventures a statement amply attested by history when he writes: "God hath set eternity into the heart of man."

This fact could hardly be put down in a more trenchant phrase. True — the metaphor belongs rather to the jewelry shop than the psychology lecture hall — but when one remembers that thirty centuries ago men knew more about the setting of precious stones than of the maneuvers of the mind, the figure is adequate. God hath set eternity into the heart of man! The thing is an authentic fact! The story of mankind does not reach back to an era when this was not true.

All races in all ages have possessed this definite fixation. People of all colors and climates, however little they may have known about the world they lived in, have borne about with them some pattern of a world outside and beyond themselves where compensation might be expected for the hungers and dreads and costly courage of this present life.

Indeed, the very dissimilarity of the techniques pursued to establish a right to future happiness, and the multitude of variant views as to what form that happiness would wear, serves only to add point to the main issue which — when everything irrelevant and phenomenal had been stripped away — was the universal expectation of everlasting life.

And — but for this instinctive hope, which explained and justified and ennobled so large an area of human suffering, it is very doubtful whether, on certain agonizing occasions, when every other reliance but this faith had been driven into complete rout — it is doubtful if men and women could or would have carried on.

It is probably no exaggeration to say that whatever any one of us may choose to think about the survival of our own personality after death, had it not been for the sure hope of that ultimate reward in the opinion of our hard-pressed ancestors — you and I would not be here at all to think about this matter, either one way or the other.

It becomes us, then, on Easter, to give this time-worthy theory the full respect due to a motive-ideal which sustained our forebears in crucial periods when every other reason for striving had been swept away — and furnished the one imperative vision without which the people must have perished.

And were we to spend this hour in meditation upon no other feature of Easter than the fact that God hath set eternity into the heart of man, it would be of profit — for nothing is more promotive of our general culture than a reverential examination of the aims and motives which have determined the course of human progress.

However — I have it in mind to talk with you about Immortality, today, in a more practical mood. It is not quite enough to speak of immortality as an instinct, and therefore meritorious. An instinct is not necessarily a virtue or an adornment. The most unbeautiful conduct we ever exhibit is prompted by our instincts.

In the order of their urgency, our instincts are (1) self-preservation, and (2) reproduction of ourselves biologically, and (3) control of personalities weaker than we are, and (4) conciliation with personalities stronger than we are.

There is very little idealism in an instinct. Indeed — most ideals are had at the cost of disciplining and defying instincts. So — to say that mankind has an Instinct for Immortality doesn't really make a virtue of it, any more than it makes a virtue of avarice to say that mankind is instinctively greedy — which fact probably applies to even more people than feel the urge to be immortal.

I therefore invite you to come along to another investigation of immortality more significant than a reaffirmation of its instinctive grip upon men's imagination.

In the tenth verse of the first chapter of Paul's second letter to his young disciple Timothy, the thoughtful man of Tarsus makes use of a phrase which deserves our intensive study. Paul writes: "Jesus Christ hath brought Immortality to light through his gospel."

In other words: Jesus is not to be thought of as the Discoverer of Immortality. . . . We know this is not true. . . . Immortality was a built-in heart-hunger, deep-rooted in all the ancient ethnic faiths, and accepted in one form or another, ages before Jesus was born. Ten centuries before he broke the bondage of his tomb, wise men of his own race believed that God had set eternity into the heart of man. And even longer before that, Homer had inspired his fellow Greeks with poems beautifully describing a land of rest and peace beyond the grave.

No — Jesus had not discovered immortality . . . but he had evaluated it in new terms which lifted it from the estate of a mere nebulous wistfulness into the exalted position of a luminous ideal. Paul says: "Jesus Christ, through his gospel, hath brought Immortality to *light.*"

One of the remarkable distinctions of Jesus' teaching resides in the fact that eternity, in his opinion, was forever — counting in both directions.

In almost everything the other great prophets and mystics and seers have had to say about eternity, it was something that began for them when time played out. Jesus considered himself to be from Everlasting to Everlasting, and counseled his disciples to share with him this conception of immortality.

To him, time that is measured in terms of so many sunrises and sunsets per month, and so many months per year, is more of an obstacle than a convenience to straight thinking. What happens today — of good or ill — and what may happen tomorrow — of good or ill — is of very small consequence to people who are (as we would say, in our common vernacular) "Eternity-minded."

Not long ago I heard a minister say, in a sermon — for I am a layman now, finding out how it feels to be preached to, and not have a chance to talk back — I heard this minister say that our world had fallen upon evil times, indeed. He quoted some radiant passages from a great religious leader's sermon on the Sunday after Armistice Day, 1918, to the effect that the world had now come to an unprecedented realization of its duties; that we had arrived, as a race, into a time when social justice could be expected as a natural corollary of what everybody had suffered. We humans had had enough of the ghastliness of war, and would stoutly resent any talk of another. The world had stepped up onto higher ground.

And then — this minister viewed with regret the predicament of the world today; a breakdown of disarmament plans, a tightening up of nationalistic egotisms, a sullen suspicion across borders, the exposure of great depravity on the part of men the public had trusted — in all civilized countries. It was — he thought — a complete repudiation of the idealism of 1918. In fact, the things that were going on today made what we were saying in 1918 seem silly and ridiculous.

I presume — if we stopped to look at both dates squarely, 1918 and 1934, we would discover that the inspired optimist who caroled of a new and illumined world in 1918 was no more in error than the defeated pessimist who today sees greed and savagery in the saddle and the whole social order galloping a mad tam-o'-shanter to the devil. The optimist in 1918 was hoping for too much. The pessimist of today is not hoping for enough. Each of them is surveying the whole world and the course of human destiny from what little he can see of it at some given moment through whatever small keyhole he happens to have applied his eye to.

He may have a vague notion about eternity . . . as a pleasant future expectation . . . but he needs *light* on this fact of immortality.

That Light is turned on in the gospel. Jesus handles exactly this situation I am talking about when he says: "Some say, 'Here comes the Kingdom!' and others 'There goes the Kingdom!' But I say, 'The Kingdom is within you!'"

In other words, if it really needs any other words to apply it to our own affairs, people have a hard time being Kingdom-conscious. They can't get themselves oriented to eternity. They say: "Here comes a new day of justice and peace. We have suffered long. We have shed blood and tears. It is over now. And here comes the Kingdom! Hooray!"

And, next day, or next year, or sixteen years afterward, when the fog settles, and hungry people are discouraged, and the erstwhile well-to-do's who have been well-to-done are trying to get it all back quickly, and wastrel institutions are discredited for their former extravagances — then how easy it is for the shortsighted to whine: "Well — there goes the Kingdom! That's all there's going to be, and there isn't going to be any more. . . . Might as well give it all up. . . . Lo — there goes the Kingdom!"

Now — when the fact of immortality is actually illuminated by the Jesus-conception of time in the large — the people who accept it are neither kited to an hysteria of exultation over the splendid sacrifices and high aims of one triumphant day — nor plunged into the nether suburbs of the doldrums by the rampant selfishness and disorders of one depression day.

Eternity never says: "Lo here, Lo there." Eternity deals with the long haul. Eternity adds things up and strikes a general average. Eternity doesn't expect the world to be saved or lost by Thursday. It isn't quite that simple. The people who believe such things, are.

The belief in immortality, therefore, when illumined by the Gospel of Christ, is a challenge to one's philosophic attitude toward the world and human destiny. It counsels us against permitting ourselves to be swept off our feet by some temporary gust of mass-exuberance over mighty battles won and painful sacrifices justified: and it counsels us, with equal insistence, against a spiritual collapse on occasions when men's purposes seem questionable and battles are lost because they are not worth winning.

If you believe in immortality as Jesus believed in it, you cannot say, of any particular period: "Now — we have solved our problems," or "Now — we have lost our grip." Some very good people have made this mistake. Twenty-five years ago, a great wave of evangelism swept this continent, promoted largely by earnest college men. The movement adopted a stirring slogan, "The evangelization of the world in this generation." Many of us, in those days, heard the most noted and influential leaders of the Christian Church summoning young men and women into Foreign Missionary service with the declaration that if we gave this cause the best that was in us, we might be alive to see the day when all the kingdoms of the world had become the kingdoms of our Lord.

Now — however well intentioned this campaign may have been, and however sincere its promoters, it is clear that no one of them was acquainted with the Jesus-idea of immortality. . . . All they could see was the short section of road immediately before them.

The same sort of people are making an even more grievous mistake today. They see the whole institution of Missions undergoing reconstruction, bewildered, discouraged, and quite obviously losing ground.

But the ultimate evangelization of the world is no more a lost cause today than it was a victorious cause in the first decade of this century. . . . Jesus said that his kingdom of world fellowship would grow like a tree. Some seasons it would seem to make great progress; some seasons it would record very little growth. Some seasons it would blossom and bear fruit. Some seasons it would be barren; but (and this was a promise) the tree would continue to grow. The leaven in the meal of human society would work slowly but it would eventually leaven the lump. Not all the people would make use of the opportunity to enter the kingdom, but the kingdom had been made permanently accessible — and nothing that could ever happen, in periods of doubt and dismay, would have the power to close that avenue to eventual victory. "Behold," he said, "I have set before you an open door . . . which no man can shut."

Now, this aspect of immortality gives it — I think — a practical value for many a man who cannot find much satisfaction in it when phrased in terms of a disembodied existence in some future abode of the soul beyond the grave.

If immortality has to do only with vague speculations about that mysterious bourne from whence travelers do not return, it is a subject that permits very little discussion for the reason that there is almost nothing that can be said of it with any degree of precision; a matter that cannot be submitted to reason, but only to the emotions. Immortality — with the light of Christ's gospel thrown upon it — becomes of immense significance to human happiness and steadiness in this present life.

If I am immortal at all, I am immortal *now*. If God's spiritual realm is to endure forever, its foreverness is a fact that should be the chief consolation and reliance to thoughtful men in their daily lives. . . . Just to be able to say to oneself, in periods of general unrest — or on occasions of personal perplexity: "The Universe is solvent. Whatever transitory losses any one generation may suffer — the divine institution as a whole is sound." Just to be able to say that — may be the salvation of many a beleaguered soul who knows he can hold on to that sure promise when every other hope has dimmed.

But let us — who call ourselves Christians — remember that when we say: "I believe in the Life Everlasting" — we are not merely looking toward some future haven for our souls, but accepting in faith and confidence the everlasting life that *now is*. . . . This enlightened view of eternity is a challenge to our optimism, a challenge to our courage. Easter asks you, "Are you brave enough, are you man enough, are you divine enough to believe and practice the life eternal?"

Sometimes one wishes that our contemporary system of Christian thought and method might have laid more stress upon the indispensibility of this high idealism. Too often our churches have made the Christian life a program of rules for conduct, rather than a motivating ideal. They have urged people to examine their weaknesses rather than their strengths, and have given more time in their liturgies to remorse over human indiscretions than to rapturous pride over their divine opportunities.

Not infrequently men and women met in the comradeship of church association to discuss what they thought were the imperatives of Christian character, and the conference turned out to be a mere trivial survey of minor matters relating to abstemiousness and self-discipline. . . . One man would get up and say that he was happy to report his steady growth in grace. He had stopped doing this, that, and the other that he had used to do — his spiritual detriment — and he asked the prayers of God's children that he might hold out faithful unto the end. . . . Another would arise to speak with splendid scorn of habits he had once thought he enjoyed — but now viewed with disgust. He, too, had quit doing a lot of things, and he would enumerate what they were: (*a*) — (*b*) — and (*c*). Sometimes, if he were particularly eloquent in confession and gifted in reminiscence, there would be trailers under these generic *a*, *b*, and *c's* detailing the specifics under (1), (2), and (3).

But apparently nobody stopped to remember that men become great because of what they are. They never become great because of what they are *not*. In the long run, sterling characters would produce worthy conduct. That was as inevitable as that healthy trees would — in the long run — produce good fruit. . . . Some blossoms might fall off before maturity — some figs might be stung by insects, blighted by frost, or otherwise made worthless — but in the long run — the sound tree promised sound fruit.

Jesus once spoke of a very beautiful tree that had produced no fruit at all for a couple of seasons. The keeper of the orchard was perplexed what to do with it. Perhaps the tree had stood there mumbling to itself — but quite audible to the neighbors — "I thank God that I am not producing bad fruit. . . . All about me are trees that might do much better than they do. Some of their figs are runty and wormy, some of them are blighted, and some are frosted and some are rotted on the tree. . . . I am glad to testify, today, that no such fruit is produced by *me*, and I hope I may hold out faithful in this unto the end." And that would have been all very nice but for the bigger fact that there wasn't any fruit on this tree at all.

What we need now — more than anything else — in our Christian living is a constructive motive. We have tried about everything else. We have talked of Christian living as a code in inhibitions and restraints, and the new generation, stall-fed on directions for keeping one's toes on some chalk line drawn by persons of cloistral minds, have come to regard it as a mere sedative for the unlucky.

We have tried to make it a system of verbal assent to dogmatic theories which have no outcome in faith, courage, hope, or culture — no matter if the theories were abundantly proved to be true — which they haven't been, and aren't going to be.

Is it not time that we should concentrate upon the belief in and practice of the Eternal Life, that views our human pilgrimage in terms of the Larger Journey, and does not permit itself to be deceived into exultation by one ecstatic mile of smooth going, or plunged into despair by a mile of rough, uphill road.

This spiritual benefit can be had only by those for whom immortality has been brought to light, through Jesus Christ our Lord.

Montreal
Easter, 1934

the garden of the sepulchre

ON CERTAIN OCCASIONS, our beloved dead seem very near. Probably not more often than once in a long lifetime would an occasion arise wherein that fact is so vividly in evidence as at this moment.

We find our emotions inarticulate; and decide that there are so many things which might be said that to say nothing and let our hearts do their work unhindered by mere words is best of all.

We are here to repledge our faith in the Life Everlasting; for the issue of this hour is Immortality.

Immortality is not something donated to mortals as they leave our world. It is not an artificial contribution to this present existence; but a natural continuation of it. If a man is immortal at all, he is immortal now.

Eternal Life is not a legacy, conferred at death; but a present endowment — the full appreciation of which deepens and beautifies and sanctifies the meaning of our earthly days; for if a man is immortal, he has already entered upon an endless course of spiritual development, with unlimited possibilities before him. He has already begun a journey in which death is but an incident.

If he really wishes to live forever, he will certify to that hope by living the kind of a life that it would be worth his while to continue living, forever.

This strange nearness of our life to their life, who have preceded us, is most beautifully — albeit simply — told in the story of Mary Magdalene's meeting with the Glorified Christ in the garden of the sepulchre.

Hurrying to the tomb, in the first faint streaking of dawn, to anoint the mangled body of her beloved friend with spices (as was the custom) Mary, finding the sepulchre vacant, looks about for someone of whom she may inquire concerning this strange occurrence.

Bending over the flowers, in the garden, was a man — presumably the gardener; and Mary approached to ask him where they had taken the body of her Master; and lo — it was he!

Doubtless if we might see them, we would find that our precious dead are not so far removed from us as we had feared. There is no reason to disbelieve that a glorified spirit would still be interested in flowers, and sunshine, and green grass, and blue sky, and spring.

Perhaps they are vitally concerned about many of the movements and issues which held their attention when they were robed with flesh — seeing that they were immortal then, exactly as they are immortal now.

For our own protection against weariness and dissatisfaction with our lives, lived under cramping conditions, we are ignorant of the Life to Come. But all the instincts of our being demand us to believe that there is a Life to Come, toward which we are tending, whether we will or no.

Where and how that life is lived, we do not know; but our hearts point the way to it. A traveler in Switzerland reports that — uncertain of his directions — he asked a small boy by the roadside where Kandersteg was; and received the reply: "I do not know, sir, where Kandersteg is; but there is the road to it."

This is our experience in contemplating immortality. It is quite beyond our comprehension. It is a destination that can never be exactly located. But we know, instinctively, that we are en route on an endless road toward an unknown perfection.

"I do not ask to see the distant scene: one step enough for me."

On this Easter morning, we shall not inquire for better proofs of immortality than the evidences engraved upon our own hearts. For we do not believe in immortality because we have proved it, but we forever try to prove it because we believe in it. And we believe in it because the Great Author of our souls has communicated this hope to His children.

By signs and tokens, He refreshes this hope within us: and if, by virtue of His genius and power, the creeping worm can fledge gorgeous wings and explore the sky; if, under His wisdom and love, somnolent Nature, cold and dead, can break forth, triumphantly, into splendor and beauty of spring — I, too, shall rise into newness of life.

As we have borne the image of the earthy, we shall also bear the image of the heavenly, for this mortal *must* put on immortality. And when this mortal shall have put on immortality, there shall be brought to pass the ancient adage: "Death is vanquished."

May the Grace of our Risen Lord, the Peace of our Father God, and the Consolation of His Holy Spirit, be upon us, and abide with us, now and ever more.

Akron, Ohio
(an Easter Address)